FOREVER
NERDY

FOREVER NERDY

LIVING MY DORKY DREAMS AND STAYING METAL

BRIAN POSEHN

Da Capo Press

Da Capo Press
Hachette Book Group
1290 Avenue of the Americas, New York, NY 10104
dacapopress.com
@DaCapoPress, @DaCapoPR

Printed in the United States of America
First Edition: October 2018

Published by Da Capo Press, an imprint of Perseus Books, LLC, a subsidiary of Hachette
Book Group, Inc. The Da Capo Press name and logo are trademarks of the Hachette Book
Group.

The Hachette Speakers Bureau provides a wide range of authors for speaking events. To find
out more, go to www.hachettespeakersbureau.com or call (866) 376-6591.

The publisher is not responsible for websites (or their content) that are not owned by the
publisher.

Editorial production by Christine Marra, Marrathon Production Services.
www.marrathoneditorial.org

Book design by Jane Raese
Set in 11-point ITC New Baskerville

Library of Congress Cataloging-in-Publication Data has been applied for.
ISBN 978-0-306-82557-6 (hardcover); ISBN 978-0-306-82558-3 (ebook)

LSC-C

10 9 8 7 6 5 4 3 2 1

To Melanie and Rhoads Posehn, my dream family.

And to my mom, thanks and sorry.

CONTENTS

FOREWORD

You're about to hang out with Brian Posehn for a few days. He's going to talk about his life and a lot of the stuff that he loves and some of the stuff he hates. He loves things in a truly lovable way. But what's better is this:

He hates stuff in a *hilarious* way.

That, to me, is the essence of being a comedian. Love lovely and hate hilariously.

Not that this book is in *any* way another "my funny struggle" rote recitation of a comedian's climb. Like Brian's career—like anyone's career, come to think of it—it advances crookedly, loops back. At one point, due to a horrific/hilarious self-inflicted injury, his career (and life) nearly comes to a full stop. *Anyone* creative, looking back with honesty and exasperation at their own journey, would cop to the same confusion.

Brian faces the confusion and disasters of his past the same way he grapples with the subjects of his stand-up— with grace, rage, style, and sloppiness. The pop culture and ephemeral wormholes he travels down in his stage act were always there, even as a kid in sun-blasted northern California. Heavy metal, horror movies, comic books, TV and films, and a dozen other escape hatches from '70s and '80s teenage boredom. Will a generation with access to everything through a screen in their pocket produce artists like Posehn—overwired minds craving stimulation that wasn't easily accessed? We'll see.

For now, you get to wade through this captivating, out-of-control historical document detailing a lost world and the comedy genius who stumbled out of it. I've known Brian for more than twenty-five years. This book, the way it's written? That's his voice. That's Brian. And once you open it, and you're in it, it's the same as hanging with him, and hearing his stories, and getting his take on life and reality.

Get ready for some hilarious hatred. You'll love it.

Lovely.

Patton Oswalt
July 30, 2018
Studio City, CA

PREFACE

Hello reader, how are you? I bet no one has ever asked you that from a thing you were reading. I am different. I'm nice. I was raised right. Mostly. You have questions: "Hey Brian Posehn, why are you writing a book?" and "Hey Brian Posehn, who the fuck are you?" Okay, maybe you should have flipped those questions. Let's start with "Who the fuck are you?" And by the way, are you always so rude to writers? Who am I? What am I known for? You ask a lot of questions . . . maybe you don't have to be a dick about it . . . or if you're a lady, the lady version of a dick.

I'm a mildly successful, not so widely known stand-up comic, writer, and actor and full-blown nerd. And by full-blown nerd, I mean I'm obsessed with a bunch of cool stuff that dumb people think is uncool, like comics, Dungeons & Dragons, action and horror movies, and HEAVY FUCK-ING METAL. I've been doing stand-up most of my life. I've written movies, TV, comic books, and a classic underground sketch show twice. I'm mostly known for playing weirdos and half-wits in sitcoms. In my stand-up act I'm known for talking about nerdiness, heavy metal, and my penis. And my balls. I think I've written way more jokes about my balls than my penis. But who's counting?

To answer your second question: Why a book? Um. Easy. Every comedian writes a book now. Comics with way less stage time than me are cobbling their stories and Twitter musings into books all over the Kindle verse—that's a thing, right? And if you must know, I recently received a message from the President of Showbiz telling me it was actually my turn to write a book. A lot of people don't know that the President of Showbiz is Tori Spelling. You would think it was someone with a better career or a grizzled old producer or ex-studio head who has seen everything. But nope, that's not how showbiz works.

Anyway, "T"—I call her "T"—anyway, "T" said, "Posehn"—she calls me Posehn—she said, "Posehn, pull your giant bird-faced noggin out of your old, stretched-out butthole and write a fucking book, you stupid, sad dick-knob." I hope that didn't shock your delicate sensibilities. I wasn't offended at all—it's how "T" and I talk to each other. I said, "Fuck you, you lucky, lizard-face dullard," and then, "Yes, I will write a book and pay one of your ex-nannies to cram it up your cob-webbed you-know-where." She typed back, "LOL, fuck you . . ." That was a year ago. And now you have my first book in your hands.

The other reason I'm writing a book is I like them. Actually, I love them. I know, what a weirdo. That's me, a fucking book-loving weirdo. I've always been entertained by autobiographies. I love reading about the details of a performer or artist's life in their voice and in their own words.

And thirdly, over the years, whenever I've known someone well and long enough to talk about our childhoods (after five minutes if whiskey is involved), people have reacted with shock and laughs at some of the shit I've been through during my fifty-plus years as a metal nerd. "Yeah, I did see a ton of car accidents on my paper route when I was twelve, and maybe I did think I was the son of Satan."

And "Yes, my sophomore year of high school was the saddest eighties movie ever. I got beaten up by a girl, a special-ed kid and a fellow nerd who used to be my friend." Oh, and "Yep, I lost my virginity at twenty-one to a twenty-eight-year-old woman I met at a comedy open-mic in a basement bar in Old Sacramento." Yep. Old Sac. Again, with the balls.

Plus, if you're actually reading this, you at least like books enough to be checking out a book from "that guy" from "that show" or "that thing." At the very least, you're in a struggling Barnes and Noble perusing my book on the new nonfiction shelf. Now, put my book back and go use the shitter because we both know that is why you're really here. Back to my deflowering story—we did it in my shitty apartment because she still lived with her ex-husband. Oh yeah, *ex-husband*.

More about him in Chapter 17 or 18. Anyway, that's how the night ended. It started in the comedy club, but it really got started in the parking lot of a cop bar downtown an hour later. You always remember your first time, especially when your first time is with a divorced rocker chick who, while we were making out against a car, she yelled at a homeless guy to "Get the fuck away from us, dude!" Or is it "divorced rocker chick whom"? Either way, super classy. Not sure why I didn't marry her in Reno that night. My wife has heard some of these stories multiple times. Actually, that last story had some details missing when I told my wife. Those details will be revealed later, and I'll tell you a secret: it rhymes with premature ejaculation.

This is not my life story. It's more like just a bunch of stories from my life. There is a difference. You'll hear (or read with your eye-ears) about when I discovered I was a nerd and how a lot of my fellow students reminded me of that fact. That's a big part of the book because it's a big part of my life. Before people said, "I identify as something or another," I identified myself as a nerd. Back when that wasn't a word you saw on T-shirts that said, "I HEART Nerds" or before nerd culture exploded beyond Comic-Con and became pop culture.

I will walk you through all my nerdy obsessions from over the years, and I'll explain why I became comfortable with that label. Sort of. You'll hear about my multiple therapists and self-prescribed medication. You'll also read how a self-hating nerd who suffered with depression was able to become successful at my dream job, TV, movies, comic books, music, and comedy, and get my dream girl to fall in love with me despite myself. You'll also, also read how even with the love of my beautiful wife and son, thousands of fans, and hundreds of dollars, I still don't feel like I quite fit in and why I'll be FOREVER NERDY.

FOREVER NERDY

ONE

POSEHN AND NERDY, THE EARLY YEARS

I wasn't born a nerd. I don't think anyone's born a nerd. I used to say that in my stand-up act: you never look at a little kid or a baby and say, "What a fucking nerd. That baby will never get laid." Hilarious joke and I stand by it. You're not born a nerd. You find it. Or fall into it. Or, in my case, grow into it. Literally. I first exhibited nerdiness or nerd-like behavior around ten years old. By age eleven I looked like a full-blown nerd—the little guy on the front of this book, full of *Star Wars* and awkwardness. In these first chapters I will take you through the first chapters of my life: my transition from a totally normal yet massive baby to an eleven-year-old nerd.

I was birthed on the sixth of July, 1966, at Sequoia Hospital in Redwood City, California. We're so proud of our trees in Northern California that we name everything after trees. Not really. Just those two places. I'm not sure what Redwood City is like now, but then it was a quaint, tree-lined little suburban town south of San Francisco and the San Francisco Airport. It was next to the more affluent Atherton (home of Stanford University and where my mom grew up).

When I was a metal-loving, "Satan"-obsessed teen I found it pretty amusing that my birthdate was 7/6/66. Birthday of the beast! Whooo! METAL! I would promise you that this is as dumb as this book is going to get, but that would be lying.

I can't start lying this early in; then you won't believe me later when I really need you to believe me. I can promise, however, that this book will get way dumber.

Both of my parents grew up in Northern California. My mom, Carole Turner, was born in November of 1939 and raised in Atherton by George and Norma Turner. She had a brother, Gary. My Grandpa George was three-quarters Irish, one-quarter English, and my Nana Norma Ziegler was, duh, German. She was also Irish and Italian. They were both born in San Francisco, California. My Nana's mom, Irene Schuler, was Italian and German. She was born in 1900, in San Francisco. So on her side I'm fourth-generation Bay Arean, which is totally different from a gay Aryan. That dude would have some shit to work through.

Being the fourth generation probably explains why, of all the places I've traveled, the bay is still my favorite and feels the most like home. My Great-Nana Irene was only fifteen when she had my Nana Norma. She had lived through the infamous 1906 earthquake that ravaged the whole city, so having a kid while being a teen was no big whoop. I heard the earthquake stories a lot as a kid. My Great-Grandpa Wes Ziegler was a German/Irish jockey from Chicago when he met my Great-Nana Irene. I spent a lot of time with my Nana Irene the first few years of my life, amazing lady and a cheap babysitter.

Great Grandpa Wes, I never met. He shot himself three days before my mom's wedding because he was dying of cancer and didn't want to ruin his granddaughter's wedding by being a cancer bummer. You do know how people with cancer always ruin weddings? Instead of ruining my mom's wedding, he shot himself. Which also ruined her wedding.

Suicide doesn't run in my family, but selfishness and bad decisions do. You'll see.

My dad, Robert, or Bob, grew up in Sacramento, California. He was born in 1942 to Edmund and Clara Posehn. He had a younger brother, Michael. My grandmother was born Clara Petersen. She was a tall, beautiful Swedish girl from Minnesota, and my Grandpa Ed was German and from Saskatoon, Canada. They had migrated from Germany to Russia to Canada to Sacramento. My Grandpa Ed was kind of an asshole, but everybody loved him. I'm kind of an asshole too. Thanks, Grandpa. My dad was a tall, skinny jokester who loved hiking and fishing and building things with my Grandpa Ed. He went to American River College in Sacramento for English and Drama.

My mom grew up a fifties nerd. She wasn't a nerd obsessed with the fifties, she was a nerd in the fifties, when they invented nerds. She says it was rough, but wait 'til you get to my high school chapters. She was working at a title agency in the South Bay when she started dating my dad. My dad was six foot eight, and my mom was six foot even. Tall lady. I always knew I was going to be freakishly tall. My grandparents were tall. Almost all my mom's close friends were tall because she belonged to a tall club.

Yep, a fucking tall club—San Francisco's premiere tall club, the Golden Gate Tip Toppers. That's where my parents met, at the Golden Gate Tip Toppers. Premiere? Like there was a shitty low-rent tall club or a thriving community of mediocre tall clubs and Golden Gate Tip Toppers was the premiere tall club. Whenever people—small, dumb people—ask me how I got so tall, I give them the short answer, "Um, my parents . . ." I had no choice. My dad had tall semen and my mom had a tall vagina. So tall was normal for me, but when I started to get really tall, normal people didn't think I was normal.

I don't remember much about the day I was born. The day after, though? Every single detail. HA HA! Not really, you guys. Babies don't remember shit. They also don't really do shit. I was one and I had one, so I know babies. I was a big baby. My mom has repeated the story of my birth a lot over the years; I think it really fucked her up, and I don't mean her hoo-haa.

Apparently I was the biggest baby in the hospital. My parents were both very tall and young. When my six-foot-eight dad looked through the nursery window at me, everybody around him knew I was his baby because I was thirty-eight inches long and weighed twenty-five pounds.

Or twenty-three inches and ten pounds, three ounces. I forget. I was actually the latter. Called my mom to confirm while writing this. Like I said, big baby. My dad died when I was two. I'll just get right to it. I don't remember that either, but it still kinda affected me. My dad died very young; I'll say it a bunch more in this book.

I've played the dead-dad card a lot over the years. Anyway, my dead dad died in 1968. Robert Edmund Posehn was twenty-five when he made the twenty-eight-year-old Carole Irene Posehn a single mom. My middle name is Edmund also, but that's not really your fucking business. (Oh wait, I guess it is.) My grandparents were around a lot those first couple of years we were alone, and my mom spoiled me when she could.

After my dad died, my mom bought me a puppy. I think I got him at my dad's funeral. A guy dressed like my dad climbed out of his casket carrying the puppy. Actually, I'm pretty sure my mom waited until my third Christmas to give me the puppy. For my second, third, and fourth Christmases she went all out. My mom said later she was trying to make me happy. Which is sweet and sad. Sorry. She tried. Apparently she burned through whatever insurance money we got from my dad pretty quickly. So there's that.

Anyway, the puppy. Puppies are fun. I super creatively named the puppy Snoopy. I was three, so let's all cut me a fucking break on naming him Snoopy. Snoopy was destructive. He ate through the phone cord, like a dumb little furry dick, while my mom was talking to her friend Anne. Because this was thirty years before cell phones, Anne got in her car and drove over immediately to see if my mom had been raped and/or murdered 1970 style.

We had also owned at least two rabbits and a turtle in Redwood City. They died. Or got out. Or both. In that order. Don't remember. Maybe I killed them. Well, this book isn't about me becoming a serial killer, so . . .

My grandparents were awesome, and I had a lot of them: five grandparents and a great grandmother. They were all incredibly cool and loving, with amazing personalities, and they're all dead now.

I don't think they were irresponsible, but I did get thrown from a horse while I was two or three while I was with my dead dad's parents in Sacramento. Mild concussion. I've had a couple of those over the years. But it must suck to be a grandma and have a horse try to murder your grandkid.

Around that same time I was at my Nana's house in Redwood City, and I fell into her apartment swimming pool while I was running around by myself at night like a dumb three-year-old in the seventies. Luckily my Nana's neighbors had their patio door open and heard my stupid little body splash into the pool. The husband ran downstairs and jumped in and saved me. Thank Satan. I don't really worship Satan—well, only on Christmas and Easter.

Some of my earliest memories that I actually remember are of TV shows I saw and nightmares I had. The first TV shows were *Batman* and *Sesame Street*. That says a lot about me. Not sure what. Maybe that I still love Batman and look like a Muppet.

I must've also seen the Universal horror classic *Dracula*, because the first bad dream I remember happened when I was around three. It was a Dracula dream. I think he was trying to kill me. You know, killing kids, just like Dracula, the famous kid killer. I guess I really was a dumb kid or my dreams were dumb. Or maybe someone shouldn't have let a three-year-old see *Dracula*, Mom.

When I was four I guess I had had enough of my mom and her *Dracula* shit, so I ran away. Really. At four. I grabbed my dog, Snoopy, and my tricycle and wagon and joined up with my friend Timmy, the kid from across the street, and we ran away. Sure, "Timmy" sounds like a bullshit name, but I know for a fact that was his name. And if your name is Timmy, yep, your name is bullshit. Anyway, we grabbed our stuff, Snoopy, and maybe some snacks, and we ran away.

Of course, my mom freaked out—she was having a rough couple of years. My Nana Norma knew a cop and called him directly. I guess he owed her a favor—don't ask. My Nana was single for the late sixties and early seventies and kind of a partier. I think she may have fucked Frank Sinatra. I hope she fucked Frank Sinatra. Anyway, the cop found us at the park. Of course, he did. We went to the park like a couple of four-year-old assholes. Where else were we going to go? Ice Cream and Puppy Land was closed, so we went to the park.

I'm not sure how serious I was about running away, after all. That was my first run-in with the cops.

I used to joke that I was raised by women. A whole village of them. It's kinda true. When we lived in Redwood City I was around women almost exclusively. My mom had a couple of close friends who lived nearby and were always around, Sherry and Anne. They were both tall, of course. Anne was my first crush when I was a little bit older. Tall and thin with perfect porcelain complexion, and because it was the late sixties, she had impossibly long Rapunzel-length brown hair. More like Cher. I thought Anne was more beautiful than Marlo Thomas. That's saying a lot: Marlo Thomas was pretty attractive when I was seven.

My two Nanas and my Grandma Grace were around a lot. Grandma Grace was my Grandpa George's new wife. I didn't know that my Nana and Grandpa had a rough divorce; I just thought everybody had three grandmothers. I saw my Sacramento grandparents a couple of times a year; as I got older I would make longer and more frequent trips. I loved being around my Grandma Clara. She was a cool lady and a great listener.

Until she died. Sorry to drop it like that. That's some Stephen King shit, a trick I learned from reading Stephen King. He's done it forever, and it can be devastating. He'll describe characters or an action a character did, then in the next sentence say, ". . . and that was their last day on earth." It's true: she died. But not until a couple of chapters from now.

I do remember my mom being sad pretty often. I recall telling her stories or jokes to make her laugh, and this is the first "really clever" one she remembers: I was four years old, and my mom had just briefly dated a man named Miles. Apparently, good old Miles had taken money from my mom.

That was the thing: he was a scam artist. He grifted my mom for some cash and bailed.

So my mom is relating this to Anne and a couple of her friends at breakfast at a little Redwood City diner. I'm sure it was an uncomfortable situation, and I think I sensed it, so when Anne asked about Miles, I said, with impeccable timing, I'm sure, "Miles is miles away by now." Her friends all laughed and couldn't believe that this weird little four-year-old had just said that. I'm glad my mom noted that in her memory bank as the beginning of me saying a lot of shitty, kinda mean things under the guise of wordplay.

I was mostly a happy kid, considering I was dadless. I didn't really know what I was missing. I didn't have a lot of friends with dads at first. When I later lived in apartments, most of the other kids who lived there also had single parents. The few dads I knew were not great examples of dadness, and by the time I was in high school and college it was clear to me that a lot of my friends' dads were dicks.

Around age seven I was diagnosed as hyperactive. Before I was diagnosed, I was just a "spazzy" kid. And once I was around other kids on a daily basis, I was definitely disruptive. My mom once showed up at the daycare I went to and was told I was in a time-out in the closet. I had knocked over another kid's brick castle. In my defense, it was an amateurish piece of shit.

My mom freaked out when she found out I was alone in the jacket closet. I actually remember my frantic mom pulling me out of the closet darkness. Apparently that wasn't the first time I had been reprimanded that way. I tell the story not to point out abuse in the preschool or daycare system of the late sixties and early seventies but really to paint the picture that I could be disruptive.

I was exposed to death and sadness within my family at a young age, but I didn't really react to it right away. Darkness, though, was a theme in my early life I picked up on later. I felt feelings in my teen years about some of the things I went through earlier, like—SPOILER—losing my dad and my mom's boyfriend Bill and having a babysitter kill himself. Though, even at the time, I definitely missed having a dad, and seeing my great-grandfather in an open casket at age four was probably not the best move my mom could have made.

I'll try not to blame my mom for everything in this book, but I didn't have a dad to blame, remember? So around the same time, at age four, I was exposed to real darkness. A sad event made even darker by a bully. The next-door neighbor kid had died, and my neighbor across the street, Timmy's older brother, teased me about it. I was playing with Timmy, and his older brother—let's call him "Tommy"—told us that "Gary, the boogeyman" was going to get us. Oh shit, "Gary, the boogeyman,"—he's gonna get us?

Wait, who is Gary the boogeyman? Boogeymen don't usually have normal names. Well, Michael Myers. But anyway, my boogeyman was named Gary. The way my mother told me the story was that I was at my daytime babysitter's house, this nice older couple my mom knew really well. I was playing with the old man and asked him if he wears his wife's clothes. The old man said, "What now?" or "Wha-hah?" or "What in the devil?" or some other comedic response that fit the day when a child would ask surprising questions like I just had.

I think now is where his wife got involved and asked what I was going on about. I said, "My other babysitter, Gary, wears my mommy's clothes." And presumably they both collectively said, "Holy shit" or "What the fuck?" or some other colorful response. I remember them as Italian Americans and the old man wearing a wife-beater and early-seventies-style plaid pants, so maybe he said something stereotypically Italian like, "Holy cannoli!" or "Ave Maria!" or "I'mma gonna wiin! It'sa me, Mario!"

That night they talked to my mom, thinking my Uncle Gary was the creepy babysitter in this story. That is a tough conversation in 1970. My mom said, "No, my brother Gary is a lazy dipshit that lives in the Santa Cruz mountains banging this hot seventies chick named Linda." Well, my mom wouldn't say that, but I would've. Nope, the Gary in this story was a teenage boy who lived next door to us and babysat me on a couple of occasions and at least once wore my mom's clothes in front of me.

My mom freaked out. All her friends heard. My nanas and my grandparents heard. I'm sure Uncle Gary heard he dodged a bullet. She eventually told the neighbors their son Gary was cross-dressing in front of me. He killed himself. Yep. There was no easy way to get to that part. His parents confronted him, and he took his teenage life. Should I have left this out of the book? Maybe. But honestly it had a lot to do with who I am. The story and my involvement has stuck with me.

So Timmy's brother, Tommy or whatever, was a real dick because this poor kid Gary had been driven to commit the ultimate shitty act and Timmy's dumb-fuck brother was scaring other little kids with his death just a couple of months after he died. That's my take-away from that story. Timmy's brother was a giant dick. I often think of that poor fucking kid, Gary, and whatever feelings that led him to kill himself. So sad.

Now I feel nothing but empathy for Gary, but when my mom first told me the whole story at age eleven or so, I reacted differently. I was confused and angry. When I was five, my mom threw a party for me, and no kids came other than good old Timmy. It was just me, Timmy, my mom, Nana Irene, and Nana Norma along with a bunch of party favors and ice cream cake sitting around an empty table.

I am almost positive that the other kids my mom invited stayed away because the teenager next door had just killed himself and *whisper whisper* "Did you know Gary used to babysit for the Posehn widow?" *whisper whisper* "Do you think the Posehn widow or that weird little redhead had something to do with it?" *whisper whisper* "They must at least know what happened." *whisper whisper* "She did stop coming to church." *whisper whisper*

That's true. We did stop going to church around the time of Gary's death. My mom left Catholicism that year, which makes sense, considering my dead dad and a couple of rough years. I'm guessing Gary's death had something to do with it. I'm also guessing our duplex and the neighbor's house were tough sells. "It's two bedrooms and one bath, small kitchen, dogs allowed, the former tenant moved because the neighbor boy wore her dresses in front of her little son and then he hung himself right next door. Would you like to see the backyard?"

TWO

POSEHN AND NERDY, THE EARLY YEARS: PART DEUX

In the summer of 1971 I turned five, and we moved about twenty-five minutes south of Redwood City to San Jose, California. We settled into a small apartment complex in a suburban neighborhood. Soon after moving to San Jose my mom met a new guy, a tall skinny, bespectacled fellow named Bill. And I'm sure you can see this coming, of course: they met at the Golden Gate Tip Toppers.

I met short people too, but only when we would leave our tall village and go to normal-land. I liked Bill a lot. He took me to see the Harlem Globetrotters; that was the first big, live event I ever went to. More tall people. Bill brought me toys from his business trips. I remember Eskimo-related toys from Alaska and American Indian–themed paraphernalia from the Dakotas.

I thought he was going to be my new tall dad and teach me "tall dad" things. Well, he died. He got in a car accident about eight months after my mom and Bill started dating. I found out because other tall people were crying at our apartment. My mom took me aside and told me about the accident. I was very sad. I liked Bill a lot. He liked me too.

One of the shittiest things my mom ever said to me was, while I was still mourning him a couple of years later, that "Bill liked you more than he liked me anyway." Shitty thing to say to a seven-year-old, sure, but maybe that was the way my mom dealt with her grief, or maybe she was just being a fucking bitch. I'm sure I'll say some shitty things to my kid, and I will blame them on my mom too.

Speaking of being fucked up, I met my first therapist in San Jose at around six years old. He was an older British gentleman named Leonard, and I would visit his office once a week. Not sure I understood why I went to his office; not sure I even knew it was an office. I just called Leonard my friend.

Every kid has a friend who happens to be an old British guy you go see for an hour a week and you talk about life and your mom and whatever was going on that week, right? It was called "play therapy." He would get on the floor with me and play while we talked. I went to Leonard because I acted out a lot at school and at home.

I had two first-grade teachers—the first one couldn't handle my bullshit. Not sure the second one fared any better. I actually was a bit of a bully to a couple of kids. One kid, William, always had stuff in his hair, pomade or something, and also had a dumb look on his face all the time, and I teased him for both the greasy hair and his dumb face.

I also threw sand at girls and wouldn't let kids take naps. I instead tried to disrupt naptime by playing "duck, duck, goose" with my sleepy "friends." It worked, and by "worked," I mean it got me transferred to another first-grade class. This is still before I was diagnosed as hyperactive, but that duck-duck-goose-naptime shit seems pretty fucking obvious to me. I was a hyper little dildo.

My second-grade teacher, Mrs. Clark, put up with my squirrelly ass all year and didn't sit on me. That's a weird thing to write, why would a teacher sit on a kid? Oh, because my third-grade teacher fucking sat on me. Yep, my third-grade teacher actually sat on me to control me. Several times. I recall it making me more spazzy, struggling under her weight.

One day I got out from under her and ran for it. All the way home to our apartment. It wasn't far, like a block. I think my four-year-old turn as a runaway was further. The principal tracked me down at home and made me go back to school. Mom wasn't happy about that.

I saw that principal, Mr. Mason, quite a bit that year. He had me tested. My IQ was high, but I wasn't excelling. No one could figure out why. It was the beginning of that problem. Meanwhile the bedwetting hadn't stopped yet. Yep, I wet the bed too. I think someone was really hoping I'd be a serial killer. Nope, worse. Comedian. Sorry.

Not sure when the bedwetting started. I don't know if I ever mastered not sleeping in pee as a baby and then it came back as a young boy or if I just always peed the bed. It was only really an issue for my mom. I actually had a couple of accidents at camp and other boys' houses and much later when I slept with girls. And almost everybody has been cool with it. It actually felt good. For a minute warm pee feels amazing, cold pee not as much. It was, however, a big deal for my mom. And, in turn, a big deal for me.

I grew to hate peeing the bed and really stressed about it. Thank god all my friends were cool, because I was a neurotic mess about it. Early mornings on someone else's carpet or camp bunk bed, panicking while cleaning up my pajamas, my sleeping bag, and whatever else I soaked, trying to get rid of the evidence. This happened into my twenties. Remind me to tell you about my Rasta friend, Chris. You won't. So I'll just tell you, we worked together at Tower Records. I got high and boozy in his apartment and I passed out on his couch. I woke up early in the morning soaking wet. So I took the soaked blanket, stripped the covers off his couch cushions and went and did laundry in his apartment complex. I came back from the laundry room and he was awake. I was totally embarrassed and he just said, "no worries, man." We started that day with a wake and bake and he never told anybody about my accident.

In the seventies there was a Michael Landon TV movie about a kid who peed the bed every day, so his mom would hang his sheets outside to embarrass him. He would run home from school to get the sheets down before his friends could see them. He later becomes an Olympic runner. We made fun of that in a Mr. Show sketch called "The Bob La-Monta Story."

My mom didn't hang up my sheets, mainly because we didn't have a yard, I think. Instead she just nagged me about it, making me feel like shit and fearing sleep and hydration. We tried everything—pills, not drinking after a certain hour, slip-on diapers, a pad we bought from Sears that was hooked to an electric torture device that gave you a mild shock and woke you with the most annoying sound to ever come out of a small box. It was terrifying.

This, of course, happened after you peed, not before. So it didn't help you not pee; it just woke you right after or during your accident like a vindictive tattletale. Fucking useless. I eventually grew out of bedwetting. In my forties. Seriously. I just stopped peeing the bed in the last ten years. It can still happen if I'm super sleepy or drunk. My wife and my previous live-in girlfriend, both of whom you will meet later, were fucking amazingly cool for putting up with it.

There were also good times at home: my mom often wrestled with me, and she actually would get very into it. It was one of my favorite things to do with her. She was a big lady, so she could throw me around. We had seen local wrestling on Bay Area cable, so when the two of us acted out our fight we took on some of their names. I was Pat Patterson or Moondog Mane, popular local superstars from our show. She was Greasy Spoon, a name I'm pretty sure she made up. Greasy and Moondog would have weekly matches on Saturday or Sunday morning.

Even at age seven it was fairly obvious I needed a male influence, as I didn't see my grandfathers really that often and dudes who slept with my mom kept dying. Two for two—pretty strong numbers. She was undefeated at having lovers die.

For the first time in my life I just realized my mom was probably a virgin when she met my dad. I've actually never even thought about it before, and now that I have, I want to take a bleach shower. And then punch myself to death. Thanks for making me think of that. BLAARRGG!!

Anyway, male influence was needed, so my mom signed me up with the Big Brothers organization. I had two Big Brothers. I don't remember much about the first one; we only had one date or whatever you want to call it that is less creepy. I think he got a girlfriend and couldn't see me anymore. There is no way to make that sound not weird.

My second Big Brother, Doug, was actually pretty great. We went to a hockey game, watched Oakland A's games in his apartment, and ate KFC and drank soda. It was my first time eating KFC. I remember it well, and the soda sticks out because my mom wasn't letting me drink sugary drinks at the time in a misguided effort to combat my hyperactivity, but I didn't tell Doug my mom's soda rule.

We also built models, and he took me to the zoo and a boat show—yep, a boat show. Dude took a seven-year-old to a boat show. Doug and I had a deal: every other week was his turn to pick the activity. A grown man who, while giving his time to charity, still had to have "his time." WTF, right, Marc Maron? So one week we went to a circus, and next week we went to a fucking boat show. I'm sure he made someone an awesome, selfish dad one day. Plus, Doug had two cats in his apartment, so who knows what the fuck was going on with Doug.

My memories of seventies TV started with *Sesame Street*, *Electric Company*, *Mr. Roger's Neighborhood*, the awesome animated *Spider-Man* show, and both versions of *Batman*, the animated and the live-action classic. I also enjoyed *The Brady Bunch*, *The Partridge Family*, *Family Affair*, *The Courtship of Eddie's Father*, *The Munsters*, *The Addams Family*, *Nanny and the Professor*, and pretty much any cartoon I laid my eyes on.

It doesn't sound like it, but my mom kept my TV watching pretty limited. I think I got to watch my shows for an hour every day. Saturdays I got two hours. And outside of the news and PBS, she didn't watch a ton of TV. I remember her watching variety shows and specials, *Flip Wilson*, *Laugh In*, and *The Smothers Brothers*, which was my first exposure to adult comedy.

A lot of popular shows I saw were courtesy of other people's TVs. I saw Roger Moore as the Saint at my neighbor Sharon's house. She had a teenage daughter, Kathy, who babysat me sometimes. When I stayed with my grandparents in Sacramento neither one of them watched a ton of TV outside of *The Andy Griffith Show* and *Gomer Pyle*.

I saw *Gilligan's Island*, *I Dream of Jeannie*, and *Bewitched* at my Grandpa Ed's neighbor's house. She was this nice lady named Marie. I would do yard work for her, and she'd let me hang out and watch TV while she fixed treats for me. She had a son but no grandkids. Her emptiness meant snacks and TV for me.

I saw Elvis at our apartment manager's place. On TV—he wasn't hanging out in a San Jose apartment. She was this nice, heavyset lady named Liz, with a B-52s haircut and a southern accent. All I remember about Liz and her husband and son is that they were massive Elvis Presley fans. And I thought Elvis was pretty cool.

My buddy and next-door neighbor Patrick was watching *Yellow Submarine* one Sunday night. When it was time for him to go to bed, I ran home to watch the rest of it on my TV. I was blown away by the animation, songs, and weird story. I didn't even know who The Beatles were. This was my first exposure to cool popular music; my mom mostly played folk and Barbra Streisand at home and on the AM car radio.

I remember thinking Mr. Magoo was super funny and sounded like the dude on *Gilligan's Island*. It was. I honestly recall making that connection and thinking voice-acting seemed like a cool job. It is. I also thought sitcom acting looked fun and was drawn to the second-tier guys like Barney Fife and, later, guys like Schneider, Bull, and Reverend Jim.

This sounds crazy, but I also remember hearing the term "character actor" at a really young age, and my first thought was that it sounded appealing. But I didn't run around telling people, "I either want to be an astronaut or a character actor" or anything that on the nose.

Ever hear about the note Jim Carrey wrote to himself about how he was going to be a very famous comedy star one day? Dane Cook apparently did something equally gross. I didn't do that. I did write myself a letter, though, telling myself to never do anything Jim Carrey or Dane Cook ever did.

There was scary stuff on TV if you looked for it, and when I found it, I was in love. *Creature Features* was a local monster movie show with host-wrap-arounds that ran on a Bay Area UHF channel. It seemed like it was on TV all the time. I remember watching it in the middle of the day on a Saturday and later at night. I wasn't really into the British Hammer horror flicks, but *Godzilla*, *Mothra*, and the Universal monsters all blew me away, even after my Dracula nightmares.

Bob Wilkins was the host of *Creature Features*, and I was a big fan. He was a local TV weatherman who also had this as a cool side gig, hosting horror and sci-fi flicks on the same channel he did the weather. So I was pretty excited when Bob Wilkins asked my mom out on a date after judging her in a beauty contest. A tall beauty contest. I think she took second place. My mom was pretty shy and still had high school "tall girl" issues, so I'm surprised and impressed she even competed. Mom passed on the date with Bob Wilkins, but I like to think she fucked him. Not really.

When I was eight years old my Grandpa George retired from the meat business. He had owned a couple of butcher shops in the Bay Area. Before he retired, I called him Grandpa Salami or Grandpa Bologna because he always had cold cuts for me. In 1974 he moved with my Grandma Grace to Sonoma, California.

That Christmas I was very mean to my Grandpa George when he was just trying to help my mom, but of course I didn't know that 'til she told me. I threw a temper tantrum because he and my grandma didn't give me toys. They gave me a winter jacket, which I needed, and I screamed about it. What a dick. A skinny, little, spoiled dick. I've felt shitty about that my whole life. A little well-placed mom guilt goes a long fucking way.

In my defense, I didn't know my mom was struggling because she didn't start telling me that every day until I was ten or so. I loved playing with toys, but I didn't have a ton. Waah, waah! But I did have a nice winter jacket. When I was eight I really coveted the toy collection of another kid who lived in the same apartment complex as us.

He was younger and had the entire collection of Mego DC action figures, including the Batcave and Batmobile. Megos were and are awesome. They were like Barbies for boys, action figures with articulation and removable cloth costumes. And like Barbie, when you took their clothes off, they didn't have parts, just confusing bumps. Made me wonder: *Why do I have a wiener? Shouldn't I just have a weird bump like Robin?*

This kid in my building had Robin and his weird junk and every hero and villain from the DC universe. That was an early lesson in jealousy. He also had both of his parents. I had a Mego Batman and Spider-Man and that was it.

Which brings me to Evel Knievel toys. It was the seventies, so I had an Evil Knievel phase. All of America had an Evel Knievel phase. Even his failures like the Snake River Canyon were massive events and had toys created about them that you had to have. The rocket-car failed and Evel almost died, but if your mom didn't buy you the new Evel Knievel Snake River rocket-car, she was a real jerk. Hang tight, though, because I've written whole chapters about my other early nerdy obsessions.

My mom regularly took me to school with her at San Jose State. I would sit in the library while she was in class, and on nice days I would play outside in the quad by myself, totally unattended. At eight years old. My eight-year-old son doesn't do anything alone. He has never been alone ever.

One day I brought a couple of toys to the university quad with me. See, I had some. One was a rubber Dudley Do-Right figure I had from the seventies cartoon. I also had a Bullwinkle. Loved those dudes.

So I was throwing my Dudley figure at a tree, as one does. Especially if one is an eight-year-old weirdo. I got the figure stuck in a tree at one point, and a student used his Frisbee to get it down. Thank god, it was the seventies on a California college campus, so of course some dumb hippie student was winging a Frisbee around, man.

Glad it wasn't the nineties—I would have had to stand there, waiting impatiently, while he kept throwing his hacky sack, saying, "Oh dude, almost . . . one more try!"

I also went on job interviews with my mom. I remember being scared by this developmentally disabled lady at Agnews State Hospital chasing me in her pajama gown, screaming, "Kiss me! Kiss me! Kiss me!" I was terrified at the time, but maybe she was just a fan of The Cure.

The craziest, most inappropriate thing my mom did with me, though, is while she was going to San Jose State for her psychology major, she had to do volunteer work for credit and work experience. So a couple of weekends in a row she took me to a sober-living house. I didn't know what was going on with everybody there; I just thought they were weird. And chatty. Super chatty.

I guess my mom really didn't want me to have another bad babysitting experience, but she wasn't concerned about me being abducted from the school grounds while I was chucking my rubber Dudley Do-Right at a tree and raped with a Frisbee or some other generational leisure device. It was also okay to raped/murdered by a rabid patient at a state institution. Or simply terrified by said rabid patient. Can kids have heart attacks?

Mom apparently also wasn't worried about me being sold on the white kid market for drugs by a desperate druggie trying to cop one more high, seventies style, on uppers, downers, or good old heroin—that classic. I was a white male, and white males are, as everybody knows, the most valuable children. Although I had a vision problem and peed the bed, so I was worth substantially less than normal white kids.

Speaking of shit I would never do with my kid, I spent a lot of time alone in department stores while my mom shopped. I remember seeing *Kolchak: The Night Stalker* on TV at a Sears and wanting to know everything about *Kolchak: The Night Stalker*. The episode I saw at Sears in January of 1975 was "The Trevi Collection" (thanks, Google).

Kolchak, played by the brilliant Darren McGavin, was investigating a murder in the fashion industry and winds up defending himself from crazed mannequins at a high-fashion department store. He finds out that the mannequins were controlled by an evil witch. Of course they were. Notice I said *evil*, not the sexy, barefoot, Stevie Nicks kind of witch.

So there I was, sitting Indian-style (or the more current and politically correct "criss-cross apple sauce") in front of the biggest TV this seventies Sears could muster, watching something called *Kolchak: The Night Stalker*. And I was in. I couldn't have been more in. He was a reporter fighting werewolves, vamps, and possessed mannequins. I want to watch that now.

I later saw and loved the 1972 movie *The Night Stalker*. The TV movie and the show were written by Richard Matheson, a *Twilight Zone* writer and author of one of my all-time favorite books, *I Am Legend*. I would find out later he's one of Stephen King's favorite writers.

Kolchak and 1975's *Trilogy of Terror*, along with my *Dracula* dreams and the giant monsters from Japan, planted the horror seed. *Trilogy of Terror*—have you seen that shit? Holy fucknuts! It was a made-for-TV movie in 1975, and it was exactly as advertised: three short stories meant to terrify. It did. It's not something I have rewatched, though, so I doubt it holds up. To be honest, all I remember is the one story "Amelia," where a woman, Amelia (Karen Black), brings home a little creepy voodoo doll, called a Zuni fetish doll.

And oh god, is that tiny thing fucking creepy, with its crazy eyes and sharp teeth. It is tiny, though. You could totally kick the fuck out of it. When you're not shitting your pants. Fuck that thing. So Amelia brings it home and sets it down. It has a tiny spear and a gold chain around its neck. When the chain falls off, the little fucker comes to life and tries to kill Amelia. She fights it and later destroys it. She burns it up in the oven.

SPOILER: the smoke gets in her lungs, and she is taken over by the doll's spirit. She later waits to kill her mom, with a knife, crazed and panting like a monster. It's forty-three years old, so the spoiler is on you. Just thinking of that little Zuni doll still freaks me out, even as I'm writing this. That terrifying little face is burned into my memory. By the way, here is a nerdy fact (non-nerds, sit this one out): nerds, do you know who wrote "Amelia," based on his own short story "Prey"? Richard fucking Matheson, y'all.

The first movie I remember seeing in a theater was Bambi. It was a fucking bummer. SPOILER: Bambi's mom dies. Then I saw *Charlotte's Web*—you know, that cheery classic. SPOILER: oh, never mind. There was an early seventies-style multiplex (so, two theaters) in San Jose, and my mom and I would save money by going to matinees.

We saw all the Disney classic animated films like *Cinderella*, *Peter Pan*, *Aristocats*, *101 Dalmatians*, and then a bunch of those late-sixties/early-seventies live-action Disney films like *Swiss Family Robinson*, *Parent Trap*, *That Darn Cat*, *Blackbeard's Ghost*, and *The Love Bug* and its sequels. My mom didn't always enjoy the Disney comedies. I think it was when we saw *That Darn Cat*, and on the way out of the theater she was really negative about it and called it "ludicrous." A Disney kids comedy about a Siamese cat that solved crimes was ludicrous? No shit. And thanks, Mom.

Of all the Disney live-action films, my favorites were the Kurt Russell classics, *The Computer Wore Tennis Shoes*, *Now You See Him, Now You Don't*, and, in my opinion back then, the best of the bunch, *The Strongest Man in the World*. And then in 1975 I would have my mind blown by a Disney film, *Escape to Witch Mountain*.

Escape had it all—humor, magic, creepy bad guys, aliens, and cute, little Kim Richards. I remember falling in love with Kim the first time I saw that movie. I also had a crush on Haley Mills and a girl on *Star Trek* before I found out those Haley Mills movies and *Star Trek* were old, so those girls weren't kids anymore. I thought that was weird, so I stopped liking those "ladies." Now, I'll jerk it to people long dead.

But it wasn't all kids movies for this kid and my movie partner, Carole Posehn. No way. When I was older she brought me along to see anything Barbra Streisand was in. I actually liked the comedies; the ones where she sang the whole time, not so fucking much.

But the most egregious parenting slip-up happened in 1972, when she took me and my Nana Irene along to see *The Godfather* and *The French Connection* in the drive-in. Yep, my mom took me and my great-grandmother to see a violent R-rated film. Twice. Both times she thought I would sleep in the backseat. I didn't. I was six, not two, so of course I was going to stay awake.

I haven't talked to my mom about it, but I really feel like she took me everywhere because of what happened in Redwood City. Makes total sense now: she wouldn't leave me with a babysitter for a while after my last one wore her clothes and killed himself. So of course I went along for *The Godfather* and *The French Connection* as well as school, job interviews, and volunteer social work.

She thought I would sleep through two brutally violent— by early-seventies standards—classics, but no, I didn't sleep. I watched every minute. My guess is if I didn't see those gritty masterpieces when I did, I might not be who I am—a nerdy comic with a dark streak—and you might be reading a book from a real star, like a YouTuber.

At one point, in the pages coming up, when I was around ten years old, I was the lethal combo of super tall and super skinny with dorky, black-framed glasses, pimples, and braces. And my mom loved to get me bowl haircuts, and we didn't spend a lot of money on my clothes or have a real sense of what didn't make me more punchable. And I thought weird shit, so I would say weird shit. So on the outside I was a giant fucking goof, for sure. But I wasn't a true nerd yet.

As I said earlier, I've always seen nerdiness as obsession. Nerds don't like things passively. They love things obsessively. They get into things hard. It becomes their life. I feel like I didn't really get nerdy or obsess over anything 'til I was ten or eleven.

I definitely dabbled in pop culture from an early age and loved music, TV, and movies. And sixth grade is when I was exposed to the joy of true horror movies, and, yes, "joy" fits because for as long as I can remember horror movies have made me happy. Hang onto your hats and glasses and your wieners and vaginas—I don't want to get ahead of myself. I would find my first nerdy obsessions in 1976 and 1977, but first I had to endure 1975.

THREE

POSEHN AND NERDY, THE EARLY YEARS: 3D

Most of 1975 sucked. I got glasses. At the end of third grade I had to say good-bye to all my San Jose friends. Right after I could finally see them. I remember being really bummed and feeling a sense of, "Hey, I worked hard for three years to get those friends and my current position, whatever that was, and now I am going to have to start all over. No fair." My San Jose friends didn't mind my glasses when I got them, but at my new school it was just going to be another thing that made me look different or stick out.

I was in trouble a lot in third grade, but it didn't hurt my popularity. I had a lot of friends. I played soccer, and no one pointed out I wasn't great at it. Or maybe at eight years old we all sucked. Of course, we all talked about how we were as good as Pelé, the seventies soccer megastar. Whenever people talk about soccer not being an American sport, I think they're young. It was huge as shit in the seventies. Pelé was one of the biggest sports stars in the world.

Besides being a soccer star, I was in the Cub Scouts and went swimming a lot at the YMCA. What else? I had mastered a bike without training wheels, and I kissed a girl. And I liked it. Not sure if she tasted like Cherry Chapstick. I cannot even remember my first kiss's name, but she was one of the cutest girls in the third grade. She had dark hair and porcelain skin and wore really cute *Little House on the Prairie* dresses all the time, so let's call her Laura Ingalls.

Laura Ingalls and I had to kiss in the school Christmas pageant. And I think the casting was solely because we were the tallest kids in our class and that fit for the pageant director's interpretation of "I Saw Mommy Kissing Santa Claus." The shortest girl in the class played the kid in the song, the witness to Mommy's Christmas indiscretion. We, of course, had to rehearse, so I actually got to kiss her a couple of times. Got to? Had to. Because, although she was super cute, I was new to girls and still kind of terrified by them. I had only decided the previous year they weren't all carriers of cooties and worthy of sand tossing.

It would of course be many years before girls liked me back, but I started liking girls in third grade. And anyway, Laura Ingalls, if you're reading this, I had a crush on another girl, Kelly, who I remember having Farrah hair before Farrah. She also had a really cute smile and no clue who I was. I had no idea what was coming in the next couple of years. Soon I would wish I had a bunch of friends and a girl who liked me. Because behavior issues aside, third grade was not nearly the hell that fourth grade was going to be.

We moved two and a half hours north in the summer. My grandparents lived in downtown Sonoma. My mom and I moved into an apartment in nearby Glen Ellen, home of the Sonoma State Hospital, my mom's new employer. I started fourth grade about two months later. I was growing tall, but I wasn't gaining weight. And now I had glasses. I was pretty shy and introverted. I constantly entertained myself—reading, drawing, and coloring.

My mom had tried to involve me in activities in town before school started in the hopes that I would already have friends at the beginning of September. I made a couple, Larry and Monte. They were friends out of proximity. Larry lived in the apartment complex across the street from mine, and I met Monte at day camp. I don't remember much about that summer before my fourth-grade hell: I attended day camp at the school I was starting in the fall. Sure, why would I want to enjoy my summer? Let's get me on a schedule and mingling with kids to get me ready for the awkwardness and ridicule.

I joined the little-league team, I think because of Larry; he was on the team. I've blocked out the games, but I do remember the pizza and root beer. I definitely recall spending a lot of time in the two local libraries. I actually entered a reading contest at the library in downtown Sonoma.

I read a shitload of books that summer, twenty or thirty— short books, kids' books—but still a shitload of books. I won a gift certificate to the local Baskin-Robbins for reading the most books for my age group. Free ice cream, not fucking bad. And I remember my mom being proud of me; that felt good. My reading contest prowess will come into play in a minute. Well, depends on how slowly you read.

Larry and I hung out a lot at first, but he turned on me pretty quickly. He seemed to mature away from me within the course of a couple of years. We were pals for a while, playing with his *Planet of the Apes* and *Star Trek* action figures in his room, and by the seventh grade he was smoking cigarettes, hitting on girls, and calling me names.

Soon I would meet other kids in my neighborhood—two nice brothers, Russ and Darren, the Goodman brothers. For real. Plus, they were good kids. And then there was the "bad kid," my pal Hinchman. Turns out Hinchman's parents later thought I was a bad influence on him. We were bad influences on each other. He had a first name, but only his dad and his stepmom used it. Our friendship would endure vandalism with paint, snow, and fire and almost end with me getting my face stomped on.

On the first day of fourth grade at my new school, Dunbar Elementary, I was given my first nickname, Turtle. I hated it right away and still do. I think traditionally a nickname is more playful and endearing, something that maybe you liked or even hated in the beginning and later grew to love. Not with me. Turtle wasn't that kind of nickname; it didn't come from friends. It was just what a bunch of assholes called me. I took it personally, which I think is why it lasted all the way through high school.

People in high school didn't even know the origin of Turtle; they just knew I hated it, so it stuck. Kids are dicks. Here's the origin: on first day of fourth grade this real fucking asshole fifth-grader thought I looked like a turtle, so he called me Turtle. What a fucking asshole.

I never hated anyone before, but I hated the dude who coined that name for me. Drew was a black kid, one of the only black kids in my small town of Glen Ellen and actually one of the first black kids I ever met. Racist people would use that bad interaction as an excuse to be racist. Not me. That was one of the key reasons I've never understood racism. I've always judged people individually, not as a race. Because, like I said, he wasn't the only black kid I met in my formative years.

The other kid was named Marcus. He was cool as shit. We met when we were ten at a Christian summer camp in the Santa Cruz Mountains called Mount . . . something. I know it wasn't called Mount Something—that I would've remembered. Mount Hermon? Yep, Mount Hermon. Most of my memories are not great from there. I had the flu one time right after I arrived. That sucked. I got stuck in the camp infirmary for the first week of my two-week stay. I just sat there reading and rereading everything I'd brought and anything I could get from the camp library and bookstore.

The bookstore, of course, was all Christian, so comic books about Roger Staubach . . . what was his name? Coach Dingus? Tom Landry. Coach Landry and other illustrious Christian members of the Dallas Cowboys all had comic books. I think every Dallas Cowboy had a comic book about how Christian they were.

I also got introduced to *The Lion, the Witch and the Wardrobe* by C. S. Lewis (the Christian Tolkien) at Mount Hermon. Anyway, I met Marcus when I was finally released from my quarantine. He lived in Oakland in the early seventies, which would explain why he's doing the black power salute in the camp picture from that year. Of course, I'm wearing a *Happy Days* shirt and making the goofiest face possible, negating any coolness.

Back to Sonoma in 1975 and my new pal, Drew. He named me Turtle the first week I showed up wearing a green hooded jacket, the same green jacket my Grandpa George gave me. Drew saw me slouching, trying to be invisible in that stupid fucking jacket, and thought I looked like a turtle.

Drew became a Wrangler jeans–wearing, Copenhagen-chewing shit-kicker, which wasn't weird in Sonoma. He also turned out to be kind of an angry, fucked-up kid. I purposefully stayed out of his way as much as I could. He allegedly put a firecracker up a cat's butt. I don't think he really did that, but that's some fucked-up sociopathic serial killer shit.

I felt pretty picked on my fourth-grade year, but looking back on it now, it wasn't that bad. The teasing and ridicule were periodic and, other than me wearing a green jacket and resembling a shell-wearing reptile and occasionally being called names I didn't understand, not that hurtful.

And I was usually asking for it. I cried in class one day. In my defense Mr. Stork showed us an anti-animal-cruelty video. It showed reenactments of a guy throwing puppies in a bag and chucking it off the freeway and another asshole holding a dog in a bag up to his exhaust pipe. Of course, I cried. It was upsetting.

That same year I bragged about winning the library contest. I then learned you didn't brag about things like that. An older kid was making fun of me and my punch-back was to brag about winning the library reading contest. I sure proved his point.

HIM: "What a dork!"

ME: "Good sir, I will have you know I am no dork. Are you aware of the fact, I ask you, that I have read no fewer than thirty books this summer? I read more books than you or anyone here. You should bow to me, for I am the current and future king of reading in all of Sonoma. Bow to me, I say."

Of course, what I really said was, "Um, shut up, Steve. I'm not a dork. I read more books than anyone in the whole town this summer. And I won ice cream." It didn't get the response I wanted. They laughed. That was the moment everyone but me knew I was a nerd and a dork.

My close friends didn't tease me, and I actually made quite a few good pals in those first couple of years in Sonoma. I wouldn't lose them all 'til the first week of high school. Boom! Stephen King shit!

One of my many bad days, early in the fourth grade, was saved by a mom. Not my mom. I don't even remember what someone was saying to me or who was saying it, but I felt picked on and was visibly upset. Then one of the student's moms, Mrs. Murphy, who volunteered at the school, saw it, and came running over to me. She consoled me. She was a total sweetheart and helped ease the pains that fourth-grade year.

Mrs. Murphy always looked out for me when she was around. She told her son Jeff to be especially nice to me. He was. He was a mature fifth-grader to my naive fourth-grade self. He helped me make friends. I even spent quite a bit of time at their house. Jeff and I didn't have that much in common besides *Planet of the Apes* and both liking his mom's cooking. He once played me his favorite singer, Bette Midler. We listened to her whole record. It didn't stick with me. I just thought she was loud and weird.

Todd McLean was another fifth-grader who was nice to me and had me over a lot, I think because his parents worked with my mom and they were trying to help out. Todd and I didn't have much in common either except humor magazines, like *Dynamite* and *Mad*. But he was a good guy. I peed the bed when I stayed at his house and he never told anyone. I don't think I stayed there again though.

One thing I noticed during the years I was picked on is that someone else always got it worse, like the unfortunate new kid, in fifth grade, who thought it would be cool to brag about beating up his mom. But it wasn't cool to a bunch of fifth-graders—they beat him up. It was ugly gang justice. It kind of freaked me out.

Anthony Italian-Name and Brian Pittland also got it way worse than me. Anthony and his sister were both Italian— notice the last name—and during their awkward years they both had largish, noticeable noses and other prominent features. I hated Turtle—well, Anthony really hated Pinocchio, as did his sister, Fishlips. Anthony would get really upset, and the kids would lean into the teasing. I think I saw that dude scream or cry a couple of times a week the whole school year. He left the next year. I don't fucking blame him.

Brian Pittland would get super wound up when guys teased him, his spazz fuse got shorter and shorter, and bullies would feed off it. I noticed it and still would get upset when kids teased me, playing right into their hands, just like Pittland.

I used anything I could think of to get kids to like me, often resorting to bragging. Suzanne Somers, that actress and exercise equipment spokesperson, is my second cousin. Her mom is my Grandpa George's sister. Little Irish apple-cheeked people, the Turners. Not that it should have, but having a famous cousin didn't really help me that much. Kids thought it was sorta cool, then lame. Sort of cool when she was on *Three's Company*, kinda, sorta cool when I saw her open for furry, flamboyant magician Doug Henning. Not cool at all when she did *She's the Sheriff* and the thing with Bobby from *Dallas*. Lame when she pimped the ThighMaster.

My mom always encouraged me to make contact with Suzanne. I barely knew her, and I didn't want to bug her. Plus, by then, as you'll see later, I was already a comedy snob. I thought I could do better than *She's the Sheriff* and ThighMaster. I was wrong. She sent me a signed poster through Nana Norma; it was the one with the black bathing suit, which at the time I found slightly inappropriate.

That first October in Sonoma I didn't have a ton of friends. This is the excuse I'm giving my mom for the next incident. During Halloween week of 1975 she took me to the haunted house down at the Sonoma Community Center. Well, she didn't take me; she drove me and left me there. I was wearing my Casper the Friendly Ghost costume. And just like Casper, I wasn't doing the scaring. I was nine, and I guess I was too young, and most of the time random adults or even parents accompany little kids so they don't have the shit scared out of them.

It was dark. It was loud. I was fucking nine and, mind you, a fragile, immature nine. I would probably be considered a special needs kid nowadays. I've since met Dr. Drew a couple of times, and he thought I was on the autism spectrum. My therapist says he's full of shit. True story. Anyway, Casper, mask, nine years old, bad mom, dark, loud—it was super spooky. And then someone grabbed me. I had a meltdown. I screamed. I cried. I wanted my mom. Some adults took me out of there. Volunteers sat with me until my mom finally came back. Like, two hours later.

Look, I don't want to paint my mom as shitty. Or, only shitty. She did plenty of great things; she always genuinely loved me, even when I would make her insane later. She encouraged my reading and my creative writing projects I started doing outside of school during the sixth grade. She took me to San Francisco a lot; a love for that amazing city took hold.

She always tried to get me what I wanted. In the really lean years she would put gifts on lay-away until the week of Christmas. Christmas was always a big deal. She took me to the city to go to the Dickens Christmas Fair and *The Nutcracker* or *A Christmas Carol*. She usually dressed me like we had more money than we did. Not important to me, but important to her.

She did a lot of great things, a third paragraph's worth. We went camping at Big Sur, one of California's stunningly beautiful state parks. It's got majestic sequoias or redwoods, and it's right by the ocean. We went with Sherry and almost got killed by a wild boar going through our easily accessible ice chest.

But Mom also left me at a haunted house. Remember? Here's another misstep: we were in Tahoe at Alpine Meadows. I was supposed to be taking a beginning ski lesson, and again my mom left me alone. While I was waiting for the lesson to start I slipped under the lodge. Luckily a couple of adults heard me and made a human chain and got me out. Could have died. Haunted house, skiing accident, almost drowning—I'm noticing a theme. I was left alone a lot for a little guy. I think my mom was hoping I'd get lost or dead.

The upside was that she left me with my favorite people pretty often. I stayed with my Nana Irene a bunch when I lived in San Jose and when we went to Sonoma. I cherished my trips to Sacramento, and I really enjoyed the couple of times my mom would leave me at my grandpa and grandma's in Sonoma. My Grandma Grace was a character and loved cooking for me, and I loved her and always considered her my real grandmother and her four grandchildren my cousins. I always had a blast hanging out with Grandpa George, even when he retired from being Grandpa Baloney.

The big advantage to having three grandmas was that some years I had three Christmases. When I was real young it was four. We would spend Christmas Eve with Nana Norma and Nana Irene, then my mom and I would go home so Santa could visit me at my own house. I'd celebrate Christmas morning with my mom/Santa, go back to Nana's, then spend a couple of hours with my Grandpa George and Grandma Grace. And then a day or two after Christmas we'd go to Sacramento and celebrate again.

In San Jose it was a variation on that with my Grandpa George coming to see us, so I could be a thankless little brat and shit on his gifts. When we lived in Sonoma and I no longer believed in Santa or dreams, we would spend Christmas Eve and Christmas with the two nanas, then drive back to Sonoma after Christmas, see Grandpa George and Grandma Grace, and then we'd go to Sacramento—a four- or five-day holiday.

It was always stressful and chaotic with my mom and my two nanas, but it was loving. We had a lot of laughs until I got weird and moody and started shutting them out. The Christmas trips to Sacramento were always a highlight for me, especially when my mom later sent me solo. I can't tell you enough how much I cherished being with my Grandma Clara. She always had a way of engaging with me and making me feel like the most important kid in the world.

And my Grandpa Ed was pretty playful when I was young. He would get on the floor and wrestle with me, or he'd lay on his back and I'd stand on his hands and he'd lift me up while my grandma or mom steadied me. He always made me giggle when he'd surprise me with a super-dry joke or some fucked-up turn of phrase: "Colder than a well-digger's armpit" got spicier and became "Well-digger's asshole" and "witch's tit" as I got older.

As I said earlier, nerds obsess over their likes and hobbies. If you're my definition of a nerd, you don't like something passively: you like it with passion and scary obsessiveness. Since I was a kid I've obsessed over everything I've ever liked. Looking back on the first things I got into, it wasn't just "like"—it wasn't ever passive at all. Comedy was one of those first loves.

I loved sitcoms at age nine. I ate them up—*Happy Days*, *Laverne and Shirley*, *Welcome Back, Kotter*, *Barney Miller*, and *Chico and the Man*. I learned of stand-up comedy because Chico (Freddie Prinze) was a very famous seventies comic. One of the other earliest stand-up comics I saw or heard—and my favorite, by far—was Steve Martin. I memorized his material and could repeat it to anyone who cared to listen. In sixth grade I saw *The Bad News Bears* several times and quickly wound up knowing that movie backward and forward. What a useless fucking skill, huh? There is a whole chapter coming up about my obsession with comedy and how it paid off.

Before I discovered and was influenced by *Mad*, *Cracked*, and, later, *National Lampoon*, there would be another literary comedic influence. I had liked riddles and jokes and puns already at age nine and would gobble up any kids books I could find, but in fourth grade my mind would be blown when I was in a bookstore with my mom and stumbled upon the greatest book ever, *The Official Polish Joke Book*. I don't even think I knew any Polish people, but the jokes were funny and mean-spirited, so I had to own it.

The best part was when you flipped over the book, it was also *The Official Italian Joke Book*, an equal-opportunity offender. Well, just those two. The jokes were crass and simple, but crowd pleasing, like, "How do you kill an Italian when he's drinking?" "Slam the toilet seat on his head." See: harmless fun. That book changed my life. I memorized most of the book and would recite my favorite jokes back to whomever would listen, and unbeknownst to me I was working on my timing and delivery.

Music was probably the earliest general obsession. Even before I collected toys and comics, I was always obsessed with music. By the time I got to junior high school, that was my biggest hobby—collecting different albums, cassettes, and, later, CDs. All my money went to music; the other hobbies took a backseat for a little bit. Throughout the eighties I was trading albums and recording stuff for friends. I even scalped concert tickets and dreamed of working at a record store.

I only passively liked music before Elvis, though. I had three 45s and a couple of albums before I heard Elvis Presley at my neighbor Liz's house. I thought he was the coolest guy ever the first time I heard him. At eight years old, I started my Elvis Presley phase. Elvis was my first real musical love, before I ever heard of heavy metal. Most of the Elvis I was listening to was pretty dated at the time, from the fifties and sixties. He was already blowing it in real life, but I just knew his songs and his movies from when he was like a hillbilly Fonzie.

By 1976 I had a bunch of Elvis records, spanning his whole career, even one of his gospel records. I was a kid— quit judging. I even did an impression of him to entertain my mom and my grandparents. I'm sure it was spot-on; they were super discerning. I even did my impression for my friends. It didn't go as well. I had a birthday party at a pizza place in Sonoma—must've been my tenth birthday—when I fell off the stage doing the Elvis windmill.

Remember the Elvis windmill? It's different from the Pete Townsend windmill. Elvis would make that kick-ass stance with his one bell-bottomed leg forward and then windmill his arm while he looked super cool pointing at some lady in the audience. Well, I did that, except I pointed at my mom. And my new friends. Then I guess I didn't have my stance perfected or my windmill was too fast—anyway, it got out of control. I fell off the stage and broke my arm.

I took a little shit from my friends who had been there, but I think they mostly felt bad because we were pretty young. I had known a couple of these guys from little league (Larry, Karl, Seth, and Monte) and soccer (my friend Tony), and even though I was the weak spot on the teams, the real alienation hadn't started yet.

Believe it or not, I don't blame my mom for never putting too much emphasis on sports. Sure, she encouraged me to try baseball and soccer, but that was mainly to make friends and try to fit in. Of course, it had the opposite effect: it showed the other kids one of my weaknesses and made me hate sports. I blame sports for being hard and dumb.

I was always a bit behind the other kids in my grade. With my summer birthday, I was slightly younger and more immature. I still loved toys through sixth grade: Hot Wheels and Corgi die-cast cars, the '66 Batmobile, and James Bond's Aston Martin were my main obsessions at nine and ten. I still played with dolls like Big Jim and the Wolfpack, my few Megos, Evel Knievel, SSP Racers, Smash-Up Derby, and TYCO slot cars. Toys kept me young and out of trouble for a while.

Eventually I made it through fourth grade, but not with the help of my fourth-grade teacher, Mr. Stork. He didn't make learning fun; instead, he nasally droned on and ruled with an iron fist. Because I was often bored, I was in trouble with him a lot. He sent me to the principal on the regular, and it felt to me like he often tried to humiliate or embarrass me in front of the other students.

On one of the many days I had detention in Mr. Stork's class instead of recess or lunch, I peed my pants laughing. Sounds more fun than it was. Alone in the class, it was me, my "friend" Larry, Monte, and a kid named Robert, who also wore glasses. I never could figure out why Mr. Stork left all the worst students alone for about fifteen minutes.

We were laughing at some dumb thing my friend Monte was doing. I warned Monte I couldn't control myself, but he kept doing the joke. I peed. A lot. Soaked my pants. At nine. I had to slink off to the office and wear ill-fitting pants from lost-and-found. I definitely lost some cool points with Monte, Larry, and Robert, but they stayed my friends for a while.

My mouth got me in trouble several times at school with Mr. Storky Dork, which, believe it or not, is what my mom called Mr. Stork. Not bad, Mom. My smart-assed tendencies became an even bigger problem in fifth grade. It even got me in trouble at church. One morning after church, during the coffee fellowship hour, I was messing around with my pals. I guess we were too loud or having too much fun because a youth pastor, Eli, grabbed me and scolded me. He was a young dad of two kids with hippie names.

I quipped, like my TV hero that week, Fonzie, "Sit on it, nerd." And then Eli slapped me with his adult-sized hand. He smacked my ear and cheek pretty hard for a hippie Christian. I didn't go to the ground, but it hurt. I should have fallen into a ball and screamed and cried; it stung, and I was in shock. I couldn't believe an adult had just hit me. Neither could the women who witnessed it.

Church women. Elderly church women. He was so fucked. I'm pretty sure he quit that night, because he wasn't there that next week. Eli, his wife, and his kids, Double Rainbow and Jerry Garcia 2,* actually moved. Which is good, because it would have been awkward, as Eli lived in my neighborhood. Come to think of it, those old church ladies may have killed him.

Fifth grade itself wasn't super memorable other than the fact that my teacher, Mrs. Sullivan, would kiss you if you disrupted class or got an answer wrong on a verbal quiz. She didn't kiss us in an inappropriate or awesome way; she just kissed boys' faces to humiliate them. She'd even put lipstick on. Oh yeah, she made a big show of it. You knew you were in trouble when she pulled the lipstick out. It was like she was a pro wrestler, and this was her finishing move.

Needless to say, I got kissed. It was my second kiss following my legendary performance of "Mommy Kissing Santa Claus" at my third-grade Christmas presentation. After Mrs. Sullivan, it would be a little while before I would get kissed again. Mrs. Sullivan was a character. She also treated the best students in the class—like the top five kids, not me—by inviting them to her house to do yard work. Nice treat. No thanks. I'm glad I was a mediocre student.

I should tell you about the dump we lived in, the Glen Ellen Manor Apartments. There were around two hundred tenants in about fourteen buildings. We had a tiny two-bedroom, one-bathroom apartment with a tight floor plan; a narrow, small kitchen; and an adjacent seating area with a miniscule patio off the living room. It wasn't private at all.

---

*I could be totally wrong on the kid's names. It's been a while.

People could look right into our apartment from the court-yard that butted against our patio.

The owner, Mr. Corpi, lived in San Francisco and was a grouchy dick. He was a diminutive ball of a man who always wore pin-striped overalls and a matching train conductor's hat when he climbed out of his Mercedes to fix anything at your apartment. He looked like a dipshit. We never got along, and it got worse as I got older. He always hired fe-male apartment managers, and my mom usually befriended them, which worked out nice when we needed apartment maintenance or the check was late.

In the nine years we lived in Glen Ellen Manor I would make a lot of friends and only a couple of enemies. There were never kids my exact age, but I made friends with older kids and younger kids. One of the older kids, Nathan, would later bully me, and John, another older kid in my courtyard, would wind up being a bad influence on me.

My friendships with the younger kids turned out better. I met a kid named Chris who was a year younger than me, and we are still friends. Chris, unfortunately, was only there on weekends and school breaks with his younger brother when they were visiting their dad, Cliff. I had a lot of great memories hanging out in their room, cranking Van Halen and Iron Maiden and watching Chuck Norris flicks with the boys and their dad.

I was also friendly with a girl named Sophie who was a couple of years younger than me. Her mom was a hippie, and Sophie knocked on my patio sliding glass door one day to tell me her hippie mom was having sex with her dumb hippie boyfriend and the curtains were open. Sure enough, so was the window. I saw and heard everything. Not for long. I was quickly creeped out and ran back to our TV.

In 1976 I was having trouble fitting in at my new school. I still mostly listened to my mom; I wasn't rebelling hard yet. The relationship between me and my mom really started to sour when she met a guy at the pool. That man's name was Ken the Monster. He was born with a different last name. I changed it. Ken the Monster was quite a bit shorter than my mom.

I guess she'd had enough of tall guys dying on her, so she was checking out short, sarcastic, cheapskate, freeloader, asshole guys. He had a mustache and a terrible Hitler-esque hair helmet. She and the Monster dated about six years. We fought a little in the beginning of their relationship. Later he moved in, and we fought all the time. Maybe I was bummed about losing my wrestling partner. I didn't hate him at first, but by the time he moved out I hated him more than I hate homophobia and bad music.

Around 1976 was when I really got into comic books and superheroes. I always liked Marvel and DC equally. Spidey and Bats are still my two favorites. They were my first nerdy likes. I never had any nerdy friends, so I never had anyone tell me you had to pick a publisher, either Marvel or DC. I turned ten during the summer of '76 and collected those cool bicentennial issues that DC Comics did that year. Every comic did a special issue that July, and that summer I was traveling around California, Oregon, and Nevada in a camper with my grandparents, Ed and Clara. It was a great trip with my two favorite people at the time.

I remember stopping at newsstands and liquor stores during the couple-week road trip and combing the comic book section for the "stars and stripes" DC banner that indicated they were special. I think I bought around twelve of a

possible thirty, only the few heroes I was into. I wasn't a com-
plete-ist nerd yet or I would have had the whole collection.

Speaking of cool-ass grandparents who encouraged my
comic book reading. Meanwhile, in Redwood City, Nana
Irene was collecting the *Amazing Spider-Man* comic strip that
ran in the *San Francisco Chronicle*. John Romita Sr. drew it
and it's still my favorite version of Spider-Man. She bought
a scrapbook, clipped the daily strips and the Sunday edition
color version, and collected them all in a homemade comic
book. Amazing Nana is more like it.

Sometime in the summer of 1976 I got into *Jaws*. I was
hooked at the trailer and the TV ads. And then I saw it in
a dark theater in Santa Rosa. Not even a year after being
scared shitless in my town's tiny, shitty haunted house, I
was seeing a terrifying thriller. By myself. It was pretty life
changing. I didn't find the shark that scary after my first
shocking viewing; I just thought it was the coolest thing I'd
ever seen. Sure, the jump-scares got me. I think the scariest
thing I'd ever seen at that point was a TV edited version of
Psycho.

So the jump-scare with Ben Gardner's head popping at
the camera in the hull of Ben's submerged boat completely
got me. And everyone else in the theater. I'd never experienced anything like that before. That year I got really into
Jaws. I saw it a bunch of times in my town's shitty theater
because back then movies stayed in the theater for a year
if they continued to do well. And at that point *Jaws* was the
biggest movie ever. (GRANDPA VOICE) This was before
DVD or even VHS . . . snore . . . I'm old. The Sebastiani
Theatre, the only movie game in my small town, wasn't actually shitty. Not the whole time.

In the seventies the Sebastiani was awesome. It was a beautiful old theater in the middle of our quaint town square. And it became the first movie theater my mom would just drop me off at. I think she liked not having to see my "ludicrous" movies anymore. So at that point of my life, outside of the record store and anyplace that served pizza, it was my favorite place in town. Later I would take the bus and even later drive the half hour or so to see movies, and the old Sebastiani Theatre started to show its age. In the early nineties somebody restored it and made it cool again. It's still open now. No one leveled it and put in a Pottery Barn—fucking amazing. Thanks, Obama. Seriously, thanks.

I loved Bruce the shark, but it was the chemistry of the three main characters—Brody, Hooper, and ol' Quint—that kept me going back. I read the book a couple of times and wore the crap out of my powder blue T-shirt with the famous cover art. I still have a framed movie poster and often wear my new powder-blue *Jaws* T-shirt and bump the soundtrack on vinyl. There is definitely an argument for *Jaws* being the first thing I was nerdy about. I read *Jaws Log* by Carl Gottlieb, a book that came out that year describing the harrowing process of making the movie. For sure, this was the first time I read a "Making of . . ." book. After my sixth viewing I thought that Ben Gardner's head was actually an homage to Hitchcock.

I felt it could be no coincidence that the head in the biggest jump-scare of the movie was bald and pale like Hitchcock and, therefore, a winking Hitchcock cameo. Stretch, I know. But I was ten years old and alone in a movie theater a lot. I was happily edging into *Jaws* nerd territory. Fuck that "*Jaws* didn't scare me" shit. It absolutely did. Turns out, I like being scared. I was terrified of real sharks but also completely fascinated by them. I thought great whites were the coolest thing ever; they made dinosaurs look like a bunch of giant dead idiots.

Though I had no desire to swim in the ocean for a while. My fear and respect for sharks led me away from the water. Before *Jaws*, thanks to Jacques Cousteau being massive on public television, I owned and loved a collection of marine biology encyclopedias he published. My mom bought me the books through PBS: at age eight I had wanted to be a marine biologist. No longer. Thanks, *Jaws*. Sure, the marine biologist lives in the movie, but fuck that—the shark cage scene with Richard Dreyfuss is terrifying.

That year I wrote about great whites as much as possible. *Jaws* even made it to school. I wrote a fifth-grade book report on the Peter Benchley book, *Jaws*, and did a researched report on great whites, where I quoted the *Jaws Log* and *Jaws* screenwriter Carl Gottlieb. I even wrote short stories about shark attacks for myself. What a *Jaws* dork.

By the way, the Benchley source material, *Jaws*, had a ton of inappropriate shit in it that didn't make the Spielberg classic or my classic fifth-grade report. Way more fucking. Oral sex, cheating subplot, and fucking. Not much fucking in the film *Jaws*, unless you consider Quint's death. He gets pretty fucked.

But the book *Jaws*—lots of fucking. It's dirty. I guess I'm saying that movie could've used more fucking. I wouldn't have called myself a *Jaws* nerd at age ten, but I would now. Twelve years ago I got to live out the *Jaws* nerd dream and spend two days on Martha's Vineyard on the Comedians of Comedy tour with Zach Galifianakis and Patton Oswalt quoting the movie while we drove around the island looking at local sites. Apropos of fucking nothing, I had a Hitler mustache that day. Don't ask.

Okay, I had been shaving every day from a full beard down to a Hitler. That was the plan, and I carried it out to completion. For no one. Actually, the crew and my friends loved it.

For my fiftieth birthday my wife and Patton rented a theater and showed a great print of *Jaws* to all my friends. One of my buddies grew up in Nantucket, so he never saw *Jaws* growing up because he didn't want it scaring him out of the water. He watched it for the first time with my rowdy friends and loved it.

So, back to the summer of '76, when Steven Spielberg ruled my cinematic world. I wouldn't know true nerdy movie worship until a year later when his chubby, bearded friend from USC would make my new Best Movie Ever and dethrone Spielberg as my favorite director for a little while. And not to sell *Jaws* short, the movie easily makes my top-five films of all time. Also included are *Star Wars*: *A New Hope*, *Empire Strikes Back*, *Die Hard*, and *Halloween*. Or *Fast Times at Ridgemont High*. Or *Raiders of the Lost Ark*. Or *Goodfellas*. Or *Groundhog Day*. Or John Carpenter's *The Thing*. That fifth one is hard.

You know what all those movies could've used, though? No, not more fucking. They all could use a funny fat kid who's always sloppily eating a chocolate bar and saying, "I need this for energy!" Every movie would be better with that. Sure, I was pretty into *Jaws*, but I wasn't truly obsessed yet. *Yet*. A couple of months later I would know true obsession. It came to me in October of '76 when I found four kooks from New York City wearing makeup and superhero costumes: ABBA.

Just kidding, silly. I'm talking about the band KISS. I really, really liked *Jaws*, but, pucker up, ladies, you're about to meet a full-on KISS nerd.

FOUR

KISS: ARMY OF ONE

Most KISS fans, I assume, found KISS through the usual different routes—their older brother, the cool guy who smelled weird at the record store, that Halloween special with that one dude, or because they were on the news for scaring Christians. Not this KISS fan. I found the band that changed my life while hiding from ridicule in the school library. Like a huge fucking nerd.

I found KISS in the Dunbar Elementary school library. Actually, they found me. Brian Posehn, the rocker nerd, didn't really even exist before KISS. I hadn't heard anything heavier than Cher and Elvis pre-KISS, and I don't even think I knew "hard rock" was a thing. At that point I thought "rock" was The Beatles and "rock and roll" was fifties music.

Until KISS I was just a kid drinking the homogenized milk that is pop music, and the four larger-than-life members of KISS hit a power chord. And Paul Stanley, with his lovable New York accent, said, "Hey young milk drinker, since I guess we're sticking with that metaphor, did you know that milk could be chocolate or strawberry flavored and music doesn't have to sound like it's comin' from your granny's radio? So get on your knees and open wide for the hottest band in the world, KISS!"

So one fall day during lunch KISS found me in my nerdy hiding place. The fucking library. It had already gotten me into trouble. I know why I was drawn to the library—I loved escaping into a book. It had been my go-to for a couple of years. I went there to forget about the other kids, my annoying teachers, and my mom. Truth is, I didn't have a ton of friends, and the library wasn't helping: "Hey friendless guy, you know where you'll really not find friends? The library."

As I said in the opening, I liked music before KISS. Liked, not loved. Music such as Olivia Newton John, Cher, and Mac Davis—you know, music? I had 45s of their singles, a Mac Davis LP with "Stop and Smell the Roses" on it, an Olivia Newton John LP, and a couple of Elvis records—in 1975 that was my entire record collection. Now I have hundreds of albums. I blame KISS. Sure, I really liked Olivia Newton John for almost two years. I thought she was pretty and had a pretty voice. I was eight, remember.

I LIKED CHER for her storytelling songs. She sang of being a half-breed* and about gypsies, tramps and also thieves.† And Cher had long hair like my mom's friend Anne. I liked Mac Davis for who fucking knows why. And yeah, I liked Elvis. All of America did.

My friend Audrey, who also lived in my Nana Irene's apartment complex in Redwood City, played me her K-Tel hits album, current big songs of 1975. I dabbled in pop. Maybe even just to not look weird around her. It didn't stick. I didn't love music that felt like it was made for kids: The Osmonds, The Bay City Rollers, The Jackson Five. I knew those bands; I knew their hit songs. They just didn't move me.

---

*See Cher song, "Half-Breed."
†See Cher song, "Gypsies, Tramps and Thieves."

That was also my first exposure to The Who. Unfortunately I didn't hear their good stuff first. I heard "Squeeze Box" on one of those K-Tel records and thought they were silly. I'd also heard a couple of Beatles songs at my Nana Norma's; she had some of my Uncle Gary's records and an old record player in the guest room at her condo. My cousin Todd and I would entertain ourselves for hours. At that point "Day Tripper" was my favorite.

Back to my library nerdhole, I don't remember what I was reading that day, but Beverly Cleary or Roald Dahl probably wrote it, or it featured the Hardy boys. Then I heard it—the greatest hard-rock song of all fucking time, "Detroit Rock City," on 45.

I was ten, and at the end of the song the car crashes and the narrator dies. Do you know how cool that was to me at the time? By the time the vocals started, I was so in. I know for a fact I had never heard anything that hard or aggressive before that, certainly not The Bay City Rollers—Mac Davis didn't rock like this. So I was all in, as they say in Vegas, Reno, Atlantic City, and really any place with legal gambling.

Then after three minutes of the best thing I'd ever heard, the song ends on a CAR CRASH! I was already a fan of story songs like Cher's work and Kenny Rogers's "Coward of the County," and this was, at the time, the coolest story song I'd ever heard. Scratch that. I didn't hear it—I felt it.

It was the coolest thing I'd ever experienced at that point. I was a KISS fan, whatever KISS was. And this was before I knew what they looked like and before I heard their other classic songs like, "Strutter," "Cold Gin," and fucking "Black Diamond."

I wish I could recreate the joy I felt when I found the KISS *Destroyer* LP. I had directed my mom to the only game in town for vinyl, the Wooden Nickel Record Store. It was near my Grandpa George's house in a mini-mall between a liquor store and a Chinese restaurant in downtown Sonoma.

The Dan Fogelberg–looking owner directed me right to the K's in the rock section. There it was: KISS: *Destroyer*. The cover, a revelation, was a comic book come to life.

The iconic cover features a painting of Paul, Gene, Ace, and Peter with their thematic face paint, matching outfits, and giant boots ruling an apocalyptic wasteland. I would later find out their mortal names, but when I learned their KISS names and roles, that's what stuck.

From left to right, it was Paul Stanley, the Star Child. Paul played rhythm guitars and lead vocals. His symbol was the star, and because of his abundant chest hair and lead singer status, he was known as the Lover and Star Man.

Next was Peter Criss, the Cat. Also known as the Cat-Man, he was the drummer. He also sang on a couple of songs. He had kitty whiskers and green cat eyes—hence the cat. No third nickname for him, though. He's just the Cat or Cat-Man. Kitty-Man didn't stick.

Next to the Cat-Man, of course, is Ace Frehley, the Spaceman. I've also heard him called the Space Ace and the Ace Man. I guess his silvery makeup looked "spacey," sure. Ace was the lead guitar player and singer of "Shock Me" and "Rocket Ride." Get it? Rocket? Space?

And who could forget little Gene Simmons, the demon? No one: Gene wouldn't let you forget him. Gene played bass and sang. Sometimes his bass looks like an axe, and demonic makeup and proclivity to blood and fire helped cement his "scar" Demon persona.

These four characters from "space" or "hell" and "two other places" looked to be traipsing around after the end of the world, and they didn't seem that bothered by it. They kinda look like they're dancing. I didn't know what to think. This feeling was new. Hero worship?

I loved Batman, Superman, and Spider-Man. I also loved Evel Knievel and *Jaws*. But before KISS I had never been obsessed with anything. KISS wasn't just a band; they were superheroes of rock. KISS could beat up Spidey, Bats, and Supes with their kick-ass guitars and punch Jaws in the nuts with their bass and drums.

My next KISS purchase was *Rock and Roll Over*. It was released later that same year. It's kind of crazy that they had two classic albums out eight months apart. *Rock and Roll . . .* came out soon after I became a KISS fan, and I went to the record store at the Santa Rosa mall on a mission to get it.

That evening in my tiny room, surrounded by KISS and Farrah Fawcett posters, while I sat on my NFL bedsheets, I excitedly listened to side one of *Rock and Roll . . .* for the first time. It started with "I Want You" and "Take Me," which provided a nice lead-in to the instant KISS klassics, "Calling Dr. Love," "Ladies Room," and then "Baby Driver."

Side two had "Love 'Em and Leave 'Em," "Mr. Speed," and "See You in Your Dreams," followed by two of my favorites, the almost pretty "Hard Luck Woman" and the ultimate sing-along ode to doin' it, "Makin' Love." And then another classic KISS album is complete, four pieces of hard-rock perfection and a couple of clunkers.

Because the members of KISS were and are the best marketers and always on brand before that was a thing, the album came with a sticker, so you know ten-year-old sticker-loving me was stoked. It went on my toy trunk. I was so young that I still had my fucking toy trunk. I wish I still had my fucking toy trunk.

In 1977 two of my favorite things collided when the guys joined with Marvel Comics to release the first KISS comic book. Of course, I had to own it forever. It was advertised as being printed in the blood of the band. Super-metal, of course—they probably only gave less than an ounce of blood.

But it was enough to make me think it was the coolest thing I'd ever heard of. The comic told a sloppy story of four New Yorkers who find a small, strange box. Of course, they open it and, of course, it turns them into KISS. Then they use their KISS powers, Gene spits fire at them, Paul tries to fuck their girlfriend, and Peter and Ace get drunk and wind up in trouble.

Actually, I think only the part with Gene shooting fire happens. Later in the book you get cameos from all the Marvel biggies, like Spidey and Cap. It also featured KISS fighting the Devil and then Dr. Doom. Because in the seventies Marvel world, Doom was scarier.

In the summer of 1977 I would go even deeper into KISS when *Love Gun* was released. I loved that record as soon as I could get it home, out of my mom's Pinto station wagon, and onto our turntable. I was still a vinyl kid at this point. *Love Gun* is maybe the second best of the bunch in my opinion.

And it came with a cardboard "LOVE GUN"—better than a sticker. Something was working; they made six great records in eight short years. Another iconic cover, in this one they're sexual superheroes. The guys are surrounded by lots of scantily clad women wearing KISS face paint. They're clearly about to be serviced.

AFTER LOVE GUN I joined the army—the KISS Army. It's the only Army I'd ever want to join, really. And it's probably the only army that would ever take me. Not probably. For certain. That said, forty years later I am still a member of the KISS Army.

The KISS Army is the shittiest army. Salvation Army would kick our asses. The army some dude made with his four angry friends to fight the leaders of their tiny village in some place I've never heard of could defeat the KISS Army.

Here are just three differences between the real US Army and the KISS Army. Real Army: you fight for a cause, learn unity, and they prepare you for life. KISS Army: Fight for a cause? To rock and roll and party every day, mother *&%er! Unity? Have you seen KISS fans? They look like me. And worse. Do you want to be a part of that group?

And how did being in the KISS Army prepare me for life? Disappointment. They taught me about disappointment. But not for another two years. It's still the fall of 1977, KISS, *Alive II* was released. I couldn't wait until KISS-mas. My mom told me it would be a great Christmas present, being that it was a double record and therefore double priced. I convinced her I would die if I had to wait 'til December 25.

We went to the Warehouse Records in Terra Linda to purchase it, like a good little member of the KISS Army. Terra Linda is a suburb of the already suburban Marin County. It's all malls, luxury car dealers, and wife swapping. It was the same Warehouse where I would later discover Randy

Rhoads. Two good things about my mom are she loved leaving Sonoma and she loved malls.

I quickly knew which malls within a fifty-mile radius had which record stores. And in the eighties some malls had more than one record store. I knew them all. And soon their employees would know me.

With *Alive II* and pretty much every other KISS record, I was first drawn to the cover. Besides *Frampton Comes Alive*, it's probably the most iconic *Live* album cover of the seventies. It's simple and perfect. Speaking of icons, you can't really beat the classic blue-and-red KISS logo, the title, *Alive II*, in blood red, and featuring four classic solo live shots of the guys. Gene won me over that time with his sweaty, bloody face—he looked absolutely demonic in that pic and pretty badass.

If you don't know that the *Live* recording starts with the announcement, "You wanted the best and you got the best . . . the hottest band in the world, KISS," then maybe we can never be friends. Well, I guess you know it now. Dammit.

My mom was always supportive of my KISS fandom— well, mostly. One day she would betray me and awaken the wrath of the KISS Army, but first this happened. In 1977 my Sunday school teacher, Miss Elaine, made my day one morning when she told us we were all going to decorate our classroom. We were allowed to each bring one poster from home. Obviously I was ecstatic and knew exactly what my poster contribution would be.

I decided not to sacrifice one of my home posters; instead, we went to my go-to Santa Rosa poster shop, International Imports. It was part Pier One and part head shop. Man, I was clueless at that age: I had no idea why it smelled like that—the air was thick with incense and patchouli. It smelled like Han Solo cut a hippy open. Who's Han Solo? Read the next chapter.

I found exactly what I had in mind, a KISS *Alive II* poster featuring two pictures of Gene in all his gory glory, spitting fire in one shot and the classic bloody, sweaty shot from the cover. I was ecstatic again. That was the poster. It was the one.

So the next weekend I took it to Sunday school for our classroom. Miss Elaine let us all put our posters up. Of course, most of the girls had posters with all the normal eleven-year-old girly things like the classic kitty on a branch saying, "hang in there, baby," a basket of puppies, and wild animals.

Cute wild animals, of course, and then the guys had, like, monster trucks and dirt bikes. I think there was a Spider-Man poster even. But I put my KISS poster up, was very proud, and didn't get much of a reaction from the other kids. And Miss Elaine clearly just tolerated it.

My Spidey sense should have warned me. Next week I came back to class and it was . . . gone. It was in the garbage, in shreds. It had clearly been ripped off the wall in frustration.

Our church was this old renovated barn because I grew up in kind of a farm town. Although it's touristy, it's mainly known for wineries and the farming industry, and it was an old barn—a huge old barn—and they gutted and renovated it just a couple of years before we got there.

We started going there in '76, once we got situated in Sonoma. My mom found the church; it was close by, I could ride my bike there, and I did. I loved it. I was really in-volved, but this was kind of the beginning of the end with me and organized religion. This story and the youth leader, Eli, hitting me made me not really trust some adults at the church and question their Christianity.

The pastor had been giving a tour of the church, showing it to other pastors from another church. That happened all the time. Our pastor was really proud of the renovations and showed our room, which had been a horse stall or something like that, before we sat in there and learned about Noah and everything else.

So I guess the pastor walks in and shows these people this room, " . . . for the kids, these rooms used to be horse stalls and . . . what the, what the devil?" Kinda comical, when you think of it. Walks in, puppies, kitties, trucks, motorcycles, devil. There is the devil, or the Demon, Gene Simmons covered in blood and sweaty and looking evil, which was awesome to me, but scary to these people. And then in the other shot he's shooting fire, another thing associated with the devil: fire and heat sources.

I kind of understand the situation now, but at eleven years old I was pissed to see my poster torn to shreds in a garbage can. So I guess he walked in, they were shocked at the travesty, and he flipped out and tore it off the wall. I don't know if he made a big show in front of everybody like, "We will not have this here. . . . Oh no, Satan will not darken our doors and appear on our walls." And he ripped it into five pieces and threw it in the trash.

Clearly a show of power: "Take that shit elsewhere, Satan." Here's where Carole stepped in. I was upset, I told Carole, so she was upset. I was using my own money to decorate the room, and this happened. So it didn't matter that it was KISS, that it was blood, and that Gene was a demon, because she thought it was just entertainment and harmless. The same way she felt about TV and movies until I ruined everything and threatened Ken the Monster that I wished Starsky and Hutch would kill him, but that's later.

My mom confronted the pastor and the deacons. Our pastor at the time—I wish I could remember his name—came and apologized to me that Tuesday. Pastor Whatshisfuck gave me a fresh new poster and told me, "I'm sorry. We walked in, and it upset me." He told me the whole story and that he thought it was inappropriate for church and that he understood what Miss Elaine told us, but this was beyond the limit.

He gave me a new poster but with one rule: I had to leave it at home. Pretty shitty. And it wasn't even the same KISS poster, which was also disappointing. It was bicentennial themed, from 1976. The poster said, "Spirit of '76," and the members of KISS are all dressed like Revolutionary War soldiers.

They're in costume, but the theme is full bicentennial. Paul has a guitar around his neck, Gene is waving the American flag, who knows what the fuck Ace is doing, and Peter Criss is playing a snare drum and has a bandage around his head and there's blood on it. So when I said that's not the same poster, the pastor said, "Well, it's got blood on it."

So, thanks, Pastor Whatshisfuck. The point of the story is that I really like that my mom had my back then. That's always been one of my favorite memories of her. I know no matter what, she always thought that I was smart or mature enough to handle entertainment and know that it was just that: entertainment. She always trusted that I was a smart enough kid and didn't get into too much trouble. Until my high school years.

Released in April of 1978, *Double Platinum* was my next KISS vinyl purchase. I went to the state hospital store to get it. My buddy Russ worked at a state hospital restaurant connected to the store. Residents and employees shopped and ate there. I did too. I would visit Russ on my bike; the burgers and fries were classic diner style and frigging awesome.

The hospital store always had a decent vinyl and cassette section. *Double Platinum* was their first greatest hits record, and at that point I had most of their records, so it didn't have a ton of songs I didn't already have. The highlight for me was "Strutter 78," an update of a three-year-old song that I actually find superior to the '75 original.

It was the first time I owned a couple of their songs like "I Wanna Rock and Roll All Night . . ." When I originally heard the lyrics "I wanna rock and roll all night . . . and party every day," my dumb ass thought they said, "And part of every day." Which initially made me question their dedication to rock and roll. And, yeah, I know that joke is in the movie *Role Models*, but this is my real life.

In the summer of 1978 I met another kid in my apartment complex through my friend John. John, who lived across from us, was two years older than me. So was this other kid. We went to his apartment to listen to KISS. He was a bigger KISS nerd than me; he had their first double live album, *Alive!*. I had never seen it outside of a record store. Inside is the classic shot of a KISS audience in Detroit or Chicago or some other place with a local arena and seventies-style stoners.

The first thing I observed was how seventies everybody looked and how smoky it was. And how some guys in the crowd looked really happy to be there, and a lot of the kids seemed to have something small and white in their hands.

And some of them were sucking on it. What was it? It looked different from cigarettes. My mom used to smoke cigarettes, and she never looked this happy. What the heck were these cool kids smoking?

John and his friend, the KISS nerd, laughed. "Oh man, those are joints. They're smoking marijuana—grass, dope, weed." Me: "Wow, that looks cool." John: "Do you want to try some?" "Nope. No, thank you. I'm gonna head back to my apartment. I think my mom is making something mediocre." I know I've shat on my mom a lot in this book so far, but her cooking is really terrible.

I didn't know my mom's cooking sucked 'til I went to restaurants and met girls who could cook. My mom was born without a sense of smell, which would come in handy when I did smoke marijuana, grass, dope, and weed, but what it meant growing up was that the food wasn't seasoned well or even cooked properly most of the time. No sense of smell. No sense of taste.

Speaking of no sense of taste, my favorite member of KISS shifted over the years. I liked Paul first because he was the lead singer, and then I was a Gene guy because of his lead vocals on "God of Thunder." Oh, and because of the blood and fire and just being a scary-looking dude.

Then came my Ace phase. Ace was the coolest; he was from space. The original Space Ace. He was the Silver Surfer, if Norrin Radd, the surfer, ripped on a Les Paul. The solo records released in '78 solidified my Ace love. His album had "New York Groove," such a fucking catchy song.

In my opinion "New York Groove" is the best song on any of the solo discs. I'm really not sure how KISS could let a dude like that go. Oh yeah, booze and drugs. I even dressed as Ace Frehley. Tony's mom, Billie, my Cub Scout den mother, made my Ace costume. It was based on the late-seventies Ace costume, with the silver foam shoulder pads forming a "V" on the chest.

The rest of the costume was a black body suit with matching silver foam boot covers. I wore the costume twice, for Halloween 1978 and for my seventh-grade drama class lip sync, "Rocket Ride," an Ace Frehley classic. Honestly, it's a weak spot on *Alive II*, but I was an Ace guy, and it seemed like the obvious choice.

I had a cardboard Les Paul with a smoke bomb strapped to it for the drama class presentation. I lit it and smoked out the whole class. I think a kid would get sent home for that today. My drama teacher ruled, though. She was this attractive young lady who worshipped Barbra Streisand and Bette Midler and was so excited about drama and acting that she made the class super fun and inspiring.

She encouraged my silly side and helped make my junior high experience slightly less painful. Her class was a daily high point for me. And I had a crush on her. There was a rumor she fucked our principal, though, so I guess I didn't have a shot.

I wish I had pictures of me in the Ace costume. I don't have tons of pics of myself growing up outside of baby photos and holiday shots. My mom wasn't around for trick-or-treating to take an Ace Frehley picture that year. I was at Tony's house, so Billie could dress me in my kick-ass costume and apply my makeup.

I was pretty mad at my mom that week anyway, and KISS was at the core of it. October 28, 1978, was the day of one of my greatest disappointments in my life. It was the night *KISS Meets the Phantom of the Park* aired on network TV. And I fucking missed it.

They had been on other people's variety shows. They had done an appearance, I believe, on Sonny and Cher, and they did a Paul Lynde Halloween special. But they had never had their own TV movie. *KISS Meets the Phantom of the Park* was to be their first movie. I was beyond stoked. I couldn't believe I was gonna see my four heroes on TV.

I started planning that evening. I would camp in front of the TV 'til it happened—I was going to need a lot of pee jars. Then my mom announces that we're going to Snookie's house. Who's Snookie? My mom's friend Anna had a sister named Snookie. Anna worked with my mom and was the first friend she made in Sonoma.

Anna was a teacher of developmentally disabled people, so obviously she's a really nice lady and had her heart in the right place. But she actually said at one point to my mom when I started comedy that she didn't like humor or comedy, that she didn't get humor or find it funny. Humor doesn't get you either, Anna.

Anyway, that night we were going to her sister Snookie's house in the hills. Snookie was a real person, not the woman from that terrible Jersey show. This is the seventies, remember. So I'm excited. I'm a little bummed I'm gonna have to watch *KISS Meets the Phantom of the Park* on somebody else's TV, but I'll make do. At least I get to watch it, right?

Nope. We got there, the TV wasn't working, she lived in the hills, didn't get great reception, didn't have cable—I think that was cable time by '78—but the point was that it was a no-go. It wasn't happening. I threw a tantrum, had a meltdown, an epic shit-fit. I hated my mom. I'm pretty sure I told her I hated her.

I'm sure that was probably the first time I told her I hated her. I'd never really been that upset or felt those kinds of feelings at that point. Not until junior high or high school did she become really hard to get along with, when Ken the Monster stepped into our lives. Then we would really clash.

But before Ken and puberty my mom and I didn't really get heated when we would butt heads. Besides minor beefs over chores and school grades, I was an easy kid. I just read, listened to music, stayed out of her way, and enjoyed things.

But here was this thing I enjoyed, KISS, and she ruined it. She told me I was going to be able to watch it at Snookie's. And this is pre-VCR, of course: I was fucked. There was no way I was ever going to see KISS in their televised glory.

There's no way I was gonna be walking down the hallway of the convention center twenty years later and see *Kiss Meets the Phantom* on VHS. I did not think that would ever, ever happen. It did, and then of course because KISS is KISS, they put it out on DVD. I have the entire collection of *KISSology*. Brag.

But that night I didn't know I would be able to see it ever again. I was twelve and furious. And it got ugly fast. She walked outside with me because I threw a fit inside. I remember being on Snookie's patio and losing my goddamn mind—I can't believe this happened: my mom betrayed me.

She betrayed the KISS Army. It was an insurrection. I was a martyr. I wasn't sure what those words meant back then. I ruined the evening; after we ate whatever Crock Pot–made meal Snookie prepared, we left early. And I was the worst the whole ride home; I gave her the silent treatment for a while.

I didn't let her off the hook probably ever, really. I still don't know if, by telling the story, I'm actually letting her off the hook. I know she couldn't control it, but we should've stayed home and just watched it on our TV. My way or the highway.

KISS Meets the Phantom . . . was a big one for any KISS fan growing up in the seventies, and I still resent my mom because of my personal experience with that movie. I didn't see *Phantom* for a long time. It really is terrible too. Turns out, I didn't miss shit. It was totally not worth my legendary meltdown. Kids are dicks.

During the summer of '79 I finally secured my own copy of *Alive I*. It featured a bunch of great early KISS songs, including "C'mon and Love Me," maybe the greatest dumbest song ever, featuring the greatest, terrible line in an already terrible song: "You were distant, now you're nearer, I can feel your face inside the mirror. . . ." Oh boy. "The lights are out, and I can feel you, baby, with my hand"—I can't think of dumber lyrics than those. And yet I sing them to my wife all the time. I once whispered them to her as Paul Stanley walked by her. She was a champ for not peeing her pants.

Really some of the dumbest lyrics ever, like "Barbie Girl" terrible. Maybe it's not a coincidence that one of the bands I left them for in high school was Rush, writers of some of the smartest songs in rock. So, reader, I ask you: What is the DUMBER KISS SONG: "Do You Love Me" or "C'mon and Love Me" or "Dr. Love" or "Ladies Room" or "Lick It Up"?

At the same time I started with KISS, there were outside influences—school, TV, radio—that pushed music toward my easily influenced young brain. Okay, I'll get right to it: I had a disco phase. It didn't last long, just a small chunk of 1978. Disco was massive in '78. Even in my small town. I never saw *Saturday Night Fever*, but I played the shit out of the record. I also owned a K-Tel's Greatest Disco Hits, where there were thirty disco songs crammed onto one LP.

That Christmas I asked for and received a KC and the Sunshine Band album. The Bee Gees and KC and the Sunshine Band were my favorites. I would argue they were the best of the bunch. I don't know who I would argue that with. I even took a disco lesson and had my mom buy me an ugly blue silk disco shirt. Disco was pervasive, and I was young.

My disco phase didn't last long. KISS was a gateway. Without KISS I'm not sure I would have gotten into AC/DC, UFO, Van Halen, or anyone who came later. After my short disco phase I wanted my rock itch scratched. I went from the *Saturday Night Fever* soundtrack to Fleetwood Mac's *Rumours*.

I joined one of those record clubs so I could get the earlier KISS albums. I also acquired ELO, Queen, and Foreigner. By the time KISS released their disco song in '79, I was a Zeppelin fan and checking out what else hard rock had to offer. It was all over for me and anything that didn't rock. Even "Beth" was played less.

So when I heard "I Was Made for Loving You," with that slick disco production and that fabricated-sounding groove, I went through, like, twenty stages of grief. I know there's only twelve, but I went through twenty.

I'm not totally sure about my dates of KISStory, I'm not a stickler for KISStorical accuracy. No KISStorian am I. But I think KISS first lost me around '79 when they took off their makeup and fired the guy I loved the most, Ace Frehley, and did a disco song. That was followed by *Phantom Menace*–like disappointment.

Here's where KISS lost me the first time: *Dynasty*. The two biggest things in the music world in the late seventies were KISS and disco; then KISS decided to go disco—how could they lose? Well, kids like me who worshipped KISS also hated disco, that's how they lost. I have a true love-hate relationship with *Dynasty*. I used to totally hate it, but now I love it. It will forever be known as the disco record. *KISSCO*. Even the insert is disco—bright flashes of colors obscure the classic logo.

One funny thing about KISS is, besides singing about girls, they mentioned partying quite a bit—such as in "Cold Gin" and even in "Detroit Rock City"—but the main two guys, Paul and Gene, never drank or did drugs. Ace and Peter did their best to make up for it, which is why they were both booted. Apparently, during the recording of this record Ace was wasted and angry the whole time. I do not blame him. He either quit right after *Dynasty* or was fired, depends whose story you're hearing.

After *Dynasty* I was out too. That was it for me as a KISS fan. I remember a feeling of *meh* when KISS, *Unmasked* came out in 1980 and again the next year, when *The Elder* dropped. A KISS concept record? No thanks. I didn't even buy *The Elder* 'til last year so I could fill out my collection. It's actually kind of entertaining in its shittiness.

I bought *Unmasked* when it came out from the state hospital store. I returned it for credit. I didn't love the first couple of records without Ace; they wouldn't win me back for a few years until *Creatures of the Night* and *Lick It Up*.

During a time when I was getting into poppy-sounding metal like Mötley Crüe and Ratt, KISS went for their version of that sound. I'm a fan of early-eighties KISS, the Vinnie Vincent/Mark St. John era. I liked both Ace replacements, even though I was sad he was gone.

St. John had a debilitating case of arthritis, which was bad for a young guitar player. He couldn't play guitar so he only played on one record, *Animalize*, but they both made an impression on me. I actually still like the Vinnie Vincent Invasion records, because of the over the top aspect of his playing and his flamboyant persona. Vinnie has had a pretty public downslide. The dude is a mess now. But he ripped and his hair was fucking awesome in the old days. And then there is the tragic, short life of Eric Carr. There is kind of some bad luck attached to being a replacement player in KISS.

Where KISS lost me the second time: "God Gave Rock and Roll to You." Because, yes, I liked the commercial direction KISS originally took in the eighties, but after *Animalize*, like a lot of those "hair metal" bands, it got slicker and more commercial. Ugh! So cheesy, especially compared to the other shit I was listening to at the time. "Tears Are Falling" and "God Gave Rock and Roll to You" didn't stand up to Exodus and Anthrax.

I've met the guys in KISS over the years—well, three of them. I haven't run into Peter, but I have met the other three original members, Ace, Gene, and Paul. Of course, Ace was my favorite. But I'll save that for later when I discuss the good and bad sides of meeting your heroes.

Ultimately, I still love KISS. Sure, I've had problems with some of the directions they've taken over the years— touring without the original guys but using their makeup, the Rock and Roll Hall of Fame weirdness, the gross money grabs like the KISS pinball machine (which is super cool and not douchey at all, because I own one), the KISS coffin (Dimebag is buried in one, and I heard Gene didn't charge him—what a good guy) and especially KISS Hello Kitty. But I'm still KISS Army for life. (By the way, what fucking weirdos were stoked when Hello Kitty finally teamed up with KISS?)

Sure, it's been hard to be a KISS fan for forty years. I feel like I've spent more time being annoyed or disappointed with KISS than I have loving them. But nothing compares to the amount of annoyance and disappointment and out-and-out hatred I would come to feel for something I previously loved held up to the things I've felt about *Star Wars*.

FIVE

STAR WARS: MY OBSESSION WITH THE ORIGINAL TRILOGY, THE UNHOLY TRILOGY, AND SECOND AND THIRD CHANCES

Jaws made me a budding movie buff, but movies like *Star Wars* and its sequels, along with other amazing blockbusters like *Raiders*, *Blade Runner*, and the *Alien* and *Terminator* flicks, made me a full-on movie nerd. In my teens I devoured films—at movie theaters, in front of a VCR, or watching cable. I was a kid obsessed. But it started with *Star Wars*.

Star Wars also made me a *Star Wars* nerd, though I didn't know I was a *Star Wars* nerd really 'til the nineties when it came back. It would also prove to be my gateway to other science fiction films and books. And that's what I considered myself before the special editions and prequels rekindled my love and passion for *Star Wars*: just a movie buff and a sci-fi and *Star Wars* fan. I didn't really know what a nerd was when I was that young.

I had gotten hit for saying "nerd" when I told Eli the youth pastor to "Sit on it," but I'd only been following Fonzie's lead. I didn't know why "nerd" was a put-down or what it really meant. I knew a couple of older guys who were fans of movies and TV shows who would now be considered nerds. My Sacramento grandparents were in a choir group and became friends with a younger couple, June and Ray. They had a twenty-year-old son who still lived with them named Marty. When my Grandpa Ed and Grandma Clara visited the couple, Marty would usually entertain me.

Marty was a big *Planet of the Apes* fan. He loved the movie and its sequels and wasn't that happy about the new *Planet of the Apes* TV series. When I told him I liked it, he ranted against the show with an organized list of complaints. He often quoted the movies. When a local Sacramento TV station did an *Apes* marathon, Marty watched them all. And he was goofy and wore glasses and didn't have a girlfriend. Wait a minute . . . he was a fucking nerd. My first nerd.

The next nerd I would meet would be my Uncle Mike. Of course, I didn't put it together then, but he turned me onto Monty Python, and memorable holiday and birthday gifts included a bunch of sci-fi paperbacks and a mint copy of *Giant Sized X-Men #1*. He also went to UC Berkeley for engineering, worked for the government at Lawrence Livermore Labs straight out of college, invented successful business software, and was one of the first game programmers at Electronic Arts.

When I visited him once in the late seventies he showed me *Hardware Wars*, a barely funny *Star Wars* parody. Nerd flag after nerd flag so far. And yet . . . I had no idea. When I stayed with him and my Aunt Cindy once in Livermore, a bunch of guys came over and had pizza and they watched *Star Trek* together. They knew the episode before it started and were pretty precious about it. I was only allowed to talk during the commercials. So you tell me: Was my Uncle Mike a nerd? Fuck. Yes.

Star Wars changed movies in May of 1977. I would have to wait a month for it to change me. I only knew a couple of kids who got to see it in May. Screenings were sold out that first month; I had to really get on my mom to even see it when we did. Obviously there was no easy future wizard shit like Fandango or apps or cell phones. I think my pals Monte and Tony saw it early, which makes sense, because their parents were hipper than my mom and had more income.

Monte's mom was like a tan Stevie Nicks, and they had money, but not in a gross, braggy way. More in a way that, as I'm writing this and thinking about their really nice house on their huge piece of property next to a vineyard and their Mercedes, it's kind of obvious now. Not then. But they definitely had money. Monte always had cool stuff before anybody—toys, skateboards, bikes, the best bike, video games. Later on, Monte had the best weed.

Tony lived in a smaller, more modest house than Monte, but they had a backyard and a doughboy pool, so it was a suburban Taj Mahal to me. At the time I would have preferred it over the actual Taj Mahal (I was actually unclear on what it even was or where. Thanks, public school.) Tony's dad was artistic and pretty cool. Anyway, cool enough to have R. Crumb and *Fabulous Furry Freak Brothers* comics lying around and to school us on *Star Trek*. He also had on prominent display in his home office a huge, mostly nude Vampirella statue that made my parts feel weird.

Those guys didn't spoil the movie for me. That wasn't really a thing people thought about back then. No one yelled "SPOILER" at you. They didn't ruin it, but they definitely hyped it up sufficiently. I also read reviews. Yep, that's me, an eleven-year-old who read movie reviews. The *San Francisco Chronicle* was my favorite.

The *Chronicle* was a miracle, specifically the famous pink section in the Sunday edition. I think I first discovered it at Nana Norma's or Nana Irene's when I visited; they both subscribed to it, and I loved it. It had all the entertainment news for Northern California. Its reviews and lists of theaters and showtimes and later concert information would be instrumental in me following my obsessions of movies and music.

On May 25, 1977, the *Chronicle* said *Star Wars* was the most exciting sci-fi film ever. The reviewer said it was more fun than *2001: A Space Odyssey*. Most movies are more fun than *A Space Odyssey*. *A Dog's Purpose* is more fun than *2001*. *Devil's Rejects* is more fun than *2001*. *Sex and the City 2* is less fun than *A Space Odyssey*. That's it. *SATC 2* is the only movie less fun than *2001*. The reviewer also name-checked *Star Trek* and *Space 1999*. That was all I needed to read.

So one Saturday in June of '77 my mom and I went to a matinee at the Parkwood Theater in Santa Rosa. Ken the Monster wanted to go, but it was already a little strained between us. He wasn't a full-blown dick yet, but I didn't love that I was no longer getting all her attention. I was still young, so I wanted my mom to go alone with me. Weird. My mom and I grabbed sodas and popcorn and licorice and sat down. I saw the greatest movie I had ever seen. My mom fell asleep. She took one of her famous movie naps. And my life changed forever.

WHEN WE WALKED OUT of the Parkside I was in love and giddy, with soda and licorice and the best movie ever pumping through my veins. My mom had taken a nice nap, so we were both wide awake. We went to Swensen's for ice cream, and I filled her in on everything she missed. Everything. At that age that was my superpower: detail.

Star Wars took over. It was kind of all I cared about. Well, Farrah Fawcett and KISS also mattered. And my mom, but that's it. I had to see it again. And again. And as soon as possible. I went to see *Star Wars* for the second time on my eleventh birthday, July 6, 1977. Back to my favorite Santa Rosa movie theater, the Parkside with a carload of my friends— Monte, Seth, Russ, Karl, Hinchman, and Robert. *Star Wars* was sold out. Of course it was. By then it was the biggest movie in the country. People were going nuts and seeing repeat viewings like never before.

With only one option, we decided to see *The Deep* instead. Decided. It was our only choice. It was rated R, and we were eleven. Of course, we decided. *The Deep* was an adaptation of a Peter Benchley book, his *Jaws* follow-up. My mom just dropped us off—1977 ruled. She let a bunch of eleven-year-old boys see machete and barracuda attacks as well as Nick Nolte discover heroin in the bottom of the ocean and curse. We were treated to Jacqueline Bisset's tits and crazy voodoo shit. Happy birthday!

I did, of course, see *Star Wars* a second time. I was obsessed immediately; I saw it as much as I could that first year on every screen I could. It eventually played the Sebastiani, and I saw it again at the Parkside. I saw it in Sacramento while I was visiting my grandparents. I saw it in Redwood City when I was visiting my Nana's. I even saw it at the Coronet in San Francisco. Three times in one sitting. My mom dropped me off while she was hanging out with Ken the Monster.

If you were to turn me in to Child Protective Services for my mom taking me from the country to a huge city and dropping me off at a movie theater for six-plus hours, I would have been pissed at you, because it was my idea. I

was obsessed. I read the adaptation as soon as it came out.
I read everything about *Star Wars* I could get my hands on.
I picked up books on the making of Lucas's masterpiece
and one that highlighted all the ships in *Star Wars*. I bought
one about all the droids and creatures in the movie. When
Marvel Comics did a *Star Wars* adaptation, I grabbed it im-
mediately. Are you fucking kidding me? Between KISS and
Star Wars, Marvel Comics got me.

Finally, in the spring of '78 *Star Wars* invaded toy stores
when the first wave of action figures was released. They
came out late—I guess no one with the movie thought it was
going to be that big of a hit or that there would be a need.
As a kid and an OG *Star Wars* fan, I can tell you: there was
a need. Christmas of '77, when they should have come out
and ruled the season, there was nothing; instead, you could
buy a piece of paper. Genius. In lieu of getting your kid action figures of all his favorite *Star Wars* pals, Kenner offered
early bird gift certificates.

You bought the certificate, and several months later you
could get the first four figures (Leia, Chewie, R2, and Luke).
My mom didn't fall for that. Dammit. I think a lot of kids
were disappointed that Christmas. I think even if you got
the certificate, you'd say, "Thanks?" I was getting out of toys
at age twelve, but I still wanted to play with *Star Wars* figures.
Again, I only had a couple of figures. No money, remember?
By then, actually, we were doing better, but we were still on
a budget, and soon Ken the Monster would try to help my
mom with money. You can guess how I took that.

Anyway. (I use "anyway" as a transition a few times in
this book because I know when I record the audio version I
can sell the shit out of it.) Anyway. Do you like true stories?
I discovered masturbating through *Star Wars*. And not the

normal way. Not like feeling a tingling from Leia's costume. And don't get me wrong: I have whacked it to Leia. I've fantasized about Original-Costume Leia, Slave Leia, Endor-Attack Cammo Leia, even whatever that disguise was she wore at the beginning of Jedi when she brought Chewie as fake bounty. And I will continue to whack it to the princess when I feel inclined. But my intro to masturbating happened indirectly.

I was sitting in our tub. I had noticed that my penis slightly resembled a certain villain. So I brought Obi-Wan into the tub with me. So there I was, reenacting the classic scene from the first movie, the climactic battle on the Death Star between Vader and Obi-Wan. I did not have a Vader figure, so standing in for Dark Lord of the Sith was my twelve-year-old penis. He had a helmet. If I wasn't circumcised, this might have never happened. My mom walked by our bathroom and saw me going at it in the tub, midfight, "Get him, get him." Vader is winning.

She lost her mind. She screamed at me, "Stop that. What are you doing?" I was startled and confused. I said, "playing Star Wars" and held up Obi-Wan. I didn't hold up Vader—he wouldn't stretch. She looked relieved and said, "Never mind." She then went back to the kitchen. I was really confused. I didn't understand the anger or the shock. And, of course, it made me wonder, *What could I have been doing?* Fairly soon after, I found out my mom thought she caught me masturbating and that taught me about masturbating. And now I love it more than *Star Wars*.

But it wasn't all wookies and sunshine and masturbating for this *Star Wars* fan back then. Like KISS, I couldn't talk about my love of *Star Wars* without mentioning my anger and frustration with it. Because, like being a fan of that band, deciding to be a *Star Wars* devotee has definitely had its share of highs and lows. So I present to you where George Lucas first lost me: *The Star Wars Holiday Special*.

In November of 1978 George Lucas would confuse and anger me for just a second and give nerds everywhere a glimpse of how bad it could get. He plotted the terrible *Star Wars Holiday Special,* so he's only about half guilty. The other half of the blame goes to "comedy" writers like Pat Proft and Bruce Vilanch. Sure, there's no way if I were a comedy writer in the summer of '78 that I would have passed on writing a *Star Wars* special and, therefore, would have wound up being responsible for a televised tragedy on the level of Bud Dwyer.

Dwyer is the politician who shot himself during a live interview in the early nineties. The band Filter wrote "Hey Man, Nice Shot" about him. Anyway, the *Star Wars Holiday Special* is as hard to watch as a suicide. It's the most unwatchable thing ever, and yet I've seen it probably ten times and it is required fucking viewing if you call yourself a *Star Wars* nerd.

I had seen it when it came out, and even at twelve years old I thought it was corny as shit and very different in tone from the first movie. The special is notorious for its extremely negative reception. Kids like me didn't just hate the thing; we were angry and sad. It was so fucking weird that I felt scarred by the special's oddness. It was the characters I loved in a way I never wanted to see them, trapped in a horribly unfunny variety special. I had kind of blocked it out, like other moments from my childhood.

Then about fifteen years ago I stumbled upon the *Holiday Special* again at a booth at a monthly comic book convention they used to have at the Shrine Auditorium on the USC campus. It was a good time for nerds, creeps, and weirdos. A monthly Con. This was before the cosplay boom and when it was really guy heavy at those events. I don't miss it. I went a ton. Not every month, but pretty often.

And it was a legit Con at that. Great vendors, awesome guests, and Jackie Chan made an appearance there once. Another weekend they showed a preview of Affleck's *Daredevil*, so we all got to hate it before anybody. At the time I was spending my fancy TV money on everything I collected. *Star Wars* figures became an addiction of the day. I would later get rid of all of them because of *Phantom Menace*.

I kind of wish my mom had taken me to one of her dumb friend's houses that night so I stayed pure and untouched by the *Holiday Special*'s shittiness. That "special" almost ruined *Star Wars* and I actually think it ruined Christmas; Bill O'Reilly is wrong, as usual. The liberals didn't ruin Christmas. George Lucas and seventies hack-comedy writers ruined Christmas.

In June of 1980, just three short years after the original film, came *The Empire Strikes Back*, the greatest sequel ever. Hands down, 'til the *Squeakquel* followed up the *Chipmunks Movie*, *Empire* dominated the sequel world. If you had asked me before it came out if there was a chance I would like it more than *A New Hope*, I would have said, "That's a load of Bantha fodder" or "Sit on it, Ralph" and you'd say, "That's not *Star Wars*," and I'd say, "I know."

And then I saw it. And of course, I loved it. It blew me away. I returned to the Parkside theater. You could say I returned to the Parkside to watch Vader try to get Luke to turn to the dark side. And if you said that, I'd have to elbow your face off.

Empire was exactly what I wanted from a sequel. Luke was less whiny and more of a badass, and the scar from Mark

Hamill flipping his Corvette helped the tough-guy look. The tauntauns were another cool creature design, like a snow kangaroo you could ride. Don't try riding a kangaroo, though—they'll kick your dick to death. Han was back and better than ever; Leia was even tougher and sassier. The dialog made me laugh out loud in the theater: "I'd rather kiss a wookie." "I can arrange that." And the action blew the original away. Again, I went in spoiler-free. I was even more pumped for the sequel than I was for the original.

This movie cemented my love of *Star Wars*. Like the first one, *Empire* is perfect—every scene works. The characters you loved are even more well-defined. It is not even a sequel in the traditional sense because it isn't a rehash; it's a continuation of the story, the second act. And like a lot of second acts, it goes darker. A lot darker. I also still love how it ups the ante in every way.

It looks better and more expensive than the original, the set pieces are more elaborate, and the action has been kicked up a couple of notches. And I was in shock when I walked out of the Parkside after that first viewing. I had so many questions: Is Vader really Luke's dad? Is Han going to live? If Part II was better than Part I, then is Part III going to be the best? I would only need to wait another three years to find out my answers. I would also need to endure the first two years of high school. High school was way worse and soul crushing than my *Jedi* anticipation.

Fast-forward three years to 1983, when George Lucas lost me the second time with *Return of the Jedi*. Don't get me wrong: I love parts of it, but it's flawed. I thought it was imperfect when I first saw it in May of '83, my junior year, which was kind of the beginning of my partying, as you'll soon read. I remember sneaking beers into the theater. I was

also a full-blown movie buff by then. So I was more mature
. . . sort of.

That spring I was excited for *Jedi*, which, as a junior, was
rare, I guess. Most of my friends didn't care about *Star Wars*
by then. I still cared. I had actually been pumped for it for a
while because of the teaser in *Empire*, when it promised *Revenge of the Jedi*. Revenge actually sounds cooler to me than
Return. First fuck up, Lucas.

The plot is kind of a mess, not nearly as tight as the first
two. The action sequences and set pieces make up for the
comedic misfires. I still miss Irving Kirshner from *Empire*,
but it's fairly well directed.

So Brian, what scenes did you hate? The song in Jabba's
palace (the original—don't even get me started yet on the
special edition), Boba Fett's comedic death—I still hate it; I
feel nerd rage just thinking about it. Of course, I despised
some of the Ewok shit, but I do like how savage they are.
The ewoks use their environment and ingenuity and are
actually pretty bloodthirsty with their cool ways of killing
stormtroopers.

And it was hilarious when they were clumsy at times. Ha
ha. I'm kidding—it's not funny; it's just another case of the
juvenile comedic tone not working. And in the reverse, Han
and Leia are more serious in this one, so the dialog isn't as
fun; it's missing the breezy back and forth of *Empire*. The
banter isn't as strong with this one.

So Brian, what do you like about it now? Okay, I'll tell
you—you don't have to be a dick. I love the payoff of the
Vader and Luke trilogy story. Vader brings Luke to the Emperor, and when Palpatine zaps the shit out of Luke, Vader
eventually feels empathy and stops him. It fucking takes forever, though—Luke takes a shit ton of lightning damage.

He's almost dead before Vader finally turns on the Emperor and throws him down the air shaft.

The Luke/Vader light saber battle is great and shows exactly how strong Luke is getting. I love when the rebels are flying into an ambush and narrowly avoid it after Admiral Akbar said, "It's a trap." And I've totally turned around on the ewoks; they are as much a part of the *Star Wars* universe as anybody, and they actually are entertaining and pretty effective little warriors. And my kid loves them.

It's a good thing Luke isn't flying in this one—his partner would have died, for sure. In Jedi no one flies with Luke. I don't blame them: they didn't want to follow Biggs and Dak. I dig the climactic battle. It's a big one: ewoks die, fighters crash, R2 is disabled. The tide of the battle turns. And even though I miss the flirty Leia and Han, I actually enjoy when it does a call-back to *Empire* and flips it on Han when he says, "I love you." And Leia says, "I know." I don't like the special edition of *Jedi*, but that's a couple of paragraphs away. I shit on *Jedi*, I have for a while, but I still love it. Sure, I had matured a little since the first two, but not too much to where I wasn't still charmed by it.

I loved the original trilogy from the first time I saw it, but I would become more obsessed with it as the years went on. Even when I didn't have a ton of money, I spent a fair amount of cash and time on it—models, action figures, a box set of the original trilogy on VHS. Once I was able to own those movies and rewatch them whenever I wanted, it led to an insane amount of repeat viewings.

What makes me a *Star Wars* nerd? It's my favorite movie—memorable characters that are like family members, and a fully immersive world unlike anything seen before. What's kept me coming back after all these years? The action, the story, quotable lines, its rewatchability, collectable merch, and spin-off novels and comic books. I even got a *Star Wars* cat. In 1997 I adopted a cat named Waampa. She had huge front paws with six toes; they looked like little catcher mitts. Her paws were awesome and waampa-like.

Until the movies made me mad, I didn't have *Star Wars* material. My comedy always had various references to the original trilogy, but at that point it was all positive. I even cowrote a *Star Wars* parody video game. In 1996 and early 1997 I wrote and produced a CD-ROM called *Star Warped*. I worked for six months with two other comedy writers who also happened to be *Star Wars* nerds. We hired my buddy and fellow comic Mark Cohen to write jokes. He wasn't a *Star Wars* nerd, but he's funny in the room and great to get high with before lunch.

Star Warped was an interactive game featuring sketches, mini-games, parodies, and a lot of *Star Wars* trivia. The final product was super nerdy and funny enough. We finished the job right before the *Star Wars* universe went south. We were excited for what was to come. The company that produced our game wanted it out when the special editions were released. We awaited the special editions and the prequels with bated nerd breath. It was a simpler time. We had no idea how dire it was about to get.

And in 1997 the special editions came out. As fans we knew the special editions were coming, Lucas had long said that he wanted to clean up the prints and upgrade the sound on the original trilogy and to make some minor tweaks to the movies. Minor things that he always wanted to do but couldn't in the past because of financial and technology constraints. Minor tweaks—that doesn't sound bad. Which brings me to where George Lucas lost me the third time. I was excited to see the special editions. I went with a group of nerdy friends.

Two and a half hours later, I hated the special editions. All three of them. I went of course to all three of them. But they bummed me out. And like a lot of other *Star Wars* nerds and purists, I was annoyed they even existed. We didn't think they needed to be fixed or changed in any way, minor or otherwise, and it turns out that shit wasn't minor. We didn't ask for special editions, because those movies are already "special." "Special" in my heart and in my soul, where it counts.

They are pretty to look at. It's a great transfer: the frames are full. But nobody needed more Dewbacks in the background on Tatooine. And not one fucking nerd ever wanted Greedo to shoot first. We all turned out okay with Han Solo shooting first our entire fucking lives. The antihero shooting a bluish-green thing in the dick didn't hurt my decision-making process. In no way did it make me run through life shooting blue aliens in the cock. Thanks, George Lucas, but we all turned out okay. I turned out okay. Well, clearly that is debatable.

When George Lucas lost me the fourth time: the prequels. In 1999 the first prequel, *The Phantom Menace*, came out, and I viewed it as the ultimate act of betrayal. It was like your cool uncle trying to mouth rape you on Christmas. Not when you're a little kid—that's terrible and disgusting and against the law. No, I'm talking about now. You're a full-grown man. And he was your cool uncle, sold you his Mustang when you got out of high school, took you to see Scorpions and Judas Priest . . .

You're at your grandma's house, you wake up early Christmas morning, you cruise out back to have a little wake-and-bake behind the garage. You head back in to watch the best

Christmas movie ever, *Die Hard*, and your formerly "cool" uncle comes out of the guestroom with his wiener out. Gets right up by your face and touches your beard.

That's what *Phantom Menace* was like. I'm not the only nerd who felt like that. I know that because people have told me my *Phantom Menace* jokes and rants nailed their feelings. Predictably, young kids liked it, because that's who they were very clearly going for with young Anakin, the pod race, and the most hated character ever, Jar Jar Binks. He still gets a lot of shit from fans. And rightfully so. But that's like saying the fish filet sucks at McDonald's when in fact everything sucks there. Sure, Jar Jar sucks, but he was the visible sucky thing. An easy target. Where they really lost me was the beginning of the fucking movie. As soon as the scroll and theme ended, it no longer felt familiar.

What threw me off was the feel—green-screen environments instead of real sets, convoluted plots, clunky writing and directing, stiff to straight-up bad acting. Actors I love like Ewan McGregor, Liam fucking Neeson, Sam Jackson, and what's her nut, Natalie Portman. By the way, how feminists didn't climb all over the part of Queen Amidala—does she fucking do anything in that movie? Leia is such a tough, dynamic force, and Amidala is such a thinly drawn character.

At least, in my opinion. Don't come at me, nerds. And Sam Jackson is wasted as Mace Windu. Jackson is arguably one of the most charismatic and likable actors ever. In D&D terms the guy has a 20 charisma with a plus 8 in coolness and likability. And poor Mace Windu was working with a 2 charisma with a plus 10 in who gives a shit. I'm not even gonna trash the kid, for the same reason I no longer go after Juggalos or Nickelback: they are an easy target and they've taken enough shit.

I just never cared about any of the characters in the film. Even when my old pal Yoda showed up, my reaction was *meh*. Where the originals had touched me unlike any other movie, the *Phantom Menace* couldn't even engage me. Cynical? FUCK YES. But that's not why. My heart isn't made of shit—plenty of recent movies have moved me. *Wonder Woman* fucking blew me away. I've seen it five times at the writing of this, and I'm moved every time.

And then in 2002 the second one, *Attack of the Clones*, came out, and you were like, "Whew, well, that was clearly a one-time-only thing, like when my cool uncle tried to mouth-rape me—that will never happen again." And then it's Thanksgiving and you're all full of turkey and his penis flesh touches your mouth this time. "Oh my god, it totally touched my mouth!" He's like, "Is this cool?" Me: "No, it's not fucking cool. You're not my uncle anymore."

The third one, *Revenge of the Sith*, came out in 2005. And it's the least shitty. But that's like the third worst school shooting or the serial killer with the third most kills. I don't remember much about it other than what's-his-fuck becoming Vader on the stupid-ass fire planet. Actually, upon reviewing, the Anakin/Obi-Wan battle is choreographed really well, and the famous Order 66 sequence when the clones and Anakin execute all living Jedi is dark and violent. And yet I just don't care, because I'm not connected. Kenobi, Vader, and Yoda are three of my favorite characters in life, and I don't give a shit about them or what they do or even what happens to them. Anakin kills little-kid Jedis, and my reaction is *meh*.

The Vader transformation is definitely the highlight of the whole series, and even then, I don't really feel much for Vader. Because I was never engaged at the beginning of the prequels, and they never did anything to earn me back. When you look at the prequels as a whole, you see what a massive misfire it is: the three individual turds combine to make one giant, shitty, stinky mess. I guess if you had to have a Vader origin story, you could have done it in one episode without all the fat.

We all could have done without the political intrigue, midi-chlorians, trade wars, bad acting, green screen CGI fillers if there were a single, solid, boiled-down story. At least that's my opinion. That opinion has actually matured a lot since the first time I saw each of the prequels. In '99, '02, and '05, it was just blind nerd rage. I couldn't even articulate my dislike; I would just blurt profanity and gesticulate wildly like an angry potty-mouthed wookie.

I hated the prequels so much that I only saw them the opening weekend. I saw *The Phantom Menace* twice opening weekend only because I'd already bought a matinee ticket to see it at the famous Cinerama Dome. That Thursday night there was a midnight screening, so I went with Patton Oswalt from television, film, and friendship. We and some other nerdy, funny friends were giddy with excitement.

Two and a half hours later we stumbled out of the beautiful Vista Theater, gut-punched. We all expressed our dislike and frustration. I went home, got up the next morning, and saw it again. I still hated it. *Attack of the Clones* and *Revenge of the Sith* would each only earn one screening, and that was fucking enough. I rewatched the special editions of the original trilogy and the holiday special as I wrote this. I did not, however, rewatch the prequels. I have viewed them with my son. He's the only one I would take that bullet for.

After wound-healing time and multiple viewings with my kid, I hate the prequels a lot less all these years later. But at the time, though, I fucking hated them. I was so done by 2005, but I kind of went out of spite. The first two prequels turned me from the whole series. I handed in my *Star Wars* fanboy card. I didn't even watch the originals for a while. After the disappointment of the Special Editions and the prequels I purged all my *Star Wars* memorabilia.

I unloaded nearly every *Star Wars* item I owned, with the exception of a coffee table book from the nineties, *The Encyclopedia of Star Wars*, and a cherry, very hard to find copy of the VHS box set of the Original Trilogy, the true special editions because Lucas hadn't fucked with them. I got rid of everything else, though.

I passed it all on to my friend, Tom Kenny's son, Mack, and Toys for Tots. Little Mack Kenny got everything that was out of the box, and we're talking a trunk-load of stuff. Toys for Tots fared even better: some kids in greater LA scored because I gave them around seventy-five figures and toys and playsets, still in the box. I didn't even put them on eBay because I didn't want blood money.

For over fifteen years I hated those movies. I actually talked to my therapist about *Star Wars*. I spent $140.00 to tell a lady that I was mad at a movie because my wife didn't want to fucking hear about it anymore: after fifteen years she is so sick of my anti–*Star Wars* bullshit because she knows *Star Wars* is my Vietnam.

I'm the crazy old guy in the neighborhood who, after some young kid says, "I like the new *Star Wars*!" I say, "Well, clearly you don't know dick about shit, motherfucker. That's not *Star Wars*. I know *Star Wars*. Where the fuck were you in 1977? I was in the shit. I saw *Star Wars* on opening day. Where the fuck were you? My mom took me to see *Star Wars* opening weekend and it was sold out, so I saw *The Deep* instead.

I saw Jaqueline Bisset's tits at eleven years old. Made me a man. Where the fuck were you?" Insane.

I really should have listened to one of the famous messages of those movies, because I let my anger control me. I went to the dark side. Fuck that. Those movies suck, and so does Lucas. I was already mad at the entire franchise, and then I would read stories where Lucas told me and all my fellow *Star Wars* nerds to get a life, like Shatner's classic Trekkie sketch on *SNL*. I was furious when I read that. Fuck you, Lucas. Sure, you don't owe us anything, but how about making a good movie and making nerds happy? Sound hard? Talk to Joss Whedon.

I went from being one of the biggest *Star Wars* fans to a guy who couldn't even talk about the series without my blood pressure cruising to unhealthy levels. I once even got to go to Skywalker Ranch to do a sketch for Comedy Central, and we were all invited to sleep in this cool little bed-and-breakfast on the grounds. I peed the bed. Just kidding. We then had the run of the ranch the next day; our small crew got the grand tour of the grounds. Looking back, it was pretty cool. Not a lot of people get to do that. This nerd did. And it was totally wasted on me at the time.

I remember every cool moment of the day was tainted by my attitude at the time. "Sure, this is so cool that I'm walking through George Lucas's library, and there is the original model of Luke's X-Wing, and there is Han's gun, but too bad, cuz' *Star Wars* sucks now." Wish I could go again, because now I love it again. Yep, it won me back. I am once again a *Star Wars* fan. More about my growth and maturity much later. For now, back to me being eleven years old and . . .

SIX

SIXTH GRADE: MY SCHOLASTIC HIGH POINT

My third and final year at Dunbar, sixth grade, was in 1977–78. I know those are two years. It didn't take two years; that's just how the school year works. Keep up. Sixth grade was the definite highlight of my elementary school career. And like every school movie where a kid turns it around, it was due to a young, eager, idealistic teacher. Mr. Richard Cox was my young, eager, idealistic teacher. We were only his third class of students. I think he was twenty-six at the time. And he was such a cool, smart, funny guy. If all my teachers were as easy to talk and listen and relate to as Mr. Cox, I probably would have done much better in school. Way to go, other teachers.

Everybody loved Mr. Cox. I'm pretty sure not one kid in my class had a beef with him. I think the clearest example of that would be the fact that his name was Richard Cox, and no one made fun of his name—"Dick Cocks," or "Dick Cox." Twenty twelve-year-old boys saw him every day and said his name and no one thought to tease him.

When we started the year he asked us what book we wanted to read out loud. I produced my copy of the *Star Wars* adaptation. It worked—he was a fan. And to be democratic and teach us all a lesson, we did a vote. Most kids in the world were *Star Wars* crazy, so it was an easy victory. Things were starting off great; we spent the first part of sixth grade reading the *Star Wars* adaptation. I felt like I won; I was so damn happy. I even read it out loud when it was my turn. I had previously been terrified of that. For Mr. Cox and *Star Wars*, I got over my fear and shyness.

He also encouraged my imagination. When we started doing creative writing exercises, it was exactly what I needed. I loved doing those assignments—crafting stories out of thin air to fit his criteria. I wasn't a horror movie nut yet, but I loved action movies and cop shows, so most of my short stories were inspired by that stuff. I wrote a *Freebie and the Bean* buddy-cop rip-off and a *Dirty Harry* sequel. The stories all had car chases and gunplay and way too much violence for a sixth-grader, but Mr. Cox let me do whatever I wanted. Like everything else I loved, I soon became obsessed and started doing short stories all the time on my own.

Because I liked him so much, I didn't get in a ton of trouble with Mr. Cox. The maddest he ever got with me was when he caught me "being creative." He saw me drawing a dirty picture. I was copying an inappropriate greeting card. Not totally sure where I got this card; I think because I was going to liquor stores to get comic books, I found these greeting cards that had sexy seventies-style drawings on them. They were almost like *Playboy* cartoons and were all about sex and alcohol. I didn't get half the jokes because I was eleven. By half, I mean any.

I wasn't contemplating life in porn. I just thought the girls on the card were sexy. I wanted to draw like that. I had dabbled at that point with drawing Spider-Man and got pretty good at mimicking John Romita. So I would mimic these cards and draw sexy girls. I changed the jokes and made the pictures dirtier. On one I drew the girl topless and added a guy with his hands down her jeans. Who knows where I got my inspiration? Divine, I guess. A couple of kids liked my "sexy" "art" and asked me to draw one for them. I didn't charge them much, like sodas or candy. It didn't make me rich, put it that way.

When Mr. Cox saw what I was doing, I got in trouble, and it was kind of my fault for doing it in class like a dumbass. He really liked me, but he had to do something, so he sent us to the principal's office. It was me and the two kids I was drawing sexy ladies for: my friend Robert Also-Glasses and this girl Dee Dee. She had an unfortunate last name that led to a homophobic slur from the asshole boys. Dee was smart and funny and kind of different from the other sixth-grade girls, which also of course leads to name calling.

The principal wasn't there, so we met with our vice principal, Mrs. Nathan, who was really upset with me. We all got paddled. It was so weird and old-school in retrospect, more like the forties than the late seventies. Getting your twelve-year-old butt smacked by a woman who isn't your mom is more embarrassing than painful. I'll talk about my mom smacking me in a minute.

My mom was called to school after the infamous drawing. She was pretty annoyed but also actually impressed with the art. She always loved when I drew. I think that it says something that I was already pimping out my art for money.

I excelled in English and especially creative writing. I also enjoyed history, but my math and science skills were lacking. I didn't excel in physical education, and that would only get worse as my attitude and disdain for team sports grew. A third of the way through the school year Mr. Cox started an incentive program. The kids who had the most improved grades in the second half of the year would get to go on a special day trip with Mr. Cox, roller skating, a museum—whatever the five most-improved kids voted on, he would do. It later inspired a *Mr. Show* sketch, but at the time I just thought it sounded cool and the incentive worked: I wanted to be a better student. It would be difficult, because outside of school, I had a lot of distractions.

I watched a shit-ton of TV at that age. And I still played outside. In our tiny living room, though, I consumed every episode of *Happy Days, Welcome Back, Kotter, All in the Family, Good Times, Chico and the Man*. I loved sitcoms. I would watch anything, and I even enjoyed *I Love Lucy* reruns. One of my best memories with Nana Irene was one visit she and I watched an episode of *Barney Miller*; I think it's called "The Brownie." Nana and I both laughed our butts off at the episode. She was in her late seventies and I was eleven, and we were both crying laughing.

Our favorites were Detectives Himana, played by Jack Soo, and Fish, played by Abe Vigoda. On a show with several scene stealers, they were the best. The episode was about Barney and the guys accidentally all eating pot brownies and tripping their balls off. It was Cheech and Chong–level comedy on a prime-time sitcom—a super-popular prime-time sitcom. It was subversive at the time; I just knew it was funny. I didn't really understand what was happening, but the performances were hilarious. I showed the episode to my wife a couple of years ago, and it still holds up. And we both know a lot about pot brownies.

I feel like my mom's TV rules became lax during sixth grade because I watched a ton of it—not just sitcoms but all the prime-time shows: *Emergency, Nancy Drew* and *Hardy Boys, SWAT, Charlie's Angels, Wonder Woman, Six Million Dollar Man*, and *Bionic Woman*. They were all huge, and I was a fan too. On the playground we would reenact classic fights between Steve Austin versus Bigfoot and Cyborg. I was usually

Bigfoot. When *Six Million Dollar Man* merchandise came out I had to have a lunch box and a Steve Austin action figure. It was a huge, ungainly action figure. You couldn't play it with other action figures because they were the wrong scale. The other figures in the series were an old guy, Oscar Goldman, and Jamie Sommers, a girl. So I stuck with the one figure, the original Steve Austin.

I also loved *Starsky and Hutch*. It would wind up being one of my worst influences. I was super into *Charlie's Angels* that year; I saw every episode. I belonged to the *Charlie's Angels* fan club. I had the trading cards, the entire set, and a *Charlie's Angels* T-Shirt. I had the Farrah poster. *The* Farrah poster. Everyone had it. I also had a T-shirt with the poster design. At the grocery store I would beg my mom for magazines featuring articles on Farrah and the other Angels.

Farrah was maybe my first love. Leia was kick-ass and beautiful and smart, but to eleven-year-old me, Farrah Fawcett as Jill Monroe was the most beautiful woman alive. *Charlie's Angels* nerd? Yep. Girls weren't into me, but they didn't treat me like a pariah. Yet there were a couple in Mr. Cox's class who actually were friendly with me. One was Gina Italian-Last-Name. Super cute and very nice to me, Italian with an annoying little brother, she and I had a couple of exchanges about Lindsay Wagner and Farrah. Gina Italian-Last-Name is not related to Anthony Italian-Name from fourth grade. See, totally different.

Gina liked Farrah and Lindsay for different reasons from me, but we bonded over it in class. I feel like I had won a bunch of people over by then. I wasn't the weird new kid. I was still the weird kid, but a lot of kids thought I was the funny, weird kid, and that was enough. Unlike my other teachers, Mr. Cox encouraged me to express my sense of humor. I liked being funny or interesting. I also liked knowing all the popular shows, movies, books, and music. It had already paid off in having something in common with Gina.

I listened to a lot of radio. Around '77 is when I made the leap from AM pop to FM rock. Of course, I loved the music, but I also really liked DJs. Being a radio DJ seemed like such a cool job to me: just play and talk about the music you love. I thought that DJs played whatever they wanted. And the bigger, crazier on-air personality, the better. I loved this drive-time DJ on a San Francisco AM station, KFRC. His name was Dr. Don Rose. I'm not sure whether he was a real doctor, judging by how crazy and loud his morning show was. He might have received his doctorate in funny phone calls and slide whistles, though—that would make sense.

I loved the Dr. Don Rose show and would still check it out, even though I was getting into KMEL and KOME, two Bay Area FM stations. They played better music, and the DJs were more mature—well, most of the time. And then there was Dr. Demento, the king of the wacky DJs with a doctorate. Later I would hear Weird Al there, but first it was fun novelty songs like "The Streak" and "Junk Food Junkie" that got me listening. I loved that songs could be funny and timely and comment on things like streakers and other seventies trends like health food. I once was in a restaurant with my mom when a streaker came in and ran around the restaurant nude. It was funny and super exciting. Now cops would shoot you.

I digress. Back to FM radio. That's where I was turned on to a lot of contemporary music. I heard Foreigner's "Cold as Ice" and "Feels Like the First Time" and Thin Lizzy's "Boys Are Back in Town" and "Jail Break" and Tom Petty's "Breakdown" and "American Girl." Peter Frampton and Lynyrd

Skynyrd were also played frequently, but neither would stick. I actually bought *Frampton Comes Alive*, and it still didn't take. Then, in 1978, Elvis Presley died. That was bad and weird. You could see his dead body on the cover of every magazine the week he died. Elvis was my first hero to die.

I was exposed to other popular music and entertainment during Mr. Cox's class or on campus. Everybody was talking about *Saturday Night Fever* that year. It was huge—almost *Jaws* and *Star Wars* big. I had no interest, really. The trailer did nothing for me. A teenager in New York or somewhere enters a dance contest and falls in love with some girl while dancing around a bunch. Sure, it had an R rating, which was appealing, but I knew it was for language and nudity and Italian stereotypes and not gunplay and bloody fisticuffs or monsters. I wouldn't see it for a couple of years, but I sure bought the soundtrack. I listened to it for several months. That was my super-short disco phase.

Fleetwood Mac's album *Rumours* was huge. That record or its singles were everywhere I went. And I liked it as much as America did. I also had a crush on Stevie Nicks, just like America did. I will remember for the rest of my life the first time I heard the classic Queen album *News of the World*. During lunch we would have music in the cafeteria. One day someone played "We Will Rock You" and "We Are the Champions." I had to have it. Like KISS, the album cover excited me. In addition to "We Will Rock You" and "We Are the Champions," I liked "Sheer Heart Attack" and "Get Down, Make Love."

I started to get nerdy about random things. I switched from baseball to football. I loved local teams, the Niners and the Raiders. I did reports in Mr. Cox's class on Kenny Stabler and the other champion Raiders of the mid-seventies.

And I liked America's teams, the Cowboys and the Steelers. I was also into the Civil War. I read several books about it. Civil War and football. I also liked conspiracy theories and whisky. I was an old white man.

I spent quite a lot of time in church groups. I actually belonged to two, so I was pretty busy with meetings and outings. One Saturday one of my youth leaders thought it would be fun to surprise us with mini-golfing, so they blind-folded us when we got in the van. After a while I whispered to everyone that we should put our faces against the window and pretend to be kidnapped. A couple of kids went along with me. Of course, when the grownups figured it out, we had to stop. Grownups always ruin kidnapping, except for when they are the kidnappers.

There were plenty of things I didn't like about living in Sonoma, but I loved spending more time with my Grandpa George and Grandma Grace. My mom would drop me off with my bike, and I'd hang out with them and ride around their neighborhood. I liked spending time with them, and I got to know their neighbors. There was a woman who lived across from my grandparents named Eve. She and her hus-band had never had grandkids, or regular kids, so she kind of adopted me. I did yard work for her, and she would feed me and let me take long breaks. I remember during one long break I watched the entire 1966 *Batman* movie. By the way, I sucked at yard work.

Enter Ken the Monster. A year or two after they started dating, Ken the Monster gave up his apartment and moved in with us. I remember my mom's warning being really short. She informed me he was moving in, and then he moved in. I think Ken did it to save money. He was a cheap dick. We found that out quickly. I'm not sure whether he loved my mom. I think she was mostly just lonely and liked his company and the regular sex. BLARG! Living with him was fine at first, but soon I would start acting out. She only lost it on me a couple of times. The wooden spoon was my mom's punishment of choice. I had gotten smacked with it a handful of times when I was younger, and it fucking hurt. As I got bigger, it hurt less.

She would lose it so hard, it could be funny. One time her spoon broke. And I laughed. I laughed my ass off. I pointed at her. That set her off even more. She was furious. Or, as she would say, "I am livid with you right now." Our fights would start out over shit like me not wanting to do homework or take out the garbage or her not letting me go to my friend's house. Minor shit. But they would escalate pretty quickly. She said a lot of mean things to be hurtful. They would get bad enough in junior high to send me back to therapy.

Once Ken lived with us, half our fights were about him. But it was still awkward to fight in front of him. I always felt like our lives weren't his business, and I resented him being there. By the time I got to high school I wanted to fucking kill him.

But then came the good part about Ken the Monster being in our lives: R-rated movies. We saw *Slapshot*. I loved *Slapshot*: it was violent and dirty and the Hansen Brothers were fucking hilarious. We also had family outings to see *Semi-Tough* and *Kentucky Fried Movie* together. Both inappropriate and fucking awesome. That's it. That was the best thing about Ken.

The second best thing was that Ken and my mom went out a lot. That meant I could watch whatever I wanted. I saw the horror masterpiece *Night of the Living Dead* on TV one Friday night, alone in our apartment. It freaked me out. I saw *Carrie* around then too. It wasn't scary, just fucked up. I also saw *The Omen*. I loved it. I had caught a TV edited version of *The Exorcist*, which at that point was the scariest thing I'd ever seen. Because of all the time I spent in church, movies featuring the devil freaked me out the most. And other flicks I just had the instinct to avoid. I had heard of *Rabid* and *The Hills Have Eyes*, but I was too scared to watch them.

I saw *Annie Hall* with my mom and Ken the Monster. Ken loved Woody, which makes sense, because they were both creeps. Alleged. I saw *The Spy Who Loved Me* with a church group. Yep, it's a Roger Moore Bond film—not my favorite, but still pretty enjoyable. I saw Mel Brooks's *High Anxiety*. I didn't understand a lot of the Hitchcock references, but it made me seek out more of his movies.

By my teens I had seen most of them. I loved the *Wages of Fear* remake, *Sorcerer*, with Roy Scheider. It was not what I was hoping for from Chief Brody, but it was still pretty intense. Of course, I didn't know what *Wages of Fear* was 'til I lived with Patton Oswalt. One night Ken took my mom and me to see *Oh God*. Or, more likely, he drove, my mom paid, and he bought popcorn. His popcorn.

I became obsessed with a flick called *Damnation Alley*. It was a postapocalypse action film featuring Jackie Earle Haley (Kelly Leak from *The Bad News Bears*), George Peppard (Hannibal from *The A-Team*), and Jan-Michael Vincent (famous fuck-up). I sat through multiple viewings one day in a San Francisco movie theater while my mom and Ken spent a day in the city. Not sure why. It's terrible. The effects were shitty and the story is a wet fart, but I liked it because it was about the end of the world and that fascinated me.

I worshipped Clint Eastwood and Burt Reynolds. I had seen all the *Dirty Harry* movies at that point, with *The Enforcer* being my favorite. I loved the trilogy of Harry Callahan flicks at the time, as most eleven- and twelve-year-old boys did. But I also dug the Eastwood flicks my friends didn't know, like *Play Misty for Me*, a real creeper, Clint's *Basic Instinct*–like stalker movie. My favorite was *The Outlaw Josey Wales*, a violent revenge western.

I saw a lot of Eastwood's movies on TV. But *The Gauntlet* was special. My mom dropped Hinchman and me off at the Sebastiani Theatre. She knew it was R rated, so she walked us up to the window and we saw one of the grittiest Eastwood flicks ever, complete with rapey bikers. *Smokey and the Bandit* was probably my favorite Burt Reynolds flick 'til I saw *Hooper*. Burt's movies were a little more fun than Clint's. Not counting *Deliverance*. Never count *Deliverance*, that wacky farce. It's also known as *National Lampoon's Rape Raft*.

I found *Saturday Night Live* one night while my mom was out with Ken. I was supposed to be in bed by 11:30. I wasn't. I stayed up for two reasons: because I was too scared to be alone and because I could. I was flipping around one night and found these funny people, the not-ready-for-prime-time players. I didn't know who they were, but I thought they were the funniest people I had ever seen in my life—Belushi, Chase, Aykroyd, and Morris were all amazing. The women were beautiful and funny. I fell in love with Jane, Gilda, and Lorraine instantly. The host was this really funny, mean hippie named George Carlin. I knew I wasn't supposed to be watching this, but I was hooked. I didn't tell my mom about my discovery, but I did encourage more Saturday night date nights.

I continued to dabble in sports. I played basketball under Mr. Cox's direction, and I barely remember one period. All my recollections of every time I played on a sports team are foggy, as though I played only one game, like *Rudy*. I guess I sucked the least at soccer, because I wound up with the "Most Improved" certificate at the end of the year. So that means I sucked at an unbelievable level when I started and sucked noticeably less by the end of the season. I guess Coach Billie, who was also my Cub Scout leader and my friend Tony's mom, thought it was better than giving me a "Keep Trying, Dummy" certificate. By the age of thirteen I knew sports weren't for me.

Mr. Cox made reading at school fun, but it had already been my number-one pastime for a couple of years at that point. By sixth grade I read everything I could get my hands on. I plowed through the kids' books in my school library and both public libraries in town. I started reading things a second time. Roald Dahl was a favorite. I started with the Charlie books, but *James and the Giant Peach* became my favorite. I dug *The Phantom Tollbooth* and read all the Hardy boys books, a shit-ton of Nancy Drews and then moved on to Tolkien, C. S. Lewis, Frank Herbert's *Dune*, and *Watership Down*. Fun, breezy romps.

Then I found even more mature stuff like the kinds of things you'd find on a rack at a grocery store if you were a young adventurous reader. I picked up a book called *Machete Summer* about the Miami drug world. It was as fucked up as you'd guess, and my mom had paid for it along with that week's groceries. Super discerning. I read *The Exorcist* way before I saw the movie. I started reading movie adaptations like *The Omen* and *Grizzly* whenever I could find them. Soon I would find Stephen King.

I loved magazines, whatever the topic. I read a lot of cheesy magazines and newspapers to get my Farrah and KISS news as well as kids' stuff like *Ranger Rick* and *Dynamite*, and I was becoming a nut for *Mad* magazine. I read skateboarding and BMX magazines. I wasn't very good at either, like most normal kid shit. But I loved reading about skateboarding and BMX and looking at the pictures. I also went through a car phase: hot rods, especially souped-up Corvettes, Camaros, and Mustangs.

And like half the boys in Mr. Cox's class, I liked foreign cars like Porsches, Ferraris, and Lamborghinis. I asked my mom for a *Car and Driver* subscription and would pick up *Road and Tracks* and *Hot Rod* magazines whenever I was at the grocery store. I drew a lot of cars and motorcycles. A bunch of the other guys in class drew cars too, and I was pretty good at it; it was definitely my way of bonding with the guys. I'm not really a car guy anymore. I currently drive a dad car. Let's be real: I drive a minivan. Like a fucking badass.

I saw the inside of my first dirty magazine in sixth grade. Actually, at school. I'd seen covers before, but I'd never dared to look inside until someone brought a *Playboy* to the playground. Pamela Sue Martin, TV's Nancy Drew, was on the cover and had a pictorial inside. I was pretty amazed: one, that someone brought it to·school, and two, that I got to see a star of TV and kids' mystery books naked.

That *Playboy* kid had to be outdone. Someone else—I'm pretty sure it was Larry—brought a *Penthouse* one day. One of the pretty, naked ladies had jizz loads on her. I had to ask

Larry what it was. His answer was gross. He made fun of me for not knowing. I was starting to lose Larry as a friend already and was wondering why we were even friends in the first place. He had made fun of my dad, and when I said my dad was dead, he said, "Dig him up." That made me hate him. I wanted to say, "Well, at least my dad liked me and my mom!" but I knew it was too mean and I'd get punched. I didn't always have that kind of self-control.

I liked being funny. When I sucked at basketball, I at least made it fun. As a ball circled the basket, I yelled, "Ring around the toilet." Even Mr. Cox thought it was funny—he stifled a snort and smiled as he gently reminded me to focus. One of the early manifestations of my future career was that other kids seemed to recognize my skill in repeating comedy routines or acting out sketches or scenes from funny movies. One day I talked to a kid who had never seen the *Bad News Bears*. I couldn't believe parents or other circumstances had prevented him from seeing the Walter Matthau classic.

So over the course of the day I told him the entire plot of the movie, acting out every gag and leaning into the bad words with relish. And mustard. I had seen *Bad News Bears* multiple times. I loved Tanner, the smart-ass, but I was more like Timmy Lupus, the shy, bullied kid. My friend wasn't allowed to see this flick that I thought was a comedic revelation, so I filled that hole for him. He was a great audience.

By the spring, because of Mr. Cox's incentive—or maybe just because he was a great teacher—I had improved enough to win "Most Improved." Like soccer, I had gone from shitty to less shitty, and it felt great. Mr. Cox selected me and the other four guys who had improved the most. They were all my friends—Robert Also-Glasses, Russ Goodman,

Hinchman, and Karl German-Name. It may have been rigged. Mr. Cox didn't pull some Mrs. Sullivan shit and treat us to cleaning his yard. Nope, he let us pick where we went.

We had all held a meeting. The decision was easy: we were all obsessed with cars. So we wanted to go to San Francisco and go to high-end car dealerships. We were sixth-grade boys and really wanted to look at Porsches and Ferraris. So that's what we did. Mr. Cox took us all to San Francisco. We were so stoked. It felt really good to turn it around. It was the highlight of an already great school year. The trip was not lost on me that I had worked so hard to make friends and move up the social strata during the last three years and that after the summer I would need to start all over at junior high. "No fair!" And then again for my freshman year. "No fucking fair!" I dreaded junior high and high school, and I really had no fucking idea.

The second highlight of that school year came right before graduation: my first big kid's party, a sixth-grade house party. Also known as a sixth-grade make-out party. It was at a girl's house. I think the girl's name was Sandy, and she owned a horse, so we'll call her Sandy Horse-Girl. My two crushes were Gina Italian-Name and Sandy Horse-Girl. She was cute, and her parents owned a nice piece of property in the hills.

Everybody was there. The party was fun—food and soda, dancing and games. Later in the evening the games changed. My first game of truth-or-dare—I was pretty excited. During the game I wound up kissing Sandy Horse-Girl. The kiss was awkward, but kind of sweet. It was just a quick kiss, and it wasn't like my third-grade love, Mommy in "I saw Mommy Kissing Santa Claus," or my fifth-grade love, Mrs. Sullivan.

Unfortunately, I didn't follow through. What twelve-year-old does have good follow-through? Later Karl German-Name kissed her longer, and she really seemed to like it. I went home to my apartment alone. I'm kidding. We were sixth-graders—no one was fucking. But I do remember how nervous and hopeful and, later, disappointed I was that night. It felt good until it didn't. Later my problem was that I always wanted it too much and didn't have much confidence—a great combo: lack of balls and sweaty desperation. And I had super-high, unreasonable standards. Why weren't girls flinging their vaginas at me? Well, I wouldn't find out in junior high. Or high school. Or even college.

SEVEN

JUNIOR HIGH: NERDY AND NERDIER

I was teased a bunch at the beginning of seventh grade. And hit quite a few times. The twelve-year-old passive-aggressive "accidental" bump or shove was no fun and pervasive. I never got in a real fight because I wouldn't fight back. That actually helped and hurt as I got older. I don't blame anyone. Six schools worth of seventh-graders—that's a lot of new faces when you start junior high. We were all new fish. Prison mentality. If it had actually been prison, I would have died in the first two weeks because I got shanked on the playground a lot. And by shanked, I mean I got punched, shoved, and called "homo," "queer," "faggot," "weirdo," "queer-bait," "fag," "mo," "dork," "nerd," and "loser."

Of all those names, I remember *loser* hurting the most. Not sure why, but it stung more, maybe because I thought of myself that way. I was a loser. And Turtle, my nickname—that hurt too. My close friends had stopped calling me Turtle, but it stuck with everyone else. At first, being involved in sports paid off here, because I knew a bunch of kids from playing their school in soccer or basketball. But most of them knew me as Turtle already. They had been exposed to my spazziness, so I couldn't really reinvent myself. A lot of my friends were from my neighborhood and St. Andrews, my church. My core friends, like Hinchman and Russ, were always there, even when I was shitty to them.

Then there were the eighth-graders. I don't remember my mom buying me clothes with giant targets on them when we went back-to-school shopping that summer at Penny's, Mervyn's, and Miller's Outpost, but they must have all had them. Either that, or I was just a tall, skinny dork who acted weird. PE was the worst—I felt vulnerable and terrified every time I hit the field. Whatever the sport, I knew I would be terrible at it and that I'd either be overlooked by the other kids or, worse, singled out and ridiculed. I hadn't been that bad at sports at eight years old, but the more I grew, the more uncoordinated I got. And the worse I got at sports, the more I hated them.

Dodgeball and I had had a love-hate relationship: kids loved ruining my day with the dodgeball, and I fucking hated it. I was never ever good at it, and if I did happen to get lucky and tag a kid out with my "weenie-arms" or my "pussy throw," then they would really wail on me with a concentrated effort. Dodgeball mutated into "smear the queer" or "tag the fag," which was worse because I was always the queer or fag. Not sure why they aren't played professionally; maybe their names held them back. Don't let angry twelve-year-old dicks name your sport. And then there was flag football, or "fag football" when I played it. Fuck, I hated being twelve.

On one miserable day during "fag football," eighth-grade blonde beauty Tami Baker, with the words "Leave Posehny alone!" saved my ass and became my massive crush at the same exact second. I already liked blondes from TV—Jeannie, Ellie May, Samantha, and my favorite angels, Farrah and Cheryl Ladd . . . even the tall, boring, blonde Angel was more appealing to my young brain than the dark-haired girls on the show. Once I started talking to real girls—I

mean, avoiding eye contact with real girls—I decided that
blondes were my favorite. I married a cute, petite blonde,
my dream girl, but I think one of the reasons a cute blonde
ex-cheerleader even became my dream girl is because of
Tami Baker.

Not Tammy Faye Bakker from TV religion and scaring cats with her face. No, this was Tami Baker, the cutest, most popular eighth-grader at Altamira Junior High.
Tami was a cheerleader and athletic, so when she ran
in slow motion onto the football field wearing dolphin
shorts and a half shirt to show off her impossibly tan belly
and legs, that image was instantly locked into my brain.
Her perfect Dorothy Hamill haircut bobbing around her
stunning—for an eighth-grader from a seventh-grader's
perspective—features.

She was running onto the field to stop an eighth-grade
man from fucking with me. When I was in seventh grade, all
the eighth-graders seemed a million years older, like adult
men and women. And here was this beautiful lady who was
upset that this gentleman had pulled my shorts down. It
was so brief that I wasn't even that embarrassed. I would
never be wearing a jock strap, so I had underwear on, and at
that point kids had done worse. But "Leave Posehny alone"
saved the day. She even pulled his pants down and gave me
a hug in front of everyone to really make it feel like a teen-
movie moment.

That wasn't the only time Tami was nice to me. She was
friendly whenever she saw me and, in turn, got people to cut
me a break just by her sheer popularity. Other eighth-grade
women were nice to me, which made the men try harder.
It saved seventh grade and made eighth grade bearable

because most kids knew who I was by then. Of course, I had a crush on Tami all of seventh and eighth grade and hoped she would be waiting at Sonoma High for me. Or, at the very least, there to watch out for me. She wouldn't be. I found out she had moved, and I was pretty wrecked.

I only had Tami in PE, so she wasn't able to stop all the teasing, and I had already suffered through a fall and winter of ridicule before Tami stood up for me. Most of it wasn't too hurtful; it just sucked feeling like a target all the time. It definitely made me dread school and put me on the defensive. I'm a relatively smart guy, so I tried to find a logical reason for being singled out. At Dunbar I was the new kid, but what was my problem here? We were all new kids. Of course, there could be something wrong with me. My looks were made fun of, so it made me hate the way I looked. And even as I grew bigger than a lot of kids, I had never fought back, so they knew I wasn't a threat.

In eighth grade there was a new kid—I don't know . . . Geordie? Sure, let's call him Geordie. He had picked up my scent and teased me a couple of times. He liked singing to me or at me. I walked by and he sang, "They Call Me the Lonesome Loser" by the Little River Band. I already didn't like that song, but this dick-face ruined it forever. He was normal looking and athletic, and I wasn't. He was in my PE class and early on noticed I was the weak link, so after a couple days of constant, annoying riding, I came up with a plan at home.

It was partly inspired by Richard Pryor and Gene Wilder acting nuts in *Stir Crazy* and a Steve Martin bit where he talks about deterring a mugger by acting psycho. I waited 'til the next time he messed with me—we were playing handball against the wall, and he pushed me and made a threat. I told him to go ahead and hit me, but I would get him when he didn't expect it, and I wouldn't stop.

I said I had a dream where I smashed his head against the ground until he was dead. Brutal, huh? I had no such dream, but it was pretty metal for a kid who wasn't even metal yet, so it worked. By worked, I mean, he thought I was fucking psycho and reported me to the principal's office. I'm lucky kids killing other kids was new. The "I Don't Like Mondays" girl shooter in San Diego had just happened, so they didn't take it super, super seriously. All that happened was I got the attention of the principal and the school counselor. And my mom. She was there a lot. Sometimes when I was the victim. Mostly because I was disruptive. That would lead to trouble at home: restriction and loss of allowance without really discussing my lack of social skills or that I was being bullied.

I didn't get a lot of empathy or understanding or really any help with problem solving from someone who had a master's in psychology. I think the California state colleges should work on their psychology program, specifically child psychology. Every time I complained about being picked on, she would say that she too got picked on. She always reminded me, even if I was crying, "They called me giraffe in high school." "Giraffe," to me, lacked the sting of "faggot." And my mom making it about her lacked the sympathy or empathy or really any "-thy" I was looking for.

It was never very helpful. Eventually she made me avoid bringing my bullying or really anything personal to her. I shut off. I read almost constantly. In the car I'd sit as far away as possible from her, in a ball in the far corner of her terrible Pinto station wagon, and read whatever Stephen

King or sci-fi or classic or even grocery store paperback I could get my hands on.

My grades continued to be a problem. I didn't have the positive creative writing outlet I had had in sixth grade and would again in high school. When I did get to go creative in high school, I went nuts—violent, dark, weird, really inspired by horror. Girls and guys thought I was super strange, but a lot of kids liked my routines. Like sixth grade, it made me feel good. But not in junior high. Seventh grade was the year I discovered drama and acting. Drama class was the highlight of my day. The teacher encouraged me and liked my silly side. I liked a couple of the girls in my drama class and the drama club, and I took the class seriously. But they didn't love me.

Any confidence I had with girls in sixth grade I had lost by the second day of seventh grade. They had matured. I looked weird and felt weirder. I had gotten gawkier looking with braces and a retainer. And some days even headgear. I was so fucked. I had friends who started the year in new relationships; that was not happening for me. I didn't have any female friends. I still tried: I went to the places guys met girls—roller-skating parties and school dances.

Roller-skating parties were stupid, and school dances were no fucking fun. I would hang out and joke with my friends, and then they would dance with girls. I didn't dance; I just stood against the wall and watched. It sucked. I didn't even try after a while; girls felt unattainable. I had no confidence; I thought I sucked at dancing. Asking girls to dance terrified me. All I remember is a few doses of rejection, giving up, and just making fun of the pop music the DJs spun. I liked it when they played Journey, Foreigner, or any rock. I hated Michael Jackson and other pop crap. I actually danced a couple of times in junior high, but in high school I would only dance once, and it wasn't with anyone.

During the eighth-grade homecoming dance I was distracted, to say the least. They had shown us the Zapruder film earlier that day in history class, and all I could think about was JFK losing his head and Jackie Kennedy grabbing his brains off the trunk of the car. "Back and to the left." "Back and to the left." It was horrifying, and I couldn't take my mind off it: "Back and to the left." I guess I could've turned it into a dance move or used it for conversation: "And then Jackie reached for his brain and didn't even lose her hat—isn't that cool?" "No, you're weird."

Oddly, at church youth group I didn't feel that weird. On the weekends and a couple of nights a week I continued to be involved in the church. My mom liked me being busy, so I spent a lot of time at church youth group get-togethers and ski trips. I actually liked youth group in my early teens. I belonged to two separate youth groups, one at my church and one at Russ and Darren Goodman's church. Russ and I were pretty close in junior high, so it was fun to get to hang out with him. I became friends with a lot of the kids I was exposed to through church. Most of them were cool, smart kids.

Then there was Ross Jox, a smarmy know-it-all. He was a bully and seemed to love making youth group miserable for me. A church group bully? Who the fuck? And why the fuck? I hated him so much. I think Jesus would've hated Ross. He was a colossal cock with a face God would find punchable. I would smart off to him—I wasn't that scared of getting hit at church after the last guy who hit me had disappeared so quickly. So I stopped taking his shit and dished it right back.

Ross was a year older, and I think he resented taking shit from me. Good. Fuck him.

Ski trips were fun. It was a relief to get away from my mom, and the youth leaders made it a positive experience. And once I learned not to go under the lodge, I was golden. I actually wasn't a horrible skier and had fun skiing with Russ Goodman and my other Christian pals. And I got better after a couple of winters. I don't remember any bedwetting issues at the cabins we stayed in, but that doesn't mean I didn't. If you want to pretend I peed the bed, you can. If you want to pretend I shit the bed, you can. Have at it.

In seventh grade I really wanted to play Dungeons & Dragons. I had heard about D&D from kids at school, and it sounded cool and like something I wanted to try. So when a group of eighth-graders started a D&D club at my school, I thought I'd check it out and join. They held it in a science classroom at lunch. I didn't mind the idea of missing lunch and ducking into a classroom for an hour, so I went to a meeting one day with my bag lunch, ready to play. I opened the door and heard, "Posehn? What are you doing here?" It was Ross Jox, I turned around and didn't play the game until 1991. Where did I run to? The library.

I felt like an outcast most of the time already, so I made a conscious effort to lean into the nerdy outcast role. I started working in the school library. Yep, you heard me: I actually worked in the library. I volunteered in seventh and eighth grade to help out in the library. So I wound up spending an entire period in there. I already spent most of my morning breaks and lunches in there. When I started assisting as a seventh-grader, the eighth-grade library assistant Neil gave me tons of attitude. His lofty position of power was somehow threatened by my impressive aptitude for being a library nerd, I guess. Or he was just a petty, angry dick.

The librarians wanted Neil to show me the ropes, so when we were alone he asked me if I already knew my way around the place. I did. So he just let me fuck off. And I did. I kept to myself; we divided the reshelving work, and I tried not to step on his toes. I was even an outcast in the library. Super cool. This wasn't your normal library, though. There were tons of teen sex and partying going on in there. And drugs. All the drugs.

Not really, but I read a book about drugs, *Dinky Hocker Shoots Smack*. I read everything I could in those two years. I did a whole lot of reading and hiding. Kids couldn't ridicule or threaten me in the library, so the library became my safe zone.

In my own neighborhood I only had a couple of safe zones. Well, one, really: My bedroom. And that's it. Bullies at school are one thing, but having them in your neighborhood pretty much ensures that you'll always be home or on edge. Any adventure outside of my apartment had the potential for violence and humiliation. I had several houses I tried to avoid when I was alone, for fear of running into one of two bully families. Yep: two whole families of mean assholes. Let's call them the Wilsons and the Not-Wilsons.

The Wilsons were almost all bully dicks, even the girls. Five kids. Four bullies. Doug Wilson, the middle son, wasn't a bully, just kind of a sweet stoner. He turned me on to Cheech and Chong. So, indirectly, he got me high. And saved my ass one day. There were four Not-Wilson boys, and two were bully dicks. I was actually friends with the two youngest brothers. That saved my ass from any real beating, but it didn't stop the older brothers from spooking me or intimidating me on purpose.

I inherited Hinchman's paper route. Russ and Darren had a paper route too. And they shared their customers and their payments. I paid for my movies, comic books, music, and snacks with money from my paper route as well as yard work in the neighborhood. One day I was riding home after my paper route. I guess I was super bored, because I closed my eyes while riding my bike. Remember when I said I was a smart kid? Forget that part. I closed my eyes for about five seconds, and it immediately went south on me. I felt myself swerving left, I went over a bump, and before I could figure out what was happening, I was freefalling off an embankment into a twenty-foot-deep ditch.

Doug Wilson saved me. He saw me crash. I heard him call my name from the street. I was trapped under my bike and had my paper route bag wrapped around one of my legs. He came down into the ditch and freed me; then he yanked me, my bike, and paper route bags out of the ditch. Later he died in a super-shitty way. He was flying on his motorcycle through our neighborhood on a rainy day, hit an oily patch in front of his house, and got thrown onto the roof of his mom's house. He was dead when he landed. Fucking awful. Doug was a good dude. I didn't even know people could die that horribly until that day.

By junior high I wasn't really friendly with Larry anymore. I mostly stayed out of his way because he teased me nonstop. Although it went both ways; I thought he was a loser dick by then. When I wasn't in school or at home or church, I was riding my bike around the neighborhood with Hinchman and the Goodmans. We were on bikes all the time. And when we weren't on bikes we were in the creek. And almost all those times we were getting into shit. Or just being dumb as fuck.

Both Hinchman and the Goodmans had the Sonoma Creek running behind their houses. The four of us built a fort in the creek behind Russ and Darren's. As with a million other boys in the seventies and eighties, the fort became where we hid our porn stash. In our case, mostly *Playboy*s and random *Penthouse*s. I had a bad experience with the hardcore shit like *Hustler*. Let's table that one for now.

We took rafts and inner tubes into the creek behind the Hinchmans' and could ride them down to the Goodmans'. Both the fort and the raft adventures would end badly. Hinchman would nearly die when he took a two-by-four to the skull and water tried to murder me a second time one summer day under the Madrone Road bridge.

The two-by-four story first. One day Russ, Darren, and I were hanging out at our tree fort down at the creek, eating snacks, looking at dirty magazines or motorcycle magazines or car magazines, being typical thirteen- or fourteen-year-old dorks. We heard a noise coming from the trees, and Russ, in classic tree fort fashion, yelled, "Who goes there?" because I guess he'd seen it in a movie or something. We didn't hear anything. The tree we were in was thirty feet tall and on a twenty-foot embankment. Below the embankment was a thicket of trees and bushes, so when you were in the tree fort, you couldn't see what was coming through the trees or bushes below.

Russ yelled, "Who goes there?" And no one answered, so Russ said, "Watch this." I didn't know then that those were a redneck's last words. He grabbed the two-by-four, and like we said back then, "he fricking winged it" through the trees.

The two-by-four went zipping end over end and made a direct hit on Hinchman's skull. If I had done it, nothing would have happened. I might've hit myself or not even gotten the board out of the tree. But because Russ was kind of a jock, athletic, and coordinated, he fucking nailed Hinchman. He stumbled out into the clearing and reached his arms to the sky, like Willem Dafoe in *Platoon*.

Then we saw what had happened: the board hit him right between the eyes. There was a giant two-by-four mark—well, not giant: it was two inches by four inches, and blood was dripping down his face. Hinchman took his knees dramatically and fell forward, dropping everything in his hands. He had brought us a two-liter bottle of soda and a giant bag of Ruffles. We climbed out of the tree panicking, Russ went first and was scrambling too fast down the tree.

He got his foot stuck in the ladder and then fell. He swung against the tree upside down, with his foot still caught. It was more dramatic than comedic at the time. Darren helped him down, and we all ran down and got Jim. We carried him out of the creek and home. Russ and I had to tell Jim's parents what had happened. They took him to the doctor. It was a concussion. He was never the same. Just kidding—he was fine.

The creek was where I almost died a second time. I could've/should've died in the creek one Saturday morning. It might have been karmic retribution for all the shit I had pulled at the creek. Hinchman and I experimented with Molotov cocktails because we saw it in *Dirty Mary, Crazy Larry*. Once, we threw a Molotov up onto the bridge. No one was hurt, but, fuck that would be terrifying. We always had fireworks, so that went bad—burned fingers, ringing ears. Lit a field on fire. No big deal.

Hinchman and I ghost rode other kids' bikes off cliffs. We also would fake our deaths by pushing each other off the bridge. The cliff went far enough out that it was only like a six-foot fall, but to drivers it looked like kids were dying. People would jump on their brakes at the sight of seeing a kid murder his friend, and we would scramble and giggle like evil little dicks. The Goodmans were no saints either—they hit a Cadillac with a tractor tire and got in trouble. Thank god I was with my mom in Marin for that one. Sounded fun, though, in a sketchy way. The guys and Hinchman found a giant hundred-pound tractor tire and rolled it down a hill. And of course it fucked up some dude's new caddy. He flipped the fuck out.

Anyway, back to how I almost died. The water in Sonoma Creek was really high and violent after a big winter. I went flying under the bridge—got air. My tube flipped over with my dumb ass stuck in it. I was in a whirlpool. The part that needs air to breath was under water. I remember being flipped around and thinking, *Oh man, I'm dying, I guess . . . that sucks*, or something similar and way more panicky. My older, sometime-bully neighbor Nathan saved me. Don't think he's a good guy or anything, because he later made me trade him my awesome skateboard for a piece of shit.

My mom had bought me a really nice skateboard for Christmas, a Logan Earth Ski with Tracker trucks and Kryptonics wheels. Not bad at all—the most popular board and accessories. Nathan had a cheap plastic board with cheap trucks and wheels. I knew it was a piece of shit, and yet I let him convince me that I was making out in the trade. He was a bully dick taking advantage of my need for approval and passivity.

He might have been doing my mom a favor, though: I'd taken a couple of pretty painful spills on that skateboard. I really wanted to be like Tony Alva and Stacy Peralta and the other guys in my skateboarding magazine, but I was still in the falling-every-time phase. I sprained one wrist bailing in front of my apartment. Another time I was dicking around in the apartment tennis courts by myself, skating as fast as I could, and hit a pebble and was ejected off my board. I tried to stop the ground from killing me by putting my hand out. Snap!

Two hours later we were at shitty Kaiser Hospital, and the doctor very gently lifted my arm to examine it. When he was done, he didn't warn me and just dropped my arm. It banged down on the table pretty hard. That is some quality doctoring. I said "Goddamit" or "Jesus Christ" or something else blasphemous. Not because I was falling away from Christianity but because Tanner in the *Bad News Bears* had opened me up to a new way of talking. I was dropping epithets all the time.

My worst bail would happen on Grandpa Ed's watch. At the end of the seventies skateboarding was just starting to die down. Skate parks had been very profitable for a couple of years, but insurance costs were making it hard for them to stay open. I would be part of the problem. I was visiting my grandparents in Sacramento and conned my Grandpa Ed to take me to a local skate park in the suburbs of Citrus Heights. I had a little bit of experience skating around my neighborhood and breaking my arm, so I was okay messing around on the flat area of the park. I thought I could go on the more advanced run—I couldn't. I entered the snake run with my rudimentary skills and uncoordination. It would only go badly.

I mean, sure, I had my basic beginner tic-tac turns down, and I'm not even sure I did tic-tac in the turns at all. I didn't really slow down, and it is a snake run—that's what the curves are for, to kind of slow you down and also to have fun with these big turns. I didn't take the big turns; I just made a beeline right through the thing. Somebody told me to slow down while I was going through the snake run—a dude yelled, "Hey man, slow down," as I was not even turning, just picking up speed toward the bowl at the end.

It was for intermediate and advanced skaters, and I went in there my first day at the skate park. I was flying into the bowl and zipped across the flat bottom and then up the transition. I went right to the top. I'm sure I came out of the pool because I was able to turn around at least. So my face was pointing at the ground. I doubt I was even on my skateboard when I landed. I hit the ground face first. Oh yeah, I was wearing full braces at the time and a retainer most of the day, and that braces wire stuck through my lip and out eight inches.

I remember walking out of the bowl, holding my skateboard, and I heard at least one kid going, "Oh, gnarly!" I had no idea how gnarly it was because my face was numb.

My grandpa took me home after I stumbled out of the snake run with a bloody face. They gave us a free pass for my ruined face. We never went back, and they closed soon after that because dumb fucking kids kept trying to die there. Grandpa Ed felt like he was at fault, but he wasn't. Me being an idiot and thinking I could handle it was the problem.

I GUESS THAT KIND of confidence is what eventually got me to get up and do stand-up, because I never thought of myself as being a fearless person. I am kind of a scaredy-cat. Maybe this is why banging my face hard knocked some fucking sense into me. My grandpa used wire cutters in his garage and cut the wire out of my head. He pulled it through my lip; I still have a bump. We went to a local orthodontist, and they took care of it. My grandparents were worried about what my mom would think. I'm not sure she cared. But as a result, she didn't want me skateboarding anymore.

So when Nathan forced me to trade my good skateboard for a piece of shit, he saved me from more accidents and becoming a lankier Tony Hawk. Nathan did change the words to that Kool and the Gang song "Celebration" to "Masturbation." "Masturbate tonight, come on! Let's masturbate . . . we're gonna masturbate, y'all." Never mind. Maybe Nathan was a good guy and a fucking genius. And a hero.

I sucked at skateboarding and sticking up for myself, but there were things I didn't suck at. I took photography in eighth grade. I not only didn't suck at it, but I actually enjoyed it. I made some new friends in my photography class, among them a popular kid, John Yomata. John invited me to his house and to a couple of events. I so desperately wanted to move up the social ladder that I bragged about being friends with John to Russ and Jim; I even implied I was gonna be cooler now and might be obligated to spend less time with them. Why would I think that, let alone say that to my friends? Those were some social skills. Luckily my friends were more loyal than I was being.

I had also become skilled at watching kinda shitty TV. I gobbled up every episode of *Magnum PI*, *Knight Rider*, *Incredible Hulk*, *The Greatest American Hero*, *CHiPs*, and *Dukes of Hazzard*. *Magnum* was the best of the bunch, but I was a pretty loyal watcher of *CHiPs* and *Dukes*. I don't think I missed an episode, although they didn't have the impact that comedy shows did. I still enjoyed the action, the quips, and the formula of those shows.

I would draw or build Legos while I watched TV, so it kind of didn't matter that the shows were disposable and pretty dumb. My mom had pretty much let go of the already-few rules she had about TV watching: as long as I wasn't in trouble, I could watch whatever I wanted. My mom had even fewer rules when it came to movies. In fact, in the summer of '78 she had unknowingly planted another comedy seed deep in my brain when she took me to see the R-rated college comedy *Animal House*. Did my mom suddenly turn cool when I graduated from sixth grade? Nope. She actually thought it was an animal movie.

In her defense, we had seen a lot of animal movies. But in my defense, no! It was rated R. And the ads didn't show a bunch of animals living in a house or condo; they showed college kids partying and implied nudity. I really think my mom didn't understand the rating system. The "R" in R rated could have stood for ravioli. She covered my eyes when the first breasts popped on screen. She soon gave up. I think she actually laughed, and we stayed for the whole thing. It wasn't awkward watching nudity and curse words in front of my mom because I was so into the movie that it was like she wasn't even there. And if you're keeping track, it wasn't the first R-rated film I saw with her.

My favorite movies of '78 and '79 were *Superman*, *Heaven Can Wait*, and *Up in Smoke*, although I didn't see *Up in Smoke* until a year or two later on cable. I also loved *Revenge of the Pink Panther* and *Every Which Way but Loose* with Clint Eastwood, Geoffrey Lewis, Clyde the Orangutan, and, the real star, Ruth Gordon. I really enjoyed the smart silliness of

Peter Sellers' *Pink Panther* and the dumb silliness of Clyde punching people, making fart noises, and flipping them off. And I thought Ruth Gordon as the raunchy, "Didn't give a shit" granny was one of the funniest people I had ever seen. "RuthGordon" would later be my gamer tag in the early days of X-Box Live.

But if you would've asked me then what the funniest comedy of '78–79 was, I would've said, "No duh—*Foul Play*." Sure, I was a fan of *Animal House*, but outside of Belushi, no one was that funny in it. *Foul Play*, however, had hilarious performances from Chevy Chase, Goldie Hawn, Dudley Moore, Burgess Meredith, and the manic Billy Barty. *Foul Play* was a farcical murder mystery set in San Francisco, which added to the film that it took place in my favorite city. I probably saw *Foul Play* more than six times in the theater. I was a *Foul Play* nerd. I tried turning my friends onto the movie too. It wasn't really a kid's comedy; it didn't stick with them. That was fine with me. I was cool with *Foul Play* being my thing.

Ken still lived with us, so that got worse and worse. I saw him nude once. Yep, just once. That was enough. I caught a gander of his furry, old-man cock and balls. I had gotten up to pee and was half asleep when I eyeballed the shlong of the dude that had just been inside my mommy. I looked at him and said, "Jesus, Ken, grab a towel." One of the best things I've ever said in my life for one of the worst reasons. It's hard to be funny when a dude just fucked your mom, and yet it's kind of exciting in the movie *Kramer vs. Kramer* when the little kid sees his dad's new lady and she's naked and clearly postcoitus.

I had the reverse *Kramer vs. Kramer*. Not so sexy when it's Ken the Monster and he's hairy like Wolverine without the adamantium claws. It says a lot about what a dick this

guy was to be naked in a tiny apartment in front of me and
so shameless and not giving a shit if he was scarring me or
not. Know this, dear reader: if and when I fuck your mom, I
promise to be cool about it.

Then, Easter break, 1979, my mom and Ken took me
back to Mount Hermon, that Christian camp in the Santa
Cruz Mountains. This time my pal Russ came with me. We
had a blast. Camp was way more fun with my good pal and
because he had a way higher charisma than me and made
some decent rolls, so he made some friends for us and even
kissed a girl. Making out at a Christian camp? Yep, I'm
pretty sure if you had a high enough charisma and were
in the right club, there was butt fucking. Not the vagina,
though—that's for Jesus. Anyway, a good time was had.

A week later my mom and Ken returned to pick Russ
and me up. I needed new shoes. Apparently it had already
been decided that we get the shoes at Kmart. I fought it.
I did not want to even go inside. Then we got to the shoe
department. Everything was hideous. No Nikes. No Pumas.
No Adidas. I complained. Pretty hard. It was embarrassing
in front of Russ. My mom softened. We didn't have to get
shoes here; she and I would go somewhere else when we got
home. Ken doubled down. I was going to be humiliated in
front of Russ if it was the last thing he did.

Dipshit von Fuckface reached into a barrel of shoes—a
fucking barrel—and pulled out a pair of Tiffs. I had seen
them before and hated them. Tiffs were fake Adidas. Tiffs
were the worst and would cause instant teasing. Steve Martin
had written a short story called "Cruel Shoes" about Tiffs,
because the teasing would be cruel. They were made with
faux leather and had four stripes instead of the classic three.
The good news was you could be a vegan and wear them. I

wasn't a vegan. They weren't even sold in a box—they were loose in a barrel. At least there was a plastic loop attaching each shoe to its pair. I. Threw. A. Shit-fit. He tossed out this old chestnut: "They look just like Adidas!" To which I replied, "There is an extra stripe, you dick." I won that one. I wound up with suede Pumas, and Ken griped about it. I wore the shit out of those Pumas.

Ken wasn't all bad—he loved Monty Python, I'll give him that. Ken was a dick, for sure—let's not get it twisted— but he did expose me to some cool stuff. Although I hated Monty Python in the beginning, I think because he loved it so much. But I learned about it through him and my nerdy uncle and now count it as a big influence.

At the same time, the older I got, the meaner my mom got. I was a total smartass, but telling me that my dad "didn't want a kid anyway," that he was upset when she got pregnant, so he "wasn't so great" didn't help her case. Neither did her telling me, "I bet you wish I had died instead." Which was fucked up. She also used to say, "And to think your dad and I wanted more kids before we had you." That one kind of stung. Even more when I consider my mom had a miscarriage right before my dad died, but still.

I started to enjoy making her insane—I could wind her up so easily. My mom called me a "son of a bitch" one day. She never did that again because I snapped back, "Then what does that make you?" Like any good joke or comedy routine, I would call it back by yelling, "Call me a son of a bitch." What a little dick I was. What a genius little dick.

I even threatened Ken in front of my mom: "I hope Starsky and Hutch come and kill you." Which they never once did on their show. Not one episode featured them going to some kid's apartment and killing his mom's boyfriend for no reason. My punishment was that I was no longer allowed to watch the show. Glad I didn't tell Ken, "I hope *Saturday Night Live* kills you."

But here's more from the "my mom wasn't all bad" department. She tried to bond with me by getting the two of us acoustic guitars and taking lessons. I stuck with it longer than she did, which was easy, as she didn't really try. I learned a couple of songs—the *M*A*S*H* theme (which was called "Suicide Is Painless") and "Blowin' in the Wind." When she wouldn't let me make the leap to electric, I quit. I sure showed her, not learning a skill.

My mom and I took a trip to Yosemite during the summer of '79, and I got to bring Hinchman. It was a blast, and we didn't burn down a National Park. In the summer of '80 my eighth-grade graduation gift was a trip to Los Angeles with my mom to visit Disneyland and Universal Studios. We actually had a blast and didn't fight. Maybe because she didn't bring Ken's dumb ass with us.

When handheld electronic games came out, I would play them to shut out my mom and Ken. But nothing could beat the combo of my two favorite things back then: reading and music. Growing up, I always had music on when I was reading in my room, and when cassette players became portable, the music went with me. First, I had a little Radio Shack cassette recorder my Grandma Clara had owned. When I visited her one trip, I played Cheap Trick, KISS, Queen, and Pat Benatar on it my whole vacation, so when I went home she let me take it with me. It sounds like a little thing, but everything my grandma did for me was a big thing. I just teared up thinking about her. My Grandma Clara made a huge impression on me, and I still cherish the fifteen years I was privileged to have with her.

I took that recorder everywhere I went; it had a tiny speaker, but it did the trick. Then I got a small radio/cassette player with a bigger speaker and decent sound. Soon the Walkman came out. No one ever heard me again at Thanksgiving or Christmas after the Walkman except my cousin Todd, because I'd tell him what I was listening to.

With music and books I could be alone anywhere. The older I got, the more comfortable I became with being alone. I went solo a lot. I rode my bike all over town and usually had a book and headphones with me. People thought I was a "lonesome loser." I would sure show them. I'm glad I found Iron Maiden and Stephen King instead of guns, because this book would be super different.

My visits to see my Grandma Clara and my grandpa were a safe haven from everything that sucked. Just fun and smiley-face pancakes. Grandpa Ed, the creative guy he was, made me a minibike. He fucking made it. He just welded a frame together, machined and welded a pair of handlebars, threw a lawnmower motor in it and slapped some wheels and a seat on it. I had about five years of fun on that thing, ripping up and down the street and fishtailing up his gravel driveway. The lankier I got, the goofier I looked. I didn't care.

Russ and I went to my grandparents' house for a week during the summer of '80. That was my first real taste of alcohol: we had a Posehn family reunion that featured Sacto Posehns, family from Canada and Germany, and my Uncle Mike's homemade beer. Russ and I snuck a couple of beers and hung out in my grandpa's camper drinking and playing Cheap Trick's "Dream Police" over and over on the camper's stereo. My grandpa loved entertaining relatives, and that summer they hosted a German cousin my grandpa called "the Berliner," Robert Posehn. Same name as my dad. More drunk and less dead.

"The Berliner" sounds like a spy name, but to me all it meant is that, because of the reputation of the Germans, he liked to drink even more than my grandpa. That trip they were all over my Uncle Mike's homemade brew all day, and Robert even loved American beer. He would start his morning with Budweiser tall boys. As twelve-year-old kids, Russ and I thought the Berliner was a badass. He was really just a doughy day drinker on vacation.

On one of my trips visiting Grandma Clara she and I made a movie with my second cousins; they were her sister's granddaughters and they lived in Sacto. We did it silent movie style. Even the story was old school, real Snidely Whiplash shit: I was the bad guy and captured one of my cousins and tied her to train tracks. I had a painted-on twirly mustache. Anyway, Grandma Clara made costumes and wrote all the subtitles in old timey letters. It was super fun and came out great. Fuck, I wish I had that somewhere. My first movie.

Life wasn't that bad with my Grandma Clara in it. No matter how rough it got at school, with bullies and teachers, and at home with my mom and Ken the Monster, at least my Grandma Clara was still alive. For now. I would really need her as my support system and life's biggest cheerleader for my first two years of high school. Sadly, that's all I would get.

EIGHT

1979–1981:
THE MAKING OF
A TEENAGE METALHEAD

A key event in my development as a metalhead was that second Christmas in a row when my mom asked me what I wanted for Christmas and I said, "whatever music is popular." In 1976 that record was KC and the Sunshine Band, *Part 3*. Pretty sure it was their third record. Anyway, I was ten—it was disco. I listened to it, but this book isn't about me turning into a disco nerd and meeting all my disco idols, so obviously it didn't stick. Fucking Disco Bri would not be as fun as Disco Stu.

In 1977 Disco Bri was destroyed forever by my cool cousin. That Christmas my mom asking the clerk at Warehouse Records, "What album is popular with kids?" would bite me in the ass. Because I unwrapped a vinyl masterpiece. Of shit. I got Shaun Cassidy, *Born Late*, his second record of boring pop ear garbage. My cousin Todd got *Physical Graffiti* by Led Zeppelin. I was schooled by my older, much cooler cousin. I liked what I heard. A lot.

It was my intro to Led Zeppelin. I knew who they were before, but now I connected this heavy, groovy music to them. We didn't even play Shaun that day. I took it home and gave it a shot. It was seventies pop, all right. He was related to a Partridge, and it fit: it sounded like music made for teenage girls. Back it went to the Warehouse Records in Santa Rosa, where the clerk felt for me and let me get something else. They didn't have *Physical Graffiti* or the Zep discography that was huge and confusing to my young dumb ass, so I went with more KISS. Lesson learned, though. I would find music on my own from then on.

By seventh grade, 1978–79, my metamorphosis into a rock fan had begun. Pop and disco could no longer pierce my thickening hide. I was drawn to a lot of bands in those next couple years, several styles approaching rock and hard rock, but there was one constant that drew me to rock—the guitars, the driving beat, the attitude, the big vocals, the aggression. I grew up in a perfect time to be a hard-rock fan: it was constantly changing, and it was getting more aggressive and shocking.

I knew that when rock and roll started in the fifties it was shocking and seen as rebel music. And I wanted the modern version of that, whatever was shocking or scary now. But not too scary. And as I became more and more disenfranchised from junior high, my mom, and the church and started to feel like a misfit, I became a bigger rock fan. Rock music didn't make me a misfit, but it was there for me when I felt left out.

By the way, I'm the first person ever to feel that way about rock music. I'm pretty fucking cool, you guys. I liked rock—we've established—and by eighth grade I really liked hard rock and I wanted it harder. I became obsessed with seeking it out.

I found a lot of music by listening to metal shows on the radio, reading every music magazine I could get ahold of, snooping around record stores, and just asking a record store clerk, "Hey, what is new and heavy?" and "Hey, what is that you're playing?" and "Hey, how old do I have to be to work here?" But I didn't always find bands on my own. Older kids in the neighborhood or at school passed quite a few of my favorite bands on to me.

Even with KISS, it was somebody else passing them on—though I never knew that mystery kid. I remember nothing about him, only that 45 and my intro to KISS. Maybe it was a ghost kid. Maybe it was the devil getting me to sell my soul to Satan through the music of four dorks in makeup. Lots of other music was first introduced to me by some cool, older kid. Just like I'd been schooled on comedy legends Richard Pryor and Cheech and Chong from two older neighborhood stoners, John and Doug, I'd learn about music in similar ways—well, one way—from neighborhood stoners.

I heard about a lot of my favorite bands at school. I was exposed to AC/DC, Led Zeppelin, Ted Nugent, Cheap Trick, The Cars, and Pink Floyd through other kids in junior high. Actually, my math teacher, Mr. Ross, had a Nugent poster in his class. I doubt he still does—it's pretty liberal where I grew up, and Mr. Ross wore Birkenstocks and taught math and drama. So he's not dumb, and he not only likes theater, he taught it. He probably gave kids an outlet for shit the Nuge would frown on and try to shoot at.

In seventh grade I remember the Blues Brothers and The Eagles being super popular. "Cool" kids played the Blues Brothers on their boombox at lunch. I didn't get it. I liked the Blues Brothers routine on *SNL* and would later love their movie, but I gotta be honest: outside of "Rubber Biscuit," the music didn't do much for me. They were playing old man's music. I wanted music for me.

At one point it seemed like everybody in my entire junior high loved The Eagles, but not this guy. "Hey Posehn, what is your favorite Eagles album?" Me, totally panicking, "Um, the one with 'Hotel California' on it." They all laughed. "That is *Hotel California*, dumbass. That's what the album is called." Ugh, really fun times. I got made fun of for not liking the fucking Eagles. I should have killed everyone there just for that.

Billy Joel was huge at my school too. I didn't like Billy Joel. Now I fucking hate Billy Joel. *Glass Houses* was super popular. Somebody played it during art, and I thought it sounded like beer commercial music.

I didn't dig Springsteen either or most of the shit I heard in art class. Didn't love Bob Seger or The Steve Miller Band. I didn't think his song "Rock'n Me" was very rocking at all. In fact, I found the Steve Miller Band to be rather lacking in the rock department.

It wasn't all shitty classic rock, which back then we just called rock. I also heard Led Zep's "Black Dog" through a cool kid's boombox at lunch and was stunned. The kid's name was Joel. I didn't know much about him other than the fact that he knew everyone, everyone loved him, he was a seventh-grader, and the eighth-graders didn't fuck with him. When I heard Robert Plant's opening line, "Hey, hey mama, said the way you move, gonna make you sweat, gonna make you groove," my twelve-year-old brain was trying to figure out what the heck that super-cool-sounding singer guy was saying and who he was saying it to.

Then the band kicked in with this monstrous groove. I knew about Zeppelin, but being kid-centric, I kind of saw them as an older person's band, like Black Sabbath or Deep Purple. My uncle liked Led Zeppelin. He also liked Hendrix, The Stones, and The Who. So I lumped them in together. They were cool, but not for me. I wanted current music, which is how Zep really won me over: they made a great record in '79, *In Through the Out Door*. It might not be their best record, but it was new and pretty cool, and that was enough. I bought the cassette and was officially a Zeppelin fan.

I found a couple of other bands at Altamira Junior High—Cheap Trick, The Cars, and Pat Benatar, who I instantly liked. And Pink Floyd, who I didn't click with right away. I heard quite a bit of Pink Floyd's *The Wall* during art class. I liked the single "Another Brick in the Wall, Part Two," but I thought the rest was too mellow. Now I think "Comfortably Numb" is one of the best songs ever. Pot and age will make anyone a Pink Floyd lover.

Actually, most of my musical schooling happened closer to home. Thin Lizzy was on the radio, but my friend Tony's older brother, Mike, told me "Aw, man, they don't play the good shit on the radio. You gotta listen to the whole *Jailbreak* album." He's right: that album rules. Mike had a UFO sticker on his Camaro, so he knew what he was talking about. I was aware of the band UFO, but only that I knew cool older kids with nice cars and mustaches liked them. Mike wasn't the only older sibling of a friend who influenced me.

Enter Kristi. Hinchman's cute, older sister. Kristi was only two years older than us, but like Tami Baker, she and her friends seemed like adults to me. She was like Lori Partridge, but wilder and more 1979: she made out in Camaros with dudes with mustaches. They were seventeen but looked like the teens in *Porky's*, which is to say thirty-year-olds. She lived with Hinchman's mom but still kept stuff at her dad's house. When she wasn't around we raided her record collection.

Through her or, more importantly, from rooting through her shit, I was turned on to Motörhead: *Ace of Spades*, Black Sabbath: *Paranoid*, and that terrible fucking "human" Ted Nugent's *Double Live Gonzo*. And she's responsible indirectly for turning me on to one of the single-greatest metal records ever, the sonic perfection that is Judas Priest: *British Steel*. Through Kristi I also heard about local Bay Area bands Yesterday and Today as well as Huey Lewis and the News; I stuck with one of them. Yesterday and Today became Y&T, and Huey Lewis and the News were notable for ruining the eighties.

I remember learning about Van Halen from Jamie, an older girl who lived in our apartment complex. Jamie was my sometime babysitter. And by learning, I mean she schooled me like a hard-rock professor. One night she brought over Van Halen: *I* and *II* and played them on my mom's stereo. She played "Beautiful Girls," "Running with the Devil," her favorite, "Jamie's Crying," and a couple of others. I loved all of it. The guitars. Those vocals. It was heavy and very slick and melodic at the same time.

We looked at the album covers: "This is Eddie and Alex Van Halen. Eddie is the best guitarist since Hendrix." My Van Halen lessons worked; I bought both albums immediately. So when Van Halen released their third record, *Women and Children First*, I was waiting for it. And it was awesome. One of their heaviest records. *Women and Children First* was *my* first Van Halen record. I bought it on cassette first, because of one word: Walkman.

Because I was able to have music with me at all times in 1980, my cassette buying increased. I amassed a pretty big collection quickly. I was still getting vinyl, mind you. Some stuff you could only get on vinyl, especially when I started going more metal. Jamie also turned me on to Journey, and her mom taught me what marijuana smelled like. Her house also smelled like my Uncle Gary's house and my friend Larry's mom. Jamie only babysat me a couple of times because I was getting to the age when I didn't need a sitter really, but I loved that she brought records over. Kids today don't know about bringing records over to someone's house without bringing irony and kitsch with them. And fuck irony and kitsch. Never been a fan.

The years 1980 and 1981 were great for my musical development. I got deeper into Van Halen and Journey and bought *Infinity* and *Evolution* with my sweet paper route cash. And I was properly introduced to bands I'd only heard of previously, like UFO, April Wine, Triumph, and Black Sabbath. A kid in freshman wood shop had bought *Heaven and Hell* from the record store across the street from the high school. I honestly wasn't a Black Sabbath fan before that; I think I was kinda scared of them. Actually, I know I was. As a Christian kid I thought their act seemed real and pretty scary.

He had the vinyl in class, and I looked at the art and was in. It was subtle, not overtly evil and too scary. That was my intro to Black Sabbath, the first album with the new singer, Ronnie James Dio. Black Sabbath with Dio was new, so I was fired up to check it out. Not long after I bought *Heaven and Hell*, the *Heavy Metal* soundtrack with the new Sabbath song, "The Mob Rules," was released. Which, to this day, is still one of my favorite Sabbath songs. A couple of months later the album *Mob Rules* dropped.

The more nerdy I got about music, the more I wanted to go to a live show. I wanted KISS to be my first concert; they came through San Francisco on the Dynasty tour in 1979. I didn't love that album, but I still wanted to see them. It was a big nope from my mom. She thought I was too young. I was so jealous of the kids from school who went. They were two friends, Pete and Brian, and from their details about the show, Ace Frehley sounded like the highlight. He was still my favorite in eighth grade. And then Ace left soon after, so missing the show really stung. Or Ace was fired, depends on which KISS member's book you read. I of course read them all. And, of course, Ace's was the best.

A year and a half later, in the summer of 1981, I would finally go to my first concert. It was Y&T, the Tubes, and local act 415 (the SF area code) at the Petaluma Fairgrounds. Music nerd fact, 415 featured the singer Eric Martin, who later had a solo band, The Eric Martin Band, and the song "Sucker for a Pretty Face." Anybody? Didn't think so. Eric also sang for Mr. Big with Billy Sheehan from Talas, David Lee Roth, and a million other eighties bands.

I went to the concert with Hinchman and my mom's friend's daughter. Don't even remember her name. Yep, barely knew her, but I wanted to go to that concert so bad, so when I heard my mom's friend Lynn tell my mom that her daughter was going to the Petaluma Fair, I jumped on it, did some schmoozing and finagling, and a week later we were watching Y&T with fellow teens and drunk grownups. The friend, Lynn's daughter or whatever, didn't even watch the concert; she just dropped off two young boys and picked them up four hours later. The late seventies were so awesome. There were no weirdos or murderers yet because murder wasn't invented until 1982.

The Tubes were the headliners, but Hinchman and I really wanted to see Y&T the most. We liked The Tubes—I had seen them play "White Punks on Dope" on TV—but that was as deep as I went on them. And 415, the local openers, weren't terrible, just late-eighties pop rock, like The Babies. But they were not our focus at all; we came for the middle act. That both bands didn't suck was a bonus, but these two dudes came over the hill from Sonoma to Petaluma at fifteen years old to see Y&T, as previously indicated.

And we were not disappointed. They made me a bigger fan than I already was. It was the Earthshaker Tour; I had to score the *Earthshaker* album the day after the concert. Lead singer/guitar player Dave Meniketti was putting on a guitar-shredding clinic, an impressive front-man and overall bad-ass. When they played "Rescue Me" it was super explosive and dynamic. The whole band ripped, but Dave was the star; his guitar playing was the most impressive musical feat I'd ever seen.

His tone was incredible, and still, in my mind, Dave Meniketti is one of the most underrated hard-rock guitar players around. Hinchman and I definitely both loved the live experience and wanted more of it. I had a blast being a part of this big group, and it introduced me to songs I didn't already know. At the end of the show I wanted to delve deeper into Y&T but also experience more live events. I wouldn't get to go to another live show for a whole other year, but I was hooked on concerts. Forty years of concert T-shirts and drunk dudes peeing too close for my liking at a giant piss trough awaited me.

I liked a lot of music in those years; it was a full-on obsession. But my favorites by the end of '81 were Van Halen, AC/DC, Def Leppard, Iron Maiden, and America's favorite madman, Ozzy. I also started a lifelong love affair with Rush. Those three genius Canadians have a whole chapter coming up, so hang on. I was already a fan of AC/DC after hearing

Highway to Hell. Then my freshman year *Back in Black* was released, the first album since rock god and original singer Bon Scott's death. It didn't take long to get used to Brian Johnson, Scott's replacement. The riffs were still great from the guitar god brothers, Angus and Malcolm Young. But this record somehow sounded bigger than anything they'd done before. Production was a new concept for me.

By junior high I was back in therapy; I went to the same guy for several years. When my mom and I were at our worst, we started going to a family therapist named Hank. He helped as much as he could. When high school was at its worst, I went to him by myself. He actually became a friend. Hank would let me earn AC/DC cassettes as incentives for not being a dick to my mom. He used his own money to help me—what a cool dude. More about Hank my helpful shrink later. I earned copies of *High Voltage* and *Powerage* next. AC/DC were another obsession. I blew out my mom's speakers with *Back in Black*.

Back in Black wasn't too dramatic, not like a music video or *Back to the Future*—there were no explosions. I was just cranking the iconic title track "Back in Black," and the opening riff sounded amazing so loud, and then it didn't. There was a loud buzz, followed by a sound of a playing card flapping on a bicycle wheel. The paper woofer cone on her cheap-ass JCPenney's speakers had ripped. It was like a heavy-metal rite of passage, ruining your mom's stereo. Thanks, Angus and Malcolm! Fuck you, Mom. Christmas 1981 at my Uncle Gary's in Tahoe was dominated by a gift from my mom, a cassette of AC/DC, *For Those About to Rock*. She got better at gifts when I told her exactly what to get. The title track played over and over to drown out my mom and my nana's constant bickering that holiday. Great record, but heavier stuff was taking over. I also played the crap out of my gift of Rush, *Exit . . . Stage Left*. This whole time I was getting deeper and deeper into Rush, but, like I said, more about them later.

I found Def Leppard in a Musicland, a chain record store in the Santa Rosa mall. As California chain record stores went, it wasn't the best. Tower ruled, but I didn't have one close by. I heard the Def Leppard riffs first and asked the clerk what was playing. He pointed to the cover of their second album, *High 'N' Dry*. It was brand new. I had been shopping for school clothes with my mom and ducked into the record store because it was impossible at that point for me to walk by a record store and not go in. I walked in and had to have whatever this was that was playing. I didn't know who they were, but the production sounded like AC/DC's *Back in Black*.

They were both produced by the same guy, John "Mutt" Lange. So, duh. The vocalist had a different singing style from Brian Johnson. He had a smoother voice, and the music was more melodic and slicker than AC/DC, but the opening track, "Let It Go," drew me in and didn't let me go. Sorry, I just flashbacked to writing high school music reviews. It was hard rock, not quite metal. It was the innate musicality and melody to it that I was drawn to it and had that metallic guitar tone. I loved the hooks. I liked the lyrics. Sure, they were simple, but to a young kid they reeked of cool. I was drawn to their attitude, and with the guys in the band teenagers themselves, it added to the appeal: teenage rebellion music made by teenagers. Fucking-A! Sign me up, man!

I got really into that record—cassette, rather—and played it all the time. It is a perfect record, not a bum track on the whole thing. Def Leppard wound up being such a massive band after this, and that would be hard for me and tested my fandom. I bailed on them after *Pyromania* but still think they're a great band with a unique sound and some of the biggest hooks in rock. I'm not gonna make one-armed drummer jokes. You and I are both better than that. Two years later they would have one of the biggest albums in the country, and I would start hating Def Leppard.

Of all the music I'd hear my freshman year, none would be as life changing as Iron Maiden and Ozzy Osbourne. Maiden was mind-blowing. I had never heard anything as cool and as heavy as them. The other stuff I listened to was hard rock. This was heavy metal. Maiden had this indescribable authenticity, and the whole band had chops. I didn't even know what chops were—it was so intense and complex and not like anything I'd ever heard.

I heard *Killers* before I heard Iron Maiden's self-titled debut. And though I dig *Iron Maiden*, I prefer the second record. It's heavier and better produced. *Killers* starts with "Ides of March," this metallic instrumental with marching percussion, a ripping guitar solo, then "Wrathchild" starts, Dave Murray rips a mini-solo, and heavy metal changed forever. Paul DiAnno's menacing vocals start.

And at that time I had never heard anything this fast or aggressive. The metal screams were the coolest thing ever, and the lyrics—holy shit. "Wrathchild" is revenge horror; the singer is hunting a dude down. Then comes "Murders in the Rue Morgue," which is based on Poe's "Murders in the Rue Morgue." The lyrics were always a draw for me with Iron Maiden, and I thought it was so cool that they wrote songs inspired by literary works; they would do it more and more over the years. For me it started here. I had always loved storytelling songs, and Maiden did that song after song. They don't get half the credit they deserve.

Their music may seem dumb and aggressive, but I would argue that they were and are one of the smartest and nerdiest metal bands ever. Plus, the logo kicks ass, and their mascot, Eddie—well, Eddie fucking rules.

My Maiden love would deepen even more in '82 when they'd get a new singer. I thought the twin guitar playing of Maiden's virtuosos Dave Murray and Adrian Smith was incredible. I thought Angus Young had the coolest guitar sound and that Eddie Van Halen was a badass. And then I heard Randy Rhoads. Randy was a fucking wizard among mere human guitar players.

Much like discovering Def Leppard, I owe it to a record store clerk in a mall record store. It was the Warehouse Records in the Terra Linda mall where I had bought KISS, *Alive II*, and then I had been on a KISS mission. With Ozzy I was in the right place at the right time—browsing through the vinyl when a record started on the store's sound system. It was insanely fast picking, with a driving beat and the guitar threw some black-magic wizard shit on me with this nutso-insano flourish. Then the king of nutso-insano started singing, and I made a beeline to the record store clerk. "Who is this?" "What is this?" "How much is this?" "Can I have this already?"

The song was called "I Don't Know," and the band or singer was called Ozzy Osbourne. I knew that name. "He was the singer for Black Sabbath and they kicked him out. They blew it!" He was right. They did blow it. I had heard Black Sabbath with Ozzy, and it was cool enough—"Paranoid" was catchy, but I had been scared of them. This had a scary album cover, Ozzy looked like a nut and had a crucifix in his hand, and my Christian Spidey sense was screaming, but this music was fucking incredible.

And the guitar player, this Randy Rhoads kid from California who Ozzy had found, was a metal messiah. If following this new messiah would secure my place in hell, then I was more than cool with it. Metal was becoming my religion, and Randy was my new god. The music of Ozzy and Randy Rhoads made my first couple of years of high school almost livable, and even if you are barely aware of who Randy Rhoads is, you probably know how tragically his story ends and what I and a million other teenage fans had waiting for us in 1982.

Grandma Clara and the longest baby ever. The grandma/long baby bond is strong. 1966-ish.

The Posehns: Dad, Mom, and tiny me. I was two. This was right before my dad died. Sorry to be a bummer, but it's true. July 1968.

My two grandpas. Grandpa Ed, me, Grandpa
George. This is after my dad died, but probably
before my grandpas died. 1968.

First grade, San Jose, CA.
Cute kid, pretty happy.
He has no fucking idea.

Seventh grade, Russ and I on my tiny bed. I quickly grew out of it. Wish I never grew out of that sweet Steve Martin shirt, "Best Fishes" indeed.

Seventh grade school picture. Holy shit, that's a lot of nerd. Why do I look so damn happy? Could I see me?

Eighth grade graduation, Altamira Junior High.
Man, I want to punch myself. I totally get it.

Rush nerd. I think I'm informing the viewer that Rush is number one. Still true. Summer 1984.

River's Edge. Me down at the American River with my new leather jacket and my pretty, pretty hair. So Metal! By the way, that's the river where they found my grandpa. 1988.

Straight from a surf shop to the stage. Metro Comedy,
Sacramento, CA, 1988.

My mom and I, enjoying a beer and a laugh
after a *Mr. Show* taping. 1997-ish.

Meeting heroes, with Mark Hamill and my old pal, Tom Kenny.
San Diego Comic-Con, 2004.

Just three old pals palling around on the set of our Comedy Central pilot, *Super Nerds*, with Patton Oswalt and Sarah Silverman. 2000.

Meeting heroes. Wasted and nerdy in Vegas with my buddy Scott Ian, and my favorite member of KISS, Ace Frehley. 2004-ish.

Makeup maestro Wayne Toth, a happy nerd with a bullet wound, and Rob Zombie. *Devil's Rejects* makeup trailer somewhere in the California desert. 2004.

Mr. Show Live, "Hooray for America." With Bob Odenkirk. 2002.

Meeting heroes. Ronnie James Dio in my kitchen. One of the best days ever. 2009.

The dude who got me through high school, my buddy Joel and I at our 20th reunion. 2004.

My future wife, Melanie, and I at the Emmys, 1998. *Mr. Show* didn't win, but I'm pretty sure we did stuff in a limo that night.

Happy honeymooners in Ixtapa, Mexico, 2004. I'm pretty sure we did stuff in Mexico too.

Meeting heroes, with Rush. (*From left to right*) Alex Lifeson, giant Rush nerd, my pal Dave Rath, and Geddy Fucking Lee. LA Forum, 2016.

Meeting heroes, with Carrie Fisher. She will always be my Princess. Montreal, JFL, 2016.

My tiny Jedi, Rhoads Posehn, joined our family in 2009.
Halloween has never been the same. He never had a chance
to not be a nerd.

My mom (Nana Carole), Rhoads(1½), Melanie, and a happy dad. Christmas, 2010.

Happy family. With Melanie and Rhoads (7). Tahoe, 2016.

NINE

HIGH SCHOOL: THE WORST TWO YEARS OF MY LIFE

The worst two years? Not just of school, but of life? Sure, I know that sounds dramatic as fuck, even for me. But after a brutal year and a half, by the middle of my sophomore year I felt pretty alone. I thought my situation would never improve or change. Kids thought I was a weird loser, so I felt like a weird loser.

When I would slam my door and plop onto my tiny bed and cry, it felt really shitty and hopeless. I was sad and angry a lot. I didn't think I was that ugly or weird, and I didn't understand why people would make me feel like that. And other days I agreed with everyone: I was ugly and weird. I was the ugliest weirdo to ever ugly a weirdo. Around then is when I started to question God: Why would he let a nice kid who worships him lose his dad, have a mom who hates him, and let most kids treat him like a joke or a punching bag?

It felt like everyone was against me before I started high school in September of 1980. It was about to get much worse: I would soon lose a lot of friends. A year later my best friend would be gone forever. At the end of my first week of Sonoma Valley High School I lost the guys I'd hung around with since fifth grade. I had already been singled out by quite a few older kids during the first four days of school, and my pals decided to let me go. After a rocky first week as freshmen, life was going to continue to be rough for them if they kept me as a friend.

Their solution? Wait until lunchtime, when we were walking off school grounds to a local deli to tell me. And by tell me, I mean they threw rocks and dirt clods at me to make me stop hanging around them. Like I was a weird stray dog with a milky eye and a near-constant erection and they were rednecks who decided they didn't like the "boner dog" anymore and weren't familiar with the words "Go away, boner dog."

It wasn't all my friends who threw the dirt clods and rocks and insults, but they were all there. Robert with glasses, Karl, Seth, Monte, my friends since Dunbar were the guys who were the loudest and most physical. Russ, Darren, and Hinchman were there too. They hadn't jumped in or defended me. Either way, I got the message: "Go away, Brian Posehn." I kind of prefer "boner dog."

That was the worst lunch of my life. And I'm a road comic—I've eaten lunch at IHOP. The International House of Pancakes. In the middle of the day. By myself. When you eat alone at an IHOP the waiter should just put a party hat on you and shoot you in the face. Anyway, I can't remember if I even got that sandwich that shitty Friday of that shitty first week of my shitty '80–81 school year. I do remember crying on the bus on the way home. And that went over well. Everyone wants to hang out with the crying kid: "What's the deal with the crying kid? What's he got going on? Posehn is a mystery!"

Thirty-five-plus years later, and I'm still not sure if my ex-friends had a formal meeting, but it was clearly premeditated. Ah, the days when kids had to meet and decide to ostracize another kid with a good, old-fashioned rain of dirt-clods instead of an impersonal "die, loser!" email or mean Facebook taunts. That year wouldn't get any better for me. It's a blur of awkward and sad mixed with punches and yelling.

I ended my freshman year with no one willing to sign my yearbook. Except for me. I signed my own yearbook. Yes. I did. How fucking sad. "Brian, you're a nice kid. Maybe next year will be better, Brian." Jeez. That's some sad, morose shit. And this was before I heard The Cure and The Smiths. And somehow sophomore year was worse.

In high school, just like in elementary school, even at my lowest there were several kids who had it way worse than me. A kid from my neighborhood was allegedly working it in a bathroom stall, and these dudes threw a cherry bomb in on him. So mean. I didn't see it, but I did hear the loud-ass explosion, and witnesses said he stumbled out of the bathroom holding his ears with his pants around his ankles. There was a Christian kid named Earl. Oh, man. Fucking Earl had it rough. He was poor, so he used the shower at school every day. No one did that. People noticed and made fun of him. Kids took his Bible and screamed "shut up" in his face when he would talk about God. Well, not people—just one stoner bully.

When Earl showered, a lot of guys in PE noticed he had a huge hog. In his dick's defense, you couldn't help but notice the dude had been given a large dick. People made him pay by smacking his dong with towels and throwing him in the pool in front of girls. "Take that, Earl, for being weird but really because you have a giant penis and we're the weird ones."

The special-ed kids got it worse than me. We only had about four, and I would see them get teased all the time. I tried to stick up for a kid named Flemming one day, and it blew up in my face. Flemming was mildly developmentally disabled, had a pretty drastic speech impediment, dressed like a ten-year-old, and still carried a lunch box. So he got made fun of. Of course, he did. I didn't really like the kid because he had shitty taste in music. He lived in my apartment complex and often carried a boombox around, playing the worst shit I'd ever heard, pop crap all the time.

One day in PE I saw some freshman dicks fucking with Flemming. They took his gym shoes and ran out of the locker room and chucked his Tiffs on the roof. They were the same kind of shoes Ken the Monster had tried to get me to wear, so maybe I felt bad for Flemming for having to wear fucking Tiffs. Regardless, I climbed the fence and got his shoes off the roof. Nice thing to do? The right thing to do? Yep and yep. Stupid? Totally. The second I got off the fence the several freshman jock dicks cornered me.

Paul was a popular rich kid. His parents owned a grocery store near me. Paul was a spoiled little dick and a total fucker. I already had been teased by him and hated his guts. Now he was pissed that I spoiled his shitty prank and demanded that I threw Flemming's shoes back on the roof. I wouldn't do it. So they got physical and started pushing me. I fucking hated that. I don't even like being touched. Maybe the bullying is the reason. Anyway, it didn't take me long to crumble. I did as they demanded—I threw Flemming's Tiffs back on the roof. I hated doing it, but I hated confrontation more.

Soon I would have a worse confrontation. Two hours later, as I'm walking toward the school bus I was cornered by that fucker Paul and his dumbass dick friends and Flemming. They pushed Flemming toward me, and he wanted to know why I threw his shoes on the roof. I said, "I didn't." Paul and his dickhole posse had clearly convinced him I was the bully here. Flemming was upset, and nothing I said could change that. Paul got him pumped up. Soon Flemming was pushing me. He hit me with his *Space: 1999* lunchbox. Ironically, I was probably the only other kid at my school besides Flemming who liked *Space: 1999*.

I didn't fight back. I wanted to. Then Paul said, "What's-a-matter, Posehn? Afraid to fight a retard?" YES. He was right: there was no way I was hitting this poor kid, no matter how pissed I was that he was misguidedly hitting me. I knew my mom would kill me. And I knew if I hit back, it would escalate, and I'd be the kid who hit the special-ed kid. So I took a couple of lunchbox hits. It got worse anyway. The bus arrived, and we all got on. They continued to give me shit the whole way home. Soon I was finally in my room and alone.

An hour or so later Flemming's mom showed up pissed. She informed my mom that I was a bully. I had thrown his shoes on the roof of the gym and then got in a fight with him at the bus stop. I swear to you people, that is not what fucking happened. Guess what, though? My mom believed this woman she had maybe spoken ten words to over the years over her own son. Why would she believe me? I acted up, so bullying wasn't a stretch.

The worst day of my sophomore year started like most days: I got on the school bus and rode for thirty minutes in to school. I guess I'd spent some time that morning staring at the new kid, a tough Mexican girl in Ben Davis jeans and a wife-beater T-shirt. She was wearing a ton of makeup. I'd never seen her before, and I'd never seen anyone dressed like that before. I later found out she had moved from a tough school in Vallejo, California. She said I was staring. I definitely was. I hadn't seen *Colors* yet, so I'd never seen this tough-girl stereotype on film or in real life.

Suddenly, as soon as the bus stopped, I guess, "it was on" for her. Not for me. I didn't know what was fucking happening. Her chest was puffed out and her arms at ass-kicking position; she was super-aggressively pushing and yelling at me. It was some prison shit—she was the "new fish," and I guess she thought she'd strike first on the wimpiest kid around. She had a good nose for wimps. I'd had assholes call me out before, and I always turned them down. I turned down the tough girl too. Then she started throwing fists at me. I clearly wasn't fighting her, but why would that stop her from hitting me? Luckily, right behind me was Tracy "Fucking" Ferguson. She said, "He's not doing anything. Leave him alone." The new girl then made the mistake of saying, "Stay out of it, bitch."

I've seen women in movies or on TV flip the fuck out when they get called the "bitch" word, but that was the first time I saw it in real life for sure. Tracy unloaded on her. The teachers shut it down pretty quickly, but everybody heard about it. I don't think Tough Girl ever fucked with Tracy again. And I know she never fucked with me again. In fact, eventually she apologized. At the time, though, it sucked real hard. There was no winning that fight.

Sure, I took the high road by not socking her in the mouth the second she yelled at me. But I was actually scared of her and knew repercussions would be even worse if I stuck up for myself. I'd get in trouble, and kids would make fun of me for trying to hit a girl. Instead, they just made fun of me for getting my ass kicked by a girl and having another girl save me. I wasn't mad at Tracy for stepping in, though; I actually thought it was pretty cool and, of course, developed an even bigger crush on Tracy.

Soon everybody knew of my "fight," and my reputation took another hit. Now I was Turtle, the kid who got his ass kicked by a special ed kid and a girl, and I felt what a new low felt like. At that moment no one had it worse than me at our school. Not even big-dicked Earl or the cherry-bomb beat-off guy. Only Hinchman, Russ, Darren, and the kids from my church were nice to me, presumably because their parents told them to be. Because of Christ and all.

Drew still teased me in high school sporadically. By then I didn't hate him as much; he was a straight-up Copenhagen-chewing, Wrangler jeans– and John Deer cap– wearing redneck. I thought it was funny how hard he tried to fit in with the good ol' boys at my school that I wrote off him teasing me to him trying to fit in. Actually, I do now. Not then. I fucking hated him.

Do you like weird segues? I feel like I was exposed to death more than most kids, at least kids who also grew up in a picturesque tourist town. Not if someone grew up in a known murder place like a war-torn nation, Chicago, or Santa Carla, the murder capital of California. Outside of my great-grandpa in his casket, the first dead body I ever saw was a newly deceased motorcyclist next to his wrecked bike. I was with the Hinchmans as we drove home from the rodeo. I didn't love the rodeo, so seeing a dead body was kind of the highlight of the evening. I guess I acted too curious or interested in it—his parents were rightly creeped out.

On my paper route my freshman year I would see a few crazy car accidents in the rain, some sketchy near-misses, and two resulting in fatalities. One afternoon I watched a guy try to avoid rear-ending a car; he swerved too hard at too high of a speed, and his Subaru went up on an embank-ment. He never slowed down; his car launched over a drive-way and smashed into a tree. He had a half a cord of wood in the back, and of course it crushed him on impact.

This was pre-airbag, so he just sat there pinned until the paramedics showed up. He screamed at first, but not for long. I saw him die. It was pretty terrible. But I couldn't really go back to my boring paper route without seeing this through. Because I had seen the accident and told the owner of the corner diner to call the cops, I felt a responsi-bility. And once I realized how bad it was, I couldn't really move. I just stood there terrified. And transfixed.

Same with the motorcycle accident I witnessed that same year, again on my paper route. And again the guy was try-ing to avoid hitting a car at a high speed. He skidded and then lurched his BMW bike forward. He hit a different car and was thrown off his bike. Incredibly, he cleared the car and hit the telephone pole behind it. Well, you know those metal footholds that the phone company uses when they're scaling telephone poles? Well, his helmet hit that. Hard. I was across the street, waiting out the rain under a Shell gas station overhang; the Shell station was owned by Goodman's grandpa. I stood there with a root beer in my hand and my mouth open. The guy's body soon fell to the ground. His helmet stayed up there. With most of his head. GAH! Two terrible accidents in one year. That, of course, fed my fear that I was the son of the devil. *The Exorcist* and *The Omen I* and *II* had opened my eyes. It all made sense: my dad had died, my mom's boyfriend died, my mom was evil, and peo-ple died in front of or near me all the time, just like Damien, from *The Omen*. We both had babysitters hang themselves and had random people die horribly in front of us. Only thing: my mom wasn't really evil, animals loved me, and I like to think the anti-Christ wouldn't be an apartment kid.

Because of my babysitter Gary's sad story, I actually had a homophobic period during my teen years. Here we go, SJWs. "Social Justice Warriors, Social Justice Warriors, come out and play!" Hold on. Let's all give this sad young nerd a break. I was sad and already pretty beaten down by life. Angry a lot. And when I obsessed on the Gary story, it made my mind wander and it made me mad. I only knew the story because my mom had relayed it to me for some reason. I had completely forgotten about it, and my mom refreshed my memory. Not sure why.

Anyway, even though I don't think Gary went anywhere beyond wearing my mom's clothes, I hated him. I felt confused by it and violated. I know he never touched me. I'm fucking positive he didn't. Then, I wasn't so sure. And I didn't understand why he would do even what he did in front of me. If you have to wear my mom's clothes, do it when I'm asleep. Now, I'm sure the poor kid was going through something, whether gay or trans—it was 1970, and clearly things were rough enough for him to kill himself when his parents found out his truth. It hurts my heart.

But my young, dumb teen mind wandered, and I guess I didn't know what would make someone wear my mom's clothes, and "trans" was a completely foreign concept to me. I didn't know what a pedophile was really, either. I think I lumped them all together. I thought I understood what gay was, but I didn't, so I thought he "must've been gay, and that's weird, so all gay guys are weird." Typical fucked-up angry-kid logic. Thankfully, I'd get turned around.

Around my sophomore year in high school I was seeing my therapist, Hank. I once went on a homophobic rant against him in his office. I was probably mad at my mom over some minor slight, but I took it out on Hank and called him a "faggot." I had been called it before, so I knew it would hurt. He said, "I'm not even gay." And I said, "But you wear Birkenstocks and you talk like that."

And Hank said, "Birkenstocks are a comfortable shoe and not necessarily gay, and I talk like this because I'm Jewish and from Brooklyn." I'm still embarrassed by my teenage homophobia. Now I know Brooklyn accents. And I haven't been homophobic since 1983. I don't hate anyone just for being a part of a group—except Springsteen fans.

High school dances were a goddamn nightmare. I went to most of my freshman and sophomore dances. I never danced with a girl. Not one time. The only time I did dance was when I pogoed to the Ramones with a couple of punk kids. One dance was deejayed by popular Bay Area rock DJ Dennis Erectus from KOME in San Jose. Dick joke in his name and dick jokes were his bread and butter.

He would play rock and metal and say hilarious shit like "Don't touch that dial—it's got KOME on it!" I barely knew what come was, but I thought it was funny. Sadly, this dance was the highlight of that year. I loved Def Leppard's second record *High and Dry,* so I requested that Dennis play the title track. He did, and that's as good as it got for me that whole fucking year.

Ken the Monster actually got worse as I got older. By high school he was in my face constantly. What irritated me the most was that he always seemed to be trying to do and say "Dad" things without actually being a dad to me. I know he thought I was spoiled, but when was it ever his fucking business? At least at that point there were a couple of other positive males in my life. Two of my best pals had stern dads, but they loved their boys. They both occasionally said racist shit, but at that point I already knew they were wrong.

They also called the people my mom worked with "feebs" and "tards." I knew it was wrong but found it kind of funny. Politically incorrect humor before I knew politically incorrect humor was a thing. So flawed, but present, loving dads. And there was Cliff, my friend's divorced dad. My friend Chris and his younger brother, Greg, lived in Sonoma with their mom and went to private school. They would visit their dad every other weekend. We met at the apartment complex and became friends; we bonded over music and movies. And I almost feel bad for how much I would hang out there when they were in town.

Cliff was such a cool dad. He never seemed annoyed by me, and the boys loved him. We would watch movies on HBO and Showtime, two things I didn't have right away. We'd listen to music. And we'd laugh. Chris and Greg were funny kids, probably because Cliff was so funny and cool. I kind of envied what they had with Cliff on their weekends.

At my church there was Pastor Rich. He was a really good loving guy. Initially he hired me to do yard work and projects at the church for extra money and, I think, to connect with what was clearly a troubled kid. We wound up spending a lot of time together; I would do small home improvement projects at his new house. And we'd talk. He told me I could always talk to him. We did. We talked about Ken, my mom, bullying, death, anger—everything. He was never preachy, just awesomely sincere in a sweet Nor-Cal loving way. He seemed to really care about me, and that meant a lot. He never directly said, "It gets better," but he indicated as much. He was right—it did. But first it got way worse.

So before I tell you that my Grandma Clara died, I'll give you one more story that shows how great she was. On one of my last visits, we were driving together, and she let me play the music. I put my *Back in Black* cassette in her cassette player. We listened to the whole thing while we ran her errands. She never said one negative thing. She wanted to know what I liked about AC/DC. I loved that. At that point I needed that from a relative—a bond, a connection, understanding. There you go. So she died.

In January of 1982 my Grandma Clara died after checking into the hospital because of heart palpitations. My poor mom hated telling me so much; she knew I would be heartbroken. I was. It wrecked me. I felt so alone. She was not just my favorite grandma; she was my favorite person. In those years my mom was never my friend like my Grandma Clara was; she didn't really "get me" or even try. She just yelled and pushed me away. But Grandma Clara loved me and wanted to know everything about me, and if she didn't always "get me," she was willing to try. I honestly still miss her presence. Outside of my wife and son, I have never been around somebody as loving and engaging as she was. But don't worry: it got better.

TEN

JUNIOR AND SENIOR YEAR: IT GOT BETTER

Not to co-op "it gets better" from people who have been through much worse than being an awkward nerd afraid to throw a punch, but I can attest that indeed it does. In my experience, though, a couple of factors need to happen to make it better. You need to know: it's not you that's the problem; it's usually other people's filtered view of you. You are weird to them: Maybe they don't know what weird is. Maybe they need a little weird. Maybe they'll never get weird and they just put up with you. Or maybe fuck what they think.

The good news is it gets better, and it got better for me. Even though at the time I didn't see it that way. But it did: my social life and mental outlook changed greatly. I would have several setbacks in my twenties, but at the end of it, my situation improved. Sometimes you need to make it better. I learned on my own that you can *improve* your own *situation* by changing it or moving. Getting the fuck out of Sonoma was the best thing I ever did. All three times. That *improved* my *situation* with my mom, and I found my life's passion and eventually stumbled into my dream girl and made my dream life.

My high school situation, though, would improve without me having to move. Junior year I made new friends in some of the different classes I was taking; I met cool kids in art, woodshop, drama, creative writing, and beginning computing. I also made friends in the classes I hated like al-gebra, Spanish, and history while I was fucking off. I didn't hate history; I just hated my teacher, Mr. Grace. He wore a wig, a super-obvious one that no one ever made fun of to his face.

That is, until one day during class, my old friend Rob-ert Also-Glasses, from the "boner dog" story, got in trouble with Mr. Grace. He was sending Robert to the office in a real showy way, humiliating him on purpose. I had forgiven Robert, and Mr. Grace was annoying, so I said, "Mr. Grace, have you flipped your wig?" Well, he really flipped his wig when I said that. Everybody laughed. In current social me-dia terms, I got a lot of likes. I could still hear the laughs as Robert and I walked to the office.

I walked to the office a lot. There were three guys you could talk to if you were sent to the office—the dean, the vice principal, or the principal. You usually just talked to the dean, a well-liked guy named Dean Osborne; everyone called him Ozzy, which made me like him. He was pretty even keeled and put up with my shit a lot for those last two years. He would just shake his head, "Again, Posehn?" I think he knew I was a good kid just going through shit. Obviously I wasn't throwing punches or threatening any-one like my eighth-grade Columbine freak-out. They were minor infractions, low-level class clownery, a lot of lateness, disrupting class, not participating, and general fucking off. I also ditched a lot of classes those last two years.

I paid attention to the classes I cared about, but when I was bored, I would entertain myself by drawing and writing short stories. The more popular I got, the more my grades deteriorated, which would continue to piss off my mom. The vice principal, Mr. Kruljac, was all business, but I didn't have a ton of run-ins with him. The principal, Mr. Grey, golfed with my Grandpa George during school; I even joked about it with him one day when he was rolling in late: "Hey, Mr. Grey, how's my grandpa today?" My knowledge of those weekly games kept me out of any real trouble. Thanks, Grandpa.

By the end of junior year everyone would know me, and not in a bad, "that's the kid who got his ass kicked by a girl" way. I was actually hanging out with the cool kids and got invited to parties. All of them. I suddenly knew about all the drinking spots I'd never heard of. I went cruising with two of the most popular kids in school in a cherry Camaro. I didn't win prom king or join the football team or anything ridiculous—I didn't even go to prom.

But compared to my previous time standing alone at dances or crying at home on a Saturday, light years had passed. As I got nerdier about music and film and books, I had less and less in common with my old pals. I was also actually making friends I had more in common with—my metalhead pals, some dudes who liked Rush, some kids who also liked horror movies, and my freshman skater friends who loved Iron Maiden, video games, and *Blade Runner*.

Joel Myers was one of the most popular kids at school. We weren't really friends until my junior summer, but he was always cool to me. He was not your typical jock: he was a smart, good-looking, funny, cool kid. He was a wrestler, super disciplined, and not a cocky dick like a lot of football and basketball players. In the five years I knew him from junior high and high school I'd never seen him bully anybody, and more importantly, he was always cool to me. We both wound up in summer school to make up credits that year.

We talked about music and Eddie Murphy. We both had memorized Murphy's stand-up record *Comedian*. Next thing I knew we were at his house and he was recording Pink Floyd's *Final Cut* for me because I had to "hear it on headphones to really experience it." I couldn't believe the biggest dork in town was hanging out with the coolest kid in town. My life was an awesome eighties teen movie.

Junior year I was clueless with girls and had a crush on every cute girl regardless of grade. I thought I had a better chance with freshman girls when I was a junior—because how could they know I sucked?

I guess by looking at me. Or talking to me. By senior year I had a lot of female friends. I didn't act on my crushes very often, so I only got my heart broken a couple of times. Senior year I met a really cute girl in my apartment complex, Stacey; we hit it off and talked a lot. She then met my friend Russ. A couple of days later we were at a lake with other friends, and Russ was making out with Stacey, and I was reading *Christine* in the tree. I just felt like I never had a chance. At least they were talking to me. I was in an awesome eighties teen movie, but sadly I was Duckie.

I was obsessed with Stephen King—reading all the time. I wasn't a big comic book reader at the time; Alan Moore and Frank Miller would get me back in the late eighties, but my main obsessions were heavy metal, comedy, and movies. Eddie Murphy was a god in both worlds. I loved him on *SNL*, viewed his special on repeat at Joel's, and rented *48 Hours* every weekend for a while. My mom wouldn't pay for movie channels, and she definitely wouldn't buy a VCR, so I rented one. Every weekend I would ride my bike to one of our town's many video stores. I would bring home a deck and a bunch of videos. I watched current stuff like *Taps, Bad Boys, Risky Business*—all Tom Cruise classics.

I watched everything—action and horror and comedy. I got heavy into John Carpenter; he and Kurt Russell ruled the early eighties with *Escape from New York*, *The Thing*, and *Big Trouble in Little China*. I would later draw from Russell's character, Jack Burton, and Ash from *Evil Dead II* when I wrote *Deadpool*. So how did I pay for VCR rental, movies, music, concerts, and all the beers I was drinking? Easy—five jobs in two years. I rode my paper route into the ground and stumbled into a series of menial jobs I would fuck up. Two restaurants, a French place owned by two mean hippies and a Chinese place where the owner cursed at me in Cantonese when I dropped a dish. That happened a lot. Once in front of my grandparents.

I worked at two gas stations, one for about a week. The other one was a dream job; my buddy Dan worked there and hired me. I stuck around there for almost two years. Man, was I a fuck up. Like high school, I valued fun over trying. I figured it was all temporary and really didn't fucking matter. So show up late, do a half-ass job—who cares? It would suck later when I liked my bosses, but my early bosses were all dicks, so I didn't care if I burned a bridge.

At home I was in trouble all the time as my grades got worse, and the older I got, the more mouthy I got. "Son of a bitch" story earlier? Soon Ken left us—they didn't break up, but he moved out, so I took it as a win. Things between my mom and myself did not improve miraculously after, though; it wasn't Ken who was stopping us from communicating like humans. Her strictness and anger and frustration with me continued, as did my attitude and acting out. Somehow our new Monster-free apartment made things between us even more strained and intense. I was just kidding with the "somehow"—I know how. She totally resented me for pushing that furry dick out of our apartment.

I've always done dumb shit. And so did Hinchman. When you put us together, shit got really stupid. Like when we were dicking around in his garage one day and found that you could use aerosol and the flame would be super kick-ass like Gene Simmons. And then two minutes later realized it was a can of black spray paint. Which, in case you've never used spray paint, it sprays black paint when you press the button. Two fucking dummies. We didn't even think ahead, and we royally fucked up his dad's garage.

There was paint on the ground, the counters, the fucking wall. Thank god there wasn't a car in there. At least his dad wasn't legally allowed to beat me. I felt like I was growing apart from Hinchman. As I was getting more into metal, he was getting more into country music. Our interests connected on partying: we both liked drinking. That ended badly for me one night. Spray paint, Clear Lake summer trip: I started to notice that we were growing apart. He liked activities and girls; I liked reading and being by myself.

I had my first and only fight my junior year. And it was as pathetic as you'd imagine. Worse, I bet. It was the saddest nerd fight ever. Ian lived in my neighborhood and was actually my friend. He was a funny, nerdy, punk kid on my paper route, and we became pals. I even had a crush on his stepsister; she was super cute and preppy, and they hated each other. Anyway, I don't remember exactly what happened between us, but me clearly wanting to fuck his freshmen stepsister couldn't have helped.

Anyway, we had both had enough of each other's shit at the bus stop and decided to fight. We each took our glasses

off and put them in our pockets. Then we started fighting—
well, light wrestling while standing up. No knockouts like in
YouTube fights. Fists were barely even thrown. At one point
his glasses landed on the ground. I thought I'd show him:
I was so mad at him that I stomped on his glasses. But they
were my glasses. I'm pretty sure I blamed him when I told
my mom I needed new glasses.

I really am the asshole in that story. *He* knew I liked his
stepsister. I know for a fact I jacked it to her. I fantasized
about every girl I liked at school. And a couple of the moms
on my paper route. I forgot to tell you guys earlier: for these
last two chapters I was jacking off that whole time. The sad
stories. The funny stories. All the fucking time. I probably
worked it right after I found out Randy was dead. I spanked
it in every room of our shitty apartment. Well, not my mom's
room—that would be weird.

I was a bully a couple of times to people below me. That
felt like shit even when I got laughs. And "below" me? I hate
that I ever thought that. But I wasn't intentionally bullying;
I was always going for a laugh, I swear. I didn't make a kid
throw another kid's shoes on the roof to lead him to a year
of humiliation, but I definitely made jokes at other people's
expense. I remember singing "Tomorrow" from *Annie* to a
freshman girl who looked like Annie. Not *to*, actually—more
like *at*. It was definitely not cool, but in 1983 I thought it was
at least creative bullying, better than just going classic bully
with "red" or "Carrot Top," and it was before the antiginger
moment. Plus, I sang. Automatic bonus bully points. Right?

My other big bullying moment was even meaner. And
also clever as fuck. The early part of my senior year my pal
Jon Krop and I were fucking around in journalism class; we
were supposed to be writing a column, but we were really

just sitting by the window and talking about music. We were on the second floor of the main building when I witnessed a kid hitting his high school low. Everyone called him Crazy Legs because he had a muscular disorder that caused him to have a walking impediment. So, of course, assholes called him Crazy Legs.

Crazy Legs had gotten his girlfriend pregnant, and in turn, his parents kicked him out. Everyone knew. So he was living out of his car. Fucked up, huh? Wait . . . it rained all the time and people wrecked a lot, remember. So Crazy Legs was leaving school, his car hydroplaned, and he smacked into a eucalyptus tree. So I said, "Holy shit, Crazy Legs crashed his house." Which is really funny because he was living out of his car and really fucking mean because he was living out of his car. I got laughs, but I didn't feel good about it. I definitely didn't like being the bully. Sometimes, though, I used my powers for good.

I barked at a teacher who killed a dog. Mr. Whoville—not his real last name—was kind of a dirt-bag history teacher. He slept with a senior the year before and kept his job. But she wasn't allowed to graduate with her friends. Dick. I really hated him because he made the local news when he had been dogsitting for a friend, the dog had been barking incessantly, so instead of walking it, letting it in, or maybe finding out why he was barking, he fucking killed it. What about closing your door? Or headphones? Or earmuffs? Or barking back at the dog? Or calling the police? Or, really, anything other than killing a fucking dog.

Anyway, this dickhole shot his friend's dog. It made the paper. Everyone at school knew. So one day, as my bus was leaving the school, we drove by Mr. Whoville, and I thought of barking at him. So I did. I barked. I howled. I was right at my open window, going nuts. He looked pissed. Some kids on the bus got the joke and joined in. It got around. A couple of days later, after I'd gotten compliments from kids who weren't even on the bus, other people started doing it.

Soon a lot of kids started barking at Mr. Whoville. I was pretty proud of myself when I heard barking and howling kids were disrupting his class. Ha ha. Instead of shooting us, Mr. Whoville transferred away from our school. Later, dog-killing dick. I had been a dog lover my whole life, and not a lot upsets me more than cruelty to animals. I wish I could bark in the face of every asshole who's ever abused an animal.

One of the repercussions of fucking off in school is that the grades take a hit. My grades were already bad sophomore year, but they would really start to tank my junior year. I flunked out of a couple of classes. *Cough* PE, Spanish . . . I won't blame my failing grades my sophomore and junior years on my grandma, but it couldn't have helped that I was sad about her for a while. I failed a couple of classes. I think you're allowed three, and I had four or five Fs by my senior year. At the beginning of the year my completely inept counselor informed me that I was going to have to make up credits if I hoped to graduate in the spring.

I did a year of volunteer work at the Sonoma State Hospital; my mom even helped set it up. I didn't hate it—I could ride my bike to work. I wasn't good at any of it. I sucked at the yard work and ground maintenance I did. I don't think I was much better working with the patients or residents or, as my mom called them, "clients"—I always thought that term was weird and impersonal. I see why it's better than "patients," and "clients" will always be a better term than local favorites: "tards" and "feebs." Near the end of the year the same idiot counselor informed me that my volunteer work didn't cover it and I would also need to go to summer school to make up credits.

I took a summer course in film at the Santa Rosa Junior College. It was really fun, actually. I got to do one of my favorite things: watch movies and talk about them. *One* of my favorite things—I didn't love talking about them. At that point I'd never seen *Shane, The Searchers, Nosferatu, Angels with Dirty Faces,* or *Singin' in the Rain.* And I was exposed to cool, older kids from the big city. In my class were two glam-rock dudes who I thought were super-fucking cool; one of the dudes played with that eighties glam band Vain. There was also a cool skater kid with John Hughes movie hair; he had stickers all over his skateboard for something called "The Cure." I sought out The Cure immediately because that kid seemed cool and I wanted to be cool too.

I was always bringing *Fangoria*, Stephen King, and music magazines to class. I got sent to the principal for reading about a new ghost movie by Steven Spielberg and the dude from the scariest movie ever, *The Texas Chainsaw Massacre.* That dude's name was Tobe Hooper. And the movie was called *Poltergeist.* The article got me hyped, and the pictures of the effects were awesome. But I was supposed to be working on algebra, not reading an entire article about a horror movie.

One of the classes I failed my junior year also had me actually kicked out of the class. Spanish? PE? Algebra? Not sure, something I sucked at. Anyway, I didn't mind sitting in the office for a semester; I called it my free period. Sitting in the office, drawing on my books, and not doing homework

is where I met Ricky Rat. I think he gave himself that nickname, but I didn't care. We had a bunch of punk kids at our
school, but even among them, he stuck out.

A lot of guys had shaved heads and wore Misfits and
Black Flag shirts and Vans. Hell, everyone wore Vans. I
grew up in California in the eighties—shit-kickers wore
Vans. Ricky, however, wore a leather jacket, no matter the
weather, along with motorcycle boots and a giant liberty
spike mohawk. I'm pretty sure I ditched more than one day
of sitting in the office, but I really only remember the one I
got in trouble for.

Ricky and I went downtown, which meant walking four
short blocks to our tiny town square. We probably got an
early lunch and were walking across the town square when
I saw my mom and, of course, she saw me. My mom was
having lunch with some friends from work when she saw
my dumb ass and freaked the fuck out. She made a beeline over to us. I was immediately interrogated. She was
pissed and embarrassed and told me she was embarrassed
and pissed. We walked back to school; Ricky didn't give me
any shit about it. When Ricky was twenty he spray-painted
"Dead People Suck" all over a tomb. He didn't make it to
twenty-one. Yup, he died. Creepy, right?

My favorite high school teacher—guess what she taught.
Woodshop, you say? Nope. Calculus? No sir, or madam,
stop trying. She taught English, and more importantly, she
taught creative writing. Again, my best grades, and I got
to be creative. When the assignment was to write from the
POV of an animal, I wrote the story of a young male deer
in the Sierra Nevada Mountains that got hit by a car. It was
graphic and dark and funny in a twisted way. It told his final
thoughts as his life flashed by.

For one assignment I did a letter to *Reader's Digest* from the mother of a blind kid. She told the reader how tough life has been for their family since her son went blind. They get him a dog, and he worships it. One day there was an accident, and their dog lost two legs. They didn't want to break their son's heart, so they never told him his dog was missing legs. They followed their kid and his two-legged dog to make sure he never detected the missing legs. There is another accident, and the dog loses its vision. They come to the difficult decision that the situation is too sad and they need to put the dog out of its misery, so in a hilarious misdirect, they kill the kid.

I wrote a novella for my senior project. Yup, a novella. It was a Stephen King–style revenge story. I was seventeen, and it was a complete *Creepshow* rip-off. "The Ultimate Sin." Before Ozzy's record of the same name. I paid a guy in my class, Mike Ross, the best artist at the school, to do art for it. My assignment. In my free time I wrote an anti-commercialism Christmas letter that got printed in the *Sonoma Index Tribune*. It was complete bullshit. Just an exercise to write from this conservative Alex P. Keaton POV. Grandma Grace loved that. I wrote papers for two jocks who trusted me to do a free creative writing episode. I got them Bs and pocketed a couple of bucks.

After a junior year journalism class I joined the school paper and ran the Dragon's Tale Rock and Review with my pal Jon Krop. By my senior year it was clear that I loved writing, and even though I'd spent hours with my school counselor discussing how I was going to make up my grades, we never once discussed my passions or what I was good at. I leaned toward radio because of my love of music. But Mrs. Garner had encouraged my writing, as did my Shakespeare teacher, Mr. Cole, and my second creative writing teacher, Mrs. Lale.

Mrs. Lale never directly told me to write comedy, but she made me aware that it was a possibility when she informed the class that she had been paid for writing jokes for Phyllis Diller. I thought Phyllis Diller was hilarious. My Nana Norma loved her and even dressed as her for Halloween. And this teacher in a small school had submitted jokes to her and been paid for it. A bell didn't go off right then, but I thought it was cool.

Thanks to Joel, I was also a school DJ. He had asked his friends in the student government to get the money for us to broadcast on the new school sound system. We had a PA and a cassette deck and a turntable. He and I played music during morning break and lunch. I loved being on air and writing jokes for the show, and I especially loved forcing my music on the entire school. Partly because of Joel, my senior year was, no question, my most fun. There was a shit-ton of drinking going on, we were partying every weekend senior year, the last couple of months were off the fucking rails, there were parties during school, and senior cut day was a train wreck on top of a car crash.

One night I made the mistake of hanging out with Hinchman and a couple of older kids. Hinchman drove. I drank six Mickey's big mouths—boy, are those horrible. I'll remember the terrible taste forever. I still can't drink out of a skunk's asshole. We went to 7-Eleven a couple of hours later, and I was fucking hammered. As we were loading up on munchies, I realized I was going to throw up—or blow chunks, as they said back then. I made my way for the door, yelling for people to get out of the way. I cleared the door and launched vomit everywhere. I stumbled to Hinchman's car, got in the passenger seat, and started to pass out.

But the door opened, and as I fell out, a pissed-off blurry dude yelled, "You puked on my girlfriend, mother fucker!" He socked me hard in the head. My upper torso hit the ground. He kicked me in the face. I still don't have feeling in the cheek where he kicked me. Hinchman panicked and took me home. Left me in front of my mom's. I passed out. She found me the next morning. I don't blame him, but we hung out even less after that. The dude who kicked me was a guy named Mikey. He was a sketchy motherfucker, a real angry stoner, the only one I ever met. That Monday I told Joel what had happened, and unexpectedly, he freaked out and said, "Fuck that shit. I'm gonna talk to that guy." He did. Mikey wasn't that tough when faced with a kid who knew how to throw a punch. Or take one. Joel told him to never touch me again. He didn't. Thanks, Joel. My hero. Two years later Mikey got in a fight at a party, probably with a girlfriend puker. A guy tried to break it up, and Mikey stabbed him. Thank god he didn't stab Joel—that would be a terrible ending to this chapter.

At the end of it all, I barely made it out of high school. I only graduated thanks to summer school at Santa Rosa Junior College. I wasn't able to graduate with all my friends, but I got the final credits I needed for my diploma. Lesson learned? Um. At the time, not really? I was happy to be out. Not in a big hurry to figure out what the fuck I was doing. Film, radio, newspapers, magazines all seemed potentially promising. I wasn't that concerned about my grades hurting my future because I didn't think a four-year college was really a part of it. More people liked me, and that's what was important. My sacrifice for the joke had paid off. Up next? I fucked around for a year and managed to get kicked out of my mom's apartment twice.

But first I feel like I painted what high school was like without the soundtrack. This next chapter covers all the metal (good and bad) I was obsessed with during those last two years in high school. Cue the RATT.

ELEVEN

1982–1984: THE MAKING OF A TEENAGE METALHEAD, PART TWO

By 1982 I was no longer dabbling in heavy metal—I was obsessed. Every heavy band I heard about I had to check out. And the more interest I put into metal, the more kids I met who also liked the same stuff. And soon we were turning each other on to new bands or at least bands that were new to us. I also had punk friends I was tape trading with, like Ian from the nerd fight. I may not have looked like a metalhead yet, but I was. Some of my newer friends, like Jon Krop and KC from my school bus, had long hair, the cool jeans, and denim and/or leather jackets. Sadly, I wasn't allowed to go full metal yet. Soon.

I dressed mostly the same as the previous two years—preppy on a budget. But band T-shirts were creeping into the wardrobe. Soon they would dominate. I had T-shirts, an impressive record and cassette collection, and a museum of metal on my bedroom walls. My hair was always thin and straight and never did anything. And my mom wouldn't let me grow it long like I wanted. I finally stopped getting bowl haircuts, and eventually my mom let me get a perm. It sounds worse than it was: my hair was so straight that a perm finally gave it some shape and style. Then I started growing it longer.

Two months after my favorite grandma died, my favorite guitar player lost his life along with two other people in a fiery crash. Randy Rhoads was just twenty-five and had only been in my metal world for less than two years, but he ruled it. Edward Van Halen politely stood aside in my brain the moment I heard *Blizzard of Ozz* in that Marin record store. So coming home and reading about the plane crash felt like losing a god. My Nana Norma was staying with me while my mom was in Oahu with Ken the Monster.

My mom had called to check in on me, and Nana told her I was in my room listening to my music and that I was really upset about a musician I loved dying. My mom said to her, "Oh no, I hope it wasn't someone in Ozzy Osbourne. That's his favorite." She was right. Ozzy was my favorite at that time. I was obsessed with Ozzy and his young godlike guitar player, Randy Rhoads. I took it hard. It felt personal. Even though school was mostly terrible my sophomore year, I do remember bonding with other Ozzy fans at school about the biggest tragedy in heavy metal.

There were loads of rockers who liked Nugent and Van Halen and other mainstream heavy music at my school, like Hinchman and my friends Pete and Brian, who turned me on to Dream Police and had seen KISS before Ace left. There were the stoners who seemed to only listen to AC/DC. And I knew all the Rush guys (they were the smart partiers, and half of them also played music). There were three Neil Peart wanna-bes at my school.

But there were only a handful of true metalheads at Sonoma High, and I knew all of them. Two of them were my really close friends, Baden and Krop. Those are their last names and what I always called them. Still do. Krop was a year younger than me, and we met in computer and journalism, and Baden was two years behind me; we met through some of the freshman skaters I knew as a junior. It was almost all about metal with the three of us.

We talked about metal constantly. When we were together we played it nonstop, we went on record store quests together, and we would drive to Santa Rosa and spend most of a Saturday hitting every record store in town, the corporate ones like Rainbow Records, Musicland, and the Warehouse as well as our indie standbys, the Last Record Store and Rebel Records. The Last Record Store is still in Santa Rosa and is literally the last record store in Santa Rosa. Go there and buy music now.

In the early eighties heavy metal was blowing up, and bands I liked were showing up everywhere. Quiet Riot, Randy's old band, got massive my junior year. I bought their album right away. Soon it was ubiquitous, and so I cooled on it. But for most of 1983 they were one of my favorite bands. Their two big songs, "Bang Your Head (Metal Health)" and their Slade cover, "Cum on Feel the Noize," had brought heavy metal to the mainstream. Those songs dominated MTV, the radio, and my high school. Quiet Riot were going to be on the US Festival, a massive Woodstock-like two-day festival in Southern California.

I wanted to see the headliners, Van Halen, Scorpions, Judas Priest, and even Quiet Riot, but I really was stoked to see the opening act, my new favorite band that year, LA's Mötley Crüe. But that wasn't happening: my mom would hardly let me go someplace an hour away, so she certainly wasn't gonna let me drive seven hours and sleep in a field for two days. I asked anyway. And I yelled and cursed at her when she said no. My friend KC went, as did a couple of other lucky rockers from my school. I was so jealous of any-body who got to see Mötley before me.

An older kid, Dwayne, had the first Mötley Crüe album at school. He was a senior whose band Down Syndrome (I swear to you) played our cafeteria after school one day. He played an SG, had all the cool T-shirts, and was my heavy-metal man crush before I knew that was a thing. One day I saw Dwayne carrying the record *Too Fast for Love*. It looked so cool. I had to have it. It was so metal. It had to be awesome. Soon I had it in my hand, and the cover screamed, "HEAVY METAL!" It's a close-up of singer Vince Neil's leather pants, a heavy-metal update of the Stones' *Sticky Fingers*. Turns out, I was early on the Mötley train—it was one of a limited vinyl release of twenty-five hundred. I still have it.

When I put the needle down for the first time on *Live Wire*, it was this almost punky take on hard rock—the guitar tone and the whiplash fast stops and starts. Even though I am currently a fifty-one-year-old man, when I hear that re-cord I'm sixteen and alone in my tiny shrine to heavy metal when Mötley was *my band*. A year later came their classic record, *Shout at the Devil*. Their image had changed to kind of a glammy *Road Warrior* thing. *Shout at the Devil* was bigger and slicker than the first record but still retained the gritti-ness and attitude. It was. Mötley Crüe had the attitude and the poppy metallic sound. I liked Mötley first.

I also found Mötley's pals, Ratt, that year. I was drawn to the fishnet stocking on the cover of RATT's EP *Summer of 83*. Fishnets meant metal back then. Their EP was awe-some. I could hardly wait for their next record. The cas-sette for their full-length debut, *Out of the Cellar*, was stuck in my Walkman for a while. Ratt were slick, well-produced pop metal like Mötley, and I actually stayed on board with

Ratt a little longer than I did with Mötley. Ratt had the twin guitar attack of Robbin Crosby and Warren DeMartini and the almost bratty vocal style of Stephen Pearcy.

On one of our Santa Rosa trips we stumbled on Dokken. You know, from the famous "rhymes with rockin'" joke loved by idiots. As a hard-core Dokken fan from the beginning, I always rolled my eyes at that joke. We found Dokken, *Breaking the Chains* in the import section of Warehouse Records under the freeway. We knew nothing about them, but the record jacket looked metal. According to the credits, there was a Scorpions connection, we guessed they too were German. I fell in love with the playing of George Lynch. A former rival of Randy Rhoads, Lynch shredded and had insane tone, and his feel added to every song he ripped on. We would continue to follow Dokken even as we checked out heavier shit.

Of the three of us, Krop's house was the best hangout. He lived with his single mom in a big house. His room was huge, and he had a good stereo, a Gibson Explorer, a Marshall, and a home computer. And his mom worked nights. So my mom hardly saw me because I was there a lot, as was Baden. Sometimes we were joined by other rocker friends, Krop's buddy Mike and the two Petes, Pete and Evil Pete. We also had our punk friend Erik over. We would drink, listen to music, watch Letterman, and smoke cigarettes. Those guys smoked cigarettes, not me.

But most nights it was just me and Krop and Baden. We would play music for hours. We'd spin our own collections and try out acquisitions after our record store trips. We listened to anything with guitars and distortion. All types of metal—traditional, new wave of British heavy metal, glam, thrash . . . anything: Scorpions, UFO, Michael Schenker, Gary Moore from Thin Lizzy. One night I brought a new member of my collection, Krokus, *Headhunter*. I had been a fan since their last single "Long Stick Goes Boom." It was commercial-sounding metal, so we thought of them as the Swiss AC/DC. I heard Marc Storace, the lead singer, was considered for AC/DC years later when Brian Johnson couldn't perform his duties anymore.

I finally conned my mom into letting me go to my second live show in the summer of 1983. Dan, an older kid in my neighborhood, drove me and another neighborhood kid. It was a big all-day concert at the Oakland Coliseum, Day on the Green #1. There were several Days on the Green every year; Bill Graham, the famous SF concert promoter, had organized them—Journey, Heart, Bryan Adams, Eddie Money, and Triumph from Canada. Triumph were the reason I went. I liked Journey and had really liked them a couple of years by then, but I was leaning heavier then and more interested in seeing Triumph rip it up. They did. Rik Emmet and his three-piece put on an arena rock show. I'm not sure why they didn't go bigger in America.

In my tiny metal nerd cave I spent a lot of time with Triumph, Judas Priest, Def Leppard, Scorpions, Motörhead, Girl School, Lita Ford, and local legends Y&T. I got really into an East Coast metal band called Twisted Sister. Their *Under the Blade* record delivered attitude and KISS- and Mötley Crüe–like showmanship. Like those bands and Alice Cooper, they touched on that bad-boy thing that appealed to me about metal—quite literally with "Bad Boys of Rock and Roll." I also liked "Shoot 'Em Down," "Under the Blade," and "You Can't Stop Rock and Roll."

Then I bought their next record, *The Kids Are Back*. I loved the title track, and "You Can't Stop Rock and Roll" is the album highlight. Next came *Stay Hungry*, with "We're

Not Gonna Take It," "Burn in Hell," "I Wanna Rock," and, of course, "Stay Hungry." I was stoked when they played "Burn in Hell" on *Pee Wee's Big Adventure*. I loved their music and their imagery. When Tipper Gore went after metal lyrics, Twisted was one of her first targets. I knew then that I had made the right choice in bands.

Sadly, their *Come Out and Play* record was pretty rough, with their first single a weak cover of "Leader of the Pack." A fifties doo-wop song. What in the fuck were those cornballs thinking? By then I was going way, way heavier. W.A.S.P. had a similar look and image but heavier songs, so I was a W.A.S.P. fan. For a little while. At the same time I was a Twisted MFer—I also liked fellow East Coast rockers Bon Jovi. Hold on. The first record. A lot of Bon Jovi sucks, but I played the crap out of that first record, especially "Runaway." It's super catchy. And my wife likes it, so watch your shit, cynical metalheads—she'll punch you in the mouth.

Iron Maiden changed singers, their sound, and their place in history when the punky brawler Paul Dianno was replaced by Bruce Dickenson, an operatic heavy-metal madman born to rule arenas. That was when Maiden cemented their place on my all-time favorite band list with 1982's *Number of the Beast*. I loved Maiden's more complex lyrics and musical composition. They were *no* KISS, but Maiden would basically save high school for me by putting out *Piece of Mind* in 1983 and *Powerslave* my senior year. The music dominated my Walkman. And I spent most of my junior and senior classes doodling their logo and their ever-changing undead mascot, Eddie.

This Is Spinal Tap came out in 1984. I hated it. I didn't buy it. As a metalhead, I was offended: How could these guys make fun of the coolest music ever? They probably never listened to heavy metal. I've only liked *This Is Spinal Tap* for about fifteen years. As a teenage metalhead, I didn't think it was funny. I hated that they were making fun of Black Sabbath, Led Zeppelin, Judas Priest, and Iron Maiden. My main problem was that I didn't think they earned the right to make fun of metal: they didn't get to make fun of it if they didn't love it like me.

My cousin Todd also wasn't done turning me on to new music. He played me UFO's "Strangers in the Night" while we were drinking beers in the hills of Redwood City during one visit, and I heard "Love to Love" for the first time. Fucking epic tune. Check it out right now if you've never heard it. Michael Schenker rips it. So melodic and as beautiful as heavy music gets. I was becoming a Michael Schenker fan. He had already left UFO by the time I became a fan, but he was starting a solo career, and I was into it.

I liked Ronnie James Dio because of the two albums he recorded with Black Sabbath, and I was aware of his Rainbow music and was a fan of the hit "Man on the Silver Mountain." Metal blasphemy: I thought it was a Sabbath song for a couple of months. Then I heard his solo project, *Holy Diver*, and I was officially a Dio fan. I had it on cassette at Christmas of 1983 in Tahoe, and my cousin Todd and I would take off and grab beers and hang out and talk—eventually weed became part of it. We still do that when what is left of our family gets together: at some point Todd and I will break off. I love the dude. That year Todd was already away at college at UC Santa Barbara.

He was dating college girls, so his musical contribution for the Christmas bonding session was David Bowie, *Let's Dance* and some Pat Methany. At the time I was shitting on everything that wasn't metal, and he was clearly maturing away from hard rock, or at least he wasn't all hard rock, all the time. I loved the Bowie record because I was already a fan of *Scary Monsters* and his earlier stuff. And Todd made an impression on me: it was good to mix it up and not listen to the same shit all the time.

My musical interests opened up because of him as well as the fact that the girls who actually talked to me were into new wave and early punk. I already liked punk, but wanting to talk to smart, cute girls with cool hair introduced me to Oingo Boingo, The Police, The Pretenders, and, later, Depeche Mode, The Cure, The Smiths, and a lot of other bands with "the" in their name, including The The. I still listen to way more new wave than you'd expect or be comfortable with, but I'll save that for the next book.

Heavier shit was starting to pop up. It intrigued me. Krop and Baden and I were all obsessed with seeking out the next heaviest band. Soon I discovered Armored Saint. I picked up the self-titled debut based only on its appearance. The cover featured heavy-metal knights of the round table. The back cover featured a bunch of metal dudes from LA. They looked cool, and they sounded even cooler. Heavier than other shit at the time. John Bush, later of Anthrax, is still one of my favorite singers. Next I heard British proto-thrash three-piece Raven.

Raven's record *All for One* ripped. One of my biggest regrets as a metalhead was not going to see the Kill 'Em All for One tour with Metallica. They played the Stone in SF. I didn't go because I was kinda afraid. I don't know what I thought was gonna happen. A year later I would go to any show.

Then I heard the German metal band Accept and their single "Fast as a Shark." It was my first thrash song—fast-as-shit guitars, huge chorus, ripping solo, and the vocals. I also bought other proto-thrash: Riot, *Fire Down Under* and the debut vinyl from Tokyo Blade and the leather-pouch-wearing Manowar.

We got into Yngwie J. Malmsteen through tape trading with KC. Classically influenced shredding by a flamboyant Swede. He turned us on to Metallica too. Soon Metallica would dominate our lives, so much so that they deserve their own chapter. After Metallica would come Anthrax and then the rest of the big four: Megadeth and Slayer. More about them later. Anthrax's debut cover, *Fistful of Metal*, was not slick by any means; it was a sloppy drawing of a fist coming through a dude's mouth. They would get even better after a line-up change, but I couldn't believe how fast songs like "Metal Thrashing Mad" and "Panic" were. The riffing was insanely fast. The drummer sounded nuts.

I also found some bands on my own. Zebra were one of *my bands*. Summer of '83—not super heavy but a Zep-influenced three-piece from New Orleans. They had a Zeppelin vibe and were most famous for their single "Tell Me What You Want." A lot of bands in the eighties went for the big Zeppelin sound—Kingdom Come; Bonzo's son, Jason Bonham, had his own band, Bonham; and Whitesnake added a bow to their guitars for "Still of the Night" and got as close to Zep as you can get; and Zebra was the first eighties band to do it. I played the shit out of that record and bought three T-shirts when I saw them in Oakland. By the end of my senior year I was going to concerts all the time.

I saw Rush, Van Halen, Scorpions, Judas Priest, and U2 all in one year. I was scalping tickets like Mike Damone in *Fast Times at Ridgemont High*. I started up my little ticket business at the beginning of the '83–84 school year when I noticed most kids at my school didn't even know where to purchase tickets. So I decided to buy extras when I got my own tickets, then I would sell them to other kids at a slightly higher price to finance my shows and buy more tickets. I even bought tickets for shows I wasn't going to, like The Who and Alabama, two popular bands at my school that I could give a shit about. I wanted to see The Clash open for The Who. But I didn't go. Now I really wish I did. Those shows financed all my concerts for that year and paid for alcoholic beverages, shitty food, and gas.

In 1984 I went to the Cow Palace with a few friends to see Van Halen live for the first time. My small business had paid for tickets for a couple of friends and myself and a pony keg to celebrate the radicalness of Van Halen. We pounded beers in the back of my friend Dave's truck on the drive down to SF. Like most people at the show, we were wasted when we got there. We walked onto the floor of the venue, where it was general seating, which means no seats. I saw a girl puke and then immediately pass out in her puke. Party!

Two weeks later Dave, Pete, and I went to Sacramento to see Judas Priest and Great White with two freshman girls. Dave was a rich kid, which I guess is how he knew these two super-cute, rich freshmen girls—there is a club, you know. It was an outdoor show at Cal Expo, and we were hanging out, waiting for the metal to commence. Pete was showing off—to who, I'm not sure—and he decided to push me out of the way. The freshman girls laughed. Oh, that's who. A minute later Pete was standing where I had been, and I'm seething and thinking about revenge—and then a bird shit on his shoulder. Right on his stupid, bare, tank-top-wearing shoulder. It was one of the greatest moments of my life at that time. It still is.

While I was writing this I recently flew up to Oakland to meet up with Krop and Baden to see Scorpions and Mega-deth at the Oakland Coliseum. It was nostalgic fun; we had seen the Scorps together thirty-five years ago. At the same fucking place. We were way more sober and restrained this time around, but it felt really special to still share our nerdy love of this band with each other all these years later. Those guys were a big part of me becoming the metal nerd I am. And they both would play a part in what I later became. But first we all fucked around for a little while.

TWELVE

EIGHTEEN AND NO LIFE

As I said, I barely graduated that summer of '84. When I received my final credits from the film class I took at the junior college, I had no fucking idea what I was going to do. So I didn't do much between the fall of 1984 and the spring of 1985 other than work at a gas station, have crushes on a couple of girls, go to a bunch of concerts, and attend Santa Rosa Junior College for two semesters. That spring I took a local neighborhood girl on my first date. Her name was Kathy, and she was super cute, smart, and sweet. And she was kinda nerdy and didn't hate me.

Kathy's mom was on my paper route. Her parents were divorced, and she had moved in with her mom. I had a crush the second I saw her. It would take months of talking and flirting and, I don't know, courting? She finally said yes, and her mom was cool with it. Actually, I think her mom was a fan of mine and played a part in it. Because we only had one date, and soon Kathy was seriously dating a nerdy little punk rock/new wave kid named Tony who lived across from Kathy. He was a bigger nerd than me and half my size—so I guess he was a smaller nerd than me—but he was into new wave and even more outwardly dorky than I was. He had more confidence than me, though, but so did Donkey-Dick Earl. Fittingly, Kathy and I saw the movie *Revenge of the Nerds* on our first date.

During that year I almost died getting nachos one day. But isn't everybody who dies just trying to get nachos, really? I was working a shift at the gas station with my friend Dan, and it was my turn to head to Circle K for our nacho run. It was a rainy day. It's where they shot John Carpenter's *The Fog*, so of course it was raining. So I'm heading back to work with nachos and sodas in my brown beater, a four-door Mercury Comet. I dubbed it the Turd Mobile. It hadn't always been a beater. It had been my Grandpa George's car, and I drove it into the ground in a short period of time.

"Hot for Teacher" by Van Halen was the song of the day. And I had it cranked. The guitar solo was starting as I was heading down the narrow two-lane Madrone Road, framed by vineyards on both sides. Way ahead of me a car came hydroplaning off the bridge, taking up both lanes. Everything slowed down, like you always hear, but scarier. I'd only been driving for two years, so, in a panic, I thought of the advice from Drivers Ed and things I'd read in the DMV manuals. Nothing.

At the last second I yanked the wheel to the right to avoid slamming head-on into this guy. I popped off the road at around sixty miles an hour, hit the muddy trail, and soon came to a stop as the dust settled in the rain and the other car went sliding past me. As soon as I came out of slow motion, David Lee Roth commented on the scary situation in typical Roth style: "Oh my God." The timing was perfect. I laughed and yelled, "Holy shit, I almost died." And David Lee Roth had topped the moment off with a quip. I drove back to the gas station, rattled but alive and happy as shit to have nachos for lunch.

I also went to a bunch of live shows that year—I was obsessed at that point. Yngwie Malmsteen was playing in Sacramento, so I made the road trip with Krop and Baden. We
decided to make a day of it and drive up early. On our way
to check out a couple of record stores in the suburbs, one
of them a Tower Records I would later work for, we visited
my Grandpa Ed. I remember thinking he was extra cranky
that day. I later received a note from him, questioning my
judgment for hanging out with two "boys who were clearly
questioning their sexuality." Because that's what growing
your hair and wearing a denim jacket meant.

The letter covered that old trope that people judge you
by the company you keep. He warned me that I might want
to rethink my friendships with them. I didn't. Around that
same time my nanas and Uncle Gary were visiting us for
the holidays when Krop came by to get me one night. After
we left Nana Irene said, "Boy, Brian's girlfriend wasn't very
attractive." Uncle Gary laughed and said, "Nan, that was a
guy." I guess I included those stories to show that grandparents just don't understand.

One really big thing happened that year. From age eighteen to nineteen I grew eight inches. No shit, I ended high
school at five foot ten, and by the time I was nineteen I
measured six foot six. As I have said in my act, I was six
foot six-point-six—the height of the beast. I went through
growing pains. Actual, literal growing pains. I would wake
up screaming because I could feel my bones fucking growing. It felt like I was making a horror movie transformation,
like *American Werewolf* or Jeff Goldblum in *The Fly* remake.

Then, in July of 1985, I turned nineteen, and my mom
had finally had enough of my shit. I get it: I was a fucking lying turd to her. I also was using my mom's credit card to buy

records—good ones, like Dokken, Anthrax, Yngwie. I had quit the gas station and worked at a natural juice company in Sonoma with Pete and my pal Randy. But I got fired for being late all the time. After the juice company let me go, I yelled at the owner in the parking lot and called her the C-word. Classy. Me—because I didn't call her "classy." That confrontation is on my regrets pile.

I also bought a bunch of beers. Weed wasn't my thing yet, but I drank like a fucking fish, a fucking fish that loved shitty beer, shitty vodka, and shitty tequila. My mom and Ken the Monster made the mistake of trusting me alone in her apartment while she took a trip to Hawaii. I wrecked our apartment and swallowed a cup full of chew spit. Did I puke? Sure did. Hard. I'm gagging as I write this. So in the summer of '85 I turned nineteen, and my mom said, "See ya. P.S. Wouldn't want to be ya." Nope, she didn't say that. I wish she were that funny.

All that said, I do not blame her for booting my dumb ass. Man, was I a disrespectful dick. Like a bartender, she said she didn't care where I went, but I couldn't stay there. A shitty, unoriginal bartender. My Grandpa Ed had said I could move to Sacramento to live with him. Instead, I went to crash with the Goodman brothers, who were going to a tech school in Phoenix. I went to see *The Goonies* with Pete and Joel and then headed out on an eleven-hour drive to a weird fucking summer.

Half a day later I arrived in Phoenix and needed a job. I got hired at Taco Bell and had to go buy brown polyester pants for my uniform with money I wanted to eat with. By the end of the week I had worked my way up to the drive-thru. Saying, "Welcome to Taco Hell" in my devil voice into the PA isn't what got me fired, but I'm sure it didn't help.

After ten days at Taco Bell I turned in my browns and got hired as a lot boy at a Chevy dealership. That summer in Phoenix was a hot, sticky blur of parties, concerts, booze, cocaine, speed, beat-running brand-new cars, and flirting with cute Phoenix rocker chicks who wanted nothing to do with my skinny, goofy ass. Thanks to my hard-partying friends, I had discovered the magic of crank, crystal meth, CR—it was super popular in the desert in the mid-eighties. I still wasn't a weed guy; instead, I was snorting all the go-go powder I could get.

By September I had no money and a hundred handwritten pages of my novel—I had started writing a horror novel. More importantly, though, I had no money. And the lot job was not going well. So I begged my mom to let me come home. I moved back in with mom but never finished the book. I only made it another three months with my mom before she again asked me to leave. I had quit working at McDonald's and didn't tell my mom, and my Grandpa George and Grandma Grace came to visit me one day and enjoy some terrible food. They asked my former coworkers where I was, and I'm guessing they joyfully told them I didn't work there anymore. Fuck my grandpa for checking in on me.

And yes, I worked at McDonald's. When I got back to Sonoma I went to our new McDonald's and got hired on the spot. I think I lasted two months. Over the next couple of years I got hired at about six fast-food places and three pizza restaurants. It was easy to get hired, but you had to work your ass off, so I hated it. When my mom booted me the second time, I moved in with my Grandpa Ed in Fair Oaks, a Sacramento suburb, and started over. Again.

I got hired at another McDonald's and started junior college. And not that surprisingly, my mom and I got along once I didn't live with her anymore. The situation would get even better once I found stand-up. It was also around then when she broke up with Ken the Monster. It had nothing to do with me, but I think they both realized they weren't a great fit and moved on. But I think they still did it every once in a while. BLAAARRRGGG!! BLEECCHH!!! UUCCCHHH!!

I guess here is as good a place as any to tell you how Ken's story wrapped up. My mom and I and all her friends would see him around the area and trade stories. He was really into recycling before anybody—that is to say, he would walk around Sonoma and surrounding towns collecting aluminum cans and return them for additional income.

I didn't hate Ken once he wasn't fucking my mom anymore. Weird how that works. He inherited my tan Members Only jacket when I turned into a giant after high school, and he wore it forever. My friend Dan would say, "I saw your jacket walking down Highway 12 today." Ken passed away a long time ago. And locals say you can still see him walking down Highway 12 in my Members Only jacket. Spooky!

THIRTEEN

METALLICA

Metallica is my metal *Star Wars*. I've been a fan of both forever, and yet I can't think of another movie or heavy-metal band that has let me down more and then won me back as a fan. KISS would be, but if we're going to be metal nerds about it—and we are—KISS are not metal, strictly speaking. And they haven't won me back as a listener. As I said earlier, I don't enjoy the new shit, but I'll still crank the crap out of "Detroit Rock City" or *Animalize*. Or even *Dynasty*.

Metallica, however, after twenty years of varying degrees of disappointment, won me back just last year with their latest record, *Hardwired . . . to Self-Destruct*. Amazing fucking record. As I write this, I'm heading to see Metallica play a giant rock show at the Rose Bowl. They're touring the new record, and I got a hook-up, so I couldn't say no. Put it this way: I know a dude.

Let's start at the beginning of Metallica, because that's when I got into them: 1982–83. I heard "Hit the Lights" first on a Metal Blade compilation, *Metal Massacre*; the record also featured the debuts of Ratt and Steeler featuring Yngwie. Hardly anyone at my school knew about *Metal Massacre*, but it was a hit tape among my friends, Baden and Krop. Our small Sonoma metal circle included these other guys—KC, Mike, and Tim.

Tim later created a bunch of video games and owns a successful game company. He used me in his game Brutal

Legend as a voice actor. Shortly after we heard *Metal Massacre* there was a full Metallica demo tape going around called *No Life 'Til Leather*. I'm pretty sure KC hooked us up with a copy of that; he was kind of a rich kid and must've been at the record store more than me because he always had killer shit, but this, I think, he got through tape trading with a pen pal.

"What's a pen pal, Grandpa Metal?" you ask. Well, in the old days you would make a friend just through writing letters. You'd see an ad in the heavy-metal magazines and would find someone who liked the same bands and had similar interests as you, like "I love Venom and shooting cats." Then if you also liked the British band Venom and shooting cats you would send that guy or gal a letter through the US Postal Service, and then you would start trading tapes with your weird new pal. (I don't like Venom or shooting cats—well, I've only tried one of them, so maybe I'll check out Venom. Ha! See what I did?)

Anyway, Krop and Baden and I were into Metallica the second we heard "Hit the Lights." Soon they had their first full-length album, *Kill 'Em All*. I was slightly put off by the imagery on the cover—the hammer, the blood, the garish implied violence—but I loved the music. The aggression, the riffing, the attitude, the memorable sing-along choruses, the Metallica-ness—I'd never heard or seen anything like it.

Then one night we drove to see the German metal band Accept at the famed Kabuki Theater in San Francisco. We had missed Metallica's Kabuki show a couple of nights previous, and here they were, checking out the show. We were fans, and we had to tell them. As we approached them I took the lead. Me: "Hey man, you shred." Kirk looked at us, fake confused and smart-alecky, "Shred? I don't even cook."

Ugh, we were shaken. We should have walked away, but we kept going.

Then I cornered James Hetfield, attitude pouring off the lead singer, "Hey, James, my friends are starting a band. What should they call themselves?" He looked at the three of us and Krop and Baden's new jackets and said, "Almost." I wish that story ended with me telling him to fuck off and the fact that I never listened to Metallica again. Instead, I followed them forever and spent a ton of money on them.

I knew a dude named Duncan who thought Metallica sold out in 1984. When I met Duncan, he was a shit-bag and I think I was one of the only kids in the neighborhood who would talk to him. I was the only metalhead within blocks, but every time I talked to Duncan it was a competition, an assault on my metalness. When *Ride the Lightning* came out, he cornered me and gave a lecture on what a misstep it was. They sold out, he told me. He clearly thought I was a poser and he'd school my dumb poser ass on Metallica.

He also said he fucked a girl at a Slayer show. In the pit he fucked some girl he just met. Sure, it's plausible now because I've seen some crazy shit at metal shows, but I remember at the time thinking, *No, you didn't.* Through the whole story all I could think was, *Um, nope. Wow, this never happened.* Duncan also only liked *Kill 'Em All*. And his favorite band member was Dave Mustaine. The guy they had kicked out. He said Kirk Hammett couldn't play. Two years into Metallica's career Duncan was off the Metallica train. I later wrote a song about Duncan called "More Metal Than You." It was about a famous guy too.

Most of the time when you meet another metalhead, it's like meeting a brother or sister you never met, but every once in a while you meet a dude who makes it a competition.

I like/liked a lot of metal. There isn't a lot of metal that I really didn't like. I have no guilty pleasures—I like what I like, and I don't care what you think. Okay, Warrant, and I probably like Depeche Mode more than you'd think or be comfortable with. But this is about metal.

With metal it's not about your knowledge. Yet with some guys, it is. But mostly metalness is judged by attitude and how hardcore you are, how outwardly metal you are. You can only really wear one band shirt at a time, so people show their metal in different ways—apparel, piercings, long hair. Not me. I would look fucking ridiculous still trying to "look" metal now. Those jeans are stupid, and fitted Affliction shirts would look silly as fuck on me. Certain guys can pull it off, and by that I mean, you would never say anything to them about it.

I was obsessed with finding faster and heavier bands, and soon I discovered Anthrax and Exodus, Testament and Death Angel, but I stayed loyal to Metallica because those early albums meant so much to me. They were *my* metal band. They are now everybody's metal band. And for a reason: there aren't many bands better at writing tight catchy tracks of focused aggression. And fuck Duncan: Metallica got better with each record. By *Master of Puppets* they were unbeatable; they set the bar in metal. You could be more evil, faster, and more frenetic than Metallica, but you were never gonna be better than them. Even they couldn't beat it.

The next two records, *And Justice for All* and *The Black Album*, sold more records and made Metallica the biggest metal band in the world, but they weren't better records than *Master of Puppets*. Thirty-five-plus years after their formation, Metallica—or metal's Rolling Stones—still feel like *my* band. I'll always be a Bay Area kid, and they will always be the Bay Area's best band. Even when they make three terrible records in a row. Even when they slowed down, cut their hair, and made a documentary showing all their flaws. Even when they make a record where it sounds like they tracked their drums with garbage cans. Even when they were assholes to me, I still loved Metallica.

Metal fans can be fickle, but we can also be fiercely loyal. So because I found this local band through tape trading and they made six classic albums that defined my teen years and early twenties, they will always be my band. And . . . because I saw them live tons of times, spent thousands of hours cranking their music and hundreds of nights pounding beers with friends and head-banging and screaming along to "Blackened" like fucking drunk idiots in a parking lot, they will always be my band. Could be worse. There are a million shittier bands.

FOURTEEN

HORROR NERD

I devoured film, but horror was the genre I connected with the most and is a big part of me. Horror movies are the Indian burial ground we built Brian Posehn on. The references to famous monsters and killers and the names of my favorite horror directors have been a part of my stand-up act for a long time. And during all those hours of looking for the next scare, I had no idea I would wind up in a modern horror classic.

So let's go back to the seventies, when the obsession started for me. *Dracula, Godzilla*, and *King Kong* were pretty fucking great, but they all belonged to someone else. They were old movies and had come from a different time. I would really connect with horror films when I found the stuff from my time. But first I would stumble on a truly scary classic in stark black and white on Friday night television.

I had read *Jaws*, the *Jaws 2* adaptation, and adaptation of "*Jaws* in the forest" schlock-classic *Grizzly*, but nothing would prepare me for William Peter Blatty's *The Exorcist*. I read *The Exorcist* before I saw the terrifying movie. My mom had bought the massive bestselling paperback and never finished it. It was the scary elephant in the room. I knew what it was. I had heard the movie made people shit their pants and throw up and blow their heads off or something, so I snuck it off my mom's bookshelf. I loved the novel, but

I was so terrified that I would gladly wait a couple of years to see it on a small screen.

I saw *The Omen* adaptation on the paperback rack at a grocery store with my grandma; she let me get it. More points for Grandma Clara. Both devil-themed movies, *The Exorcist* and *The Omen* would later creep me out and give me strange ideas, but what really started my horror obsession was the terrifying black-and-white intro to zombies, *Night of the Living Dead*. As I mentioned before, I'd seen it by chance on TV on one of my mom's date nights with Ken the Monster, and it stuck. The opening of that movie stirred up a sense of dread I'd never felt before and kept it going all the way to its shocking climax. And it was an important racial allegory that still holds up. George Romero's classic was my zombie bite that led to a full-blown horror infection.

I heard about my favorite horror film ever one Sunday afternoon on a church group day trip. We were driving over the hill to go mini-golfing, and an older girl in my group was telling her friend about the movie *Halloween*. I eavesdropped for a while and then just came clean: I wanted to know everything about *Halloween*. She told us most of the plot. It sounded scary and incredible. I saw it a couple of months later—she didn't sell it hard enough. It was earth shattering. The pacing, the terror, the heroine. You wanted Laurie Strode to live. Donald Pleasance rules as Dr. Loomis. But what stuck with me and made me a horror fan forever was the menacing, unstoppable villain/hero of the movie, Michael Myers. Tons of sequels and other slasher movies would follow, but *Halloween* was the original and is still the perfect horror movie.

In the next couple of years I would see hundreds of horror movies. It was a great time for them, and I wanted to see them all, good and bad. I saw *Carrie* before I read it or knew who Stephen King was, but the two instances had a lot to do with me becoming a massive Stephen King fan. Carrie's Sissy Spacek and the explosive relationship she had with her mom, Piper Laurie, made me feel normal. That movie zips by with one iconic scene after another. Great acting and direction really make a difference.

I saw *Alien* on HBO at a friend's house in the middle of the day, and we were scared shitless. I remember his parents making fun of us for being scared, and then we watched *Blues Brothers* for the tenth time to get our minds off of *Alien*. If you haven't seen *Alien*, I'm not sure we can be friends, reader. Sorry. But of course, you've seen the sci-fi horror classic.

Friday the 13th I viewed in the theater with no spoilers. Had no idea what I was in for. It scared the crap out of me. The nervous, scared energy was a lot of fun. During the famous beheading of Mrs. Vorhees, I yelled, "Don't lose your head, lady!" Everybody laughed. I liked that feeling a lot—making strangers in a dark room laugh at something I made up out of nowhere—almost more than being scared. I love the original that started it all, but the sequels became a lifelong obsession. Jason Vorhees is my spirit animal.

During the early eighties, horror movies came at me fast, and I happily devoured them. I saw *Piranha* on cable. I liked the gore and the violence, but I didn't love the cheapness of *Piranha*. I liked my horror more slick and mainstream. I saw *The Omen II* a couple of times in the theater. We even read the scene in my freshman drama class. The midnight movie *Dawn of the Dead* didn't scare me, but I couldn't believe how gory it was. Romero's follow-up to *Night of the Living Dead* would easily hold up to repeat viewings. When I first saw

Texas Chainsaw Massacre, it felt wrong, like I was watching something I wasn't supposed to see, like a snuff film. That is definitely what Tobe Hooper was going for, though. It still combines horror and dread with an unshakable sense of "ick."

I was leveled by John Carpenter's remake of *The Thing*; the combo of Kurt Russell and John Carpenter would become a big one for me. I was a fan of their first team-up, *Escape from New York*, and would later lose my shit over *Big Trouble in Little China*, but *The Thing* was where I fell in love with the Russell/Carpenter combo. It blew me away and was a repeat rental.

I've always liked it when comedy is mixed with horror. The first one I saw was *Return of the Living Dead*. Another flick I loved renting and rewatching was *Evil Dead II*—it was the perfect combo of laughs and scares. During the late eighties I watched *Evil Dead II* on video with a bunch of people dozens of times. It's so fun and completely holds up over time. There is an alternate universe where Bruce Campbell is the biggest star in the world, and I'd like to live in that universe. I totally prefer *Evil Dead II*'s sillier tone over the more serious *Evil Dead*. At the time I loved Jeff Goldblum in *The Fly* remake, although some of the "comedy" in that didn't feel completely intentional.

I liked watching horror films with friends, but I really love watching them alone, in a theater or in front of my TV, checking out new ones or repeat viewing the same flicks over and over. In the forty years I've watched horror movies I've been mostly open minded; I've checked out everything. But not everything stuck. My taste is pretty mainstream. Carpenter is still my all-time favorite horror director. I generally prefer studio horror over low budget, although *Halloween* was an independent.

And I like gore and practical effects, but not sleazy horror. I'm not a B-level or Z-grade guy; I didn't love the Spanish and Italian stuff I sampled from the seventies. I don't love the trend of torture porn, and I bum out when it feels too exploitive. The repeat-watch horror flicks, from *Halloween* to *Monster Squad* to *Near Dark*—it's strong characters, genuine scares, and great effects that have kept me a fan boy for so long.

So when my buddy was in Rob Zombie's first movie, *House of 1000 Corpses*, I have to admit I was a little jealous. I loved heavy metal *and* horror movies; my buddy didn't love either. I would never say that to him, of course. Instead, I said, "Hey, congrats on the zombie flick." He said, "Thanks, man. You know, you and Rob should meet." Me: "Okay." So the next time he got invited to Rob's, he brought me. We hit it off. Rob watched sitcoms, specifically *Everybody Loves Raymond*, so he knew who I was. What a cool dude, and I'd been a White Zombie fan since the beginning.

I played Jimmy in *The Devil's Rejects*; I was the roadie for Lew Temple and Geoffrey Lewis and their country band. It was always Rob's intention that I get killed. Originally he wrote me as a serial killer traveling Route 66 in an ice cream truck. When he decided to lose that scene, Rob said to me, "Hey, I'm not gonna have you be the ice cream truck guy, but do you want to play the comic relief and then they kill you right away?" I was so stoked this was even happening, I said, "Dude, whatever you want, I'm there."

I die a pretty brutal death: shot in the face, super-close range. And then I laid there playing dead while the *Three's*

Company lady (Priscilla Barnes) gets raped with a gun. Yuck—my mom will never see it. The shoot was so fun and easy; Rob is one of the coolest directors I've ever worked with. It might've helped that we were friends, but he was amazing with the whole cast—such a mellow, funny guy. I was on set for five days. Two days for our dialog scenes. It was a dream to act with Geoffrey Lewis, Clint Eastwood's pal in so many classic movies. I improvised a couple of lines, and they stuck. We shot my death scene on the third day.

And then I had to play dead for two days. Had to? Got to. Kane Hodder (Jason Vorhees in four *Friday the 13ths*) was the stunt coordinator, and he showed me how to take a bullet. Rob had Kane take me off set. Kane warned me how loud it was going to get and then fired a gun at my face and said, "See, it's loud," and I said, "Yep." It was crazy loud. But also very exciting. We went back on set and did it for real. I loved having an apparatus attached to me so when I got shot, blood and skull debris would be pumped from the back of my head and all over my fellow actor, Lew Temple. It was a gnarly effect, and I was in horror nerd heaven.

Of all the things I've done, *Rejects* is the one I'm still most proud of. I have a blast every time I get to be in the same room as the cast. We did a ten-year reunion screening at the Hollywood Forever Cemetery a couple of years back, and it was a total blast. Horror fans love the movie, and the cast is a staple at horror conventions.

Because I have a whole comedy career that I'll tell you about in a minute, I rarely get to attend horror cons as a special guest. I do get to go to them as a paying guest when I stumble upon one, though. Horror nerds are pretty loyal in general, but *Rejects* fans are an especially voracious group—I have signed many a poster or DVD cover in the last twelve years.

I love seeing horror T-shirts in my audience—that means I'm probably going to sign some *Rejects* merch after the show. It's an incredibly fucked-up film to have as your favorite flick, and yet most of the fans I've met seem totally normal and cool. And there's the few who make you want to bathe in bleach after meeting them, and some would like to bathe you in bleach and way worse.

FIFTEEN

RUSH:
MY OTHER OBSESSION

I fell in love with Rush in my teens, and if anything, my love has only grown stronger and more intense. Not Rush Limbaugh, of course—the Canadian power trio, Rush. You know, "Tom Sawyer"? The band with that guy? I was talking about Rush to my wife one day, and my conservative mother-in-law had the weirdest look on her face: "Not Rush Limbaugh, right?" And I was, like, "Ewww. Fucking-A right, not Rush Limbaugh." I didn't say "Fucking A," though.

My history with Geddy Lee, Alex Lifeson, Neil Peart, and the best band ever started in 1981. I was aware of them earlier, but I hadn't yet been fully exposed to the majesty that is Rush 'til "Tom Sawyer" was everywhere. It was love at first listen. I was moved, and not just by the music; Geddy's vocals, the words, and, of course, their insane instrumental acrobatics grabbed me by the head and slapped me silly. Rush had this whole amazing package. A massive impression was made. *Moving Pictures* was copped immediately. Cassette first—in the early eighties I bought most stuff on cassette. *Signals* I bought on vinyl, though, when it came out two years later. That album deserved to be savored and revered and would benefit from the sonic boost music got when I plugged my headphones into my receiver and dropped a platter on my turntable. Still have my copy.

Luckily I kept most of my collection. I wish I would have kept my cassette collection now that they are in vogue again as I write this. And because I'm a hoarder. After *Moving Pictures* I went to *Exit . . . Stage Left*, their double-live effort from the *Moving Pictures* tour. Of course, just like with my other obsessions, once I was bitten, I had to go deeper. I wanted all the songs that were on *Exit . . .* , so I purchased *Permanent Waves, Hemispheres*, and *Farewell to Kings* over the course of a couple of months. Around that same time another Rush kid in my neighborhood recommended fucking *2112*, quite possibly the greatest record ever. Unless you are a dumb dick. Perusing through Rush bins at record stores, I found their first live record, *All the World's a Stage*.

And then I had to have all the songs from that recording, so I sought out *Caress of Steel, Fly by Night*, and their self-titled debut. Their first record is one of their weakest records, though. There are some highlights, like "Working Man" and "I Think I'm Going Bald," but they lack the unique sound and focus they had later. And, really, the big thing is: no Neil Peart. He's the lyricist and drummer (the best fucking drummer) and a massive part of why Rush rules.

By the time *Signals* came out, I was in deep; they were in my top five bands. Then I heard *Signals*. At the time it felt like it was personally prepared by the members of Rush as a message to me. It was *my* record from the very first listen. It wasn't as heavy as the previous records, and it's considered the beginning of their big electronic phase, when Geddy and Neil went nutty with electronic drums and keyboards, but I didn't care about that. It was the songs. The lyrics of Rush always spoke to me in ways Van Halen and AC/DC didn't. Smart, complex, sometimes fantastical, other times political, and, like Iron Maiden and later Anthrax, with Rush there were literary references everywhere. Mostly Ayn Rand in Rush's case. They went through a "Rand" phase. Didn't we all? As a teen their lyrics challenged me. Some songs like "Subdivisions" made an emotional connection with me that will always be there. In the same way that some of my friends got a lot of their personality and point of view from being an Elvis Costello or Tori Amos fan, I was a Rush guy.

At home Rush was a soothing balm when I needed it most. "Subdivisions," with the lyrics: "in the high school halls, in the shopping malls, conform or be cast out" felt less like the best song ever written about high school and suburban conformity and more like a direct missive from the guys in Rush. Like my awesome Canadian uncles came into my room and opened my cone of sadness and sat down on my twin bed I dangled off and talked to me about growing up and life in a way that my mom, grandparents, therapists, and members of the Big Brother agency couldn't. Indirectly, they helped with my loneliness and teen depression.

One day specifically I had run into my room wanting to cry. I was a junior, and two freshman girls had teased me and embarrassed me. At school that day a girl named Cindy told me her friend Marie liked me. I had a crush on Marie, and I guess they both knew because I stared at and pined for Marie every time I was near her; they both saw that and baited me. Cindy said, "I know you like Marie—why don't you call her and tell her?" She gave me Marie's number. I thought, *Wow, that's cool of Cindy. She's making this easy for me. Awesome, no games.* But the whole thing had been a game. I got home and got up the courage to call Marie, only to have her rudely laugh in my face and tell me there was no way she would ever go out with me, let alone talk to me. I was in shock—how did this happen? How was I so misguided? And then Marie's laugh was joined by another familiar laugh, and I realized Cindy was there and I was a victim of their hilarious prank. I hung up—not angry, just sad and embarrassed. Of course, she didn't like me. Why would she? I was a loser for thinking I even had a chance with a popular freshman. I ran down our short hall and into my room, where Geddy was waiting to talk me off a ledge. "Subdivisions" didn't have any answers about how to navigate through the bullshit I was experiencing, but they told me with "Nowhere is the dreamer or the misfit so alone" that answers existed and at least I wasn't alone with that feeling. Even though I felt very alone.

At school I soon noticed that cool kids were into Rush. By my senior year it felt cool to be a part of this new club at school. Once I outed myself as a Rush fan, other kids outed themselves to me. When I played the first side of *2112* on the PA during lunch, Rush won over a few fans, and I made some cool new friends with three-quarter-sleeve *Moving Picture* shirts and feathered hair. Check out the picture of my wall of Rush in my high school bedroom (not pictured: Van Halen and Mötley Crüe walls). That kid doesn't have muscle definition or style, but he has confidence. That is the picture of a young man in love with a band and not afraid to tell anyone.

That year the *Grace Under Pressure* tour in San Francisco at the World Famous Cow Palace was to be my first Rush show. It was the same day as senior-cut day, and I got so hammered at the lake with my friends that I almost missed the show. That day was legendary—for the puking. I threw up twice on the long, winding drive home from Lake Berryessa in Napa. In my friend's car. All over. A lot. It was Pete's dad's Lincoln, and I had neglected to roll the backseat window down. And once I started yacking, I was too wasted to do anything about it. Pete's dad—or, as we all called him, Pops—handled it incredibly well. I helped him clean up the backseat while I was still drunk. We even laughed during the process. He was a drinker—it happens.

After Pete's mom attempted to sober me up with her homemade lasagna and coffee, we grabbed Baden and Krop and headed down to SF. When we got to the Cow Palace parking lot we commenced with the teen ritual of getting as wasted as you could in a short period of time. Once I was back to my earlier level of drunk teen idiot, we stumbled in. My group of shit-face teens miraculously got to our terrible seats at the top of the stadium, and Gary Moore took the stage. I don't remember any of Gary—I passed out immediately. An hour later I woke up as Rush took the stage. And it was fucking amazing—those three pals are magical on stage. The set list was composed of all the songs we wanted to hear; it was like we wrote it. Their energy and the tightness of that band is another one of the factors that made me a fan for life. And I loved the solos, when each member had their time to shine. Neil Peart, of course, gave a tutorial on being a bad-ass drummer who no one could follow.

That was the *Grace Under Pressure* tour. And I've seen every tour since. I don't even know how many times I've seen them live, but I'd say a fucking lot. In fact, Rush became an even bigger obsession of mine after seeing them in person that first time. The guys became my idols; I still wish Geddy was my uncle—my Jewish bad-ass genius uncle. Now I have an insane Rush collection—vinyl, cassettes, DVDs, and bobble heads. And MP3s. But no one ever brags about their MP3 collection.

Rush has been my favorite band through all the phases of my life: when I was listening to as much crazy heavy shit as I could, when I found new wave, dabbled with hip-hop, stumbled on the Seattle scene, bounced through the Lollapalooza era, and back through all the metal I've experienced in the last thirty years—the legendary Canadian trio has always been a constant. My wife loves Rush too—she'd have to. Melanie had seen Rush and the Scorpions multiple times before we met. She once said, "All my boyfriends liked Rush." To which I say, "Great—all." Some of my friends didn't like Rush, were dismissive of them. That didn't stop me from talking about their greatness to that person every chance I got. More than any other band I can think of, Rush has always been divisive. Like the 2016 election. With Rush it's either full-blown love, obsession, and loyalty or sheer, ugly hatred. Rush fans will hurt you if you cross our band. Okay, well, we will hurt your feelings, for sure. See you later, feelings. Suck it up, snowflake!

My friend Pearl's dad is Meatloaf. Not the thing, the guy. I have never ever been a fan of Meatloaf the guy. I love the food. As a matter of fact, the combo of Margaret Cho, potent weed, ecstasy, a sketchy cab driver, and the song "Bat Out of Hell" made it so I could never hear Loaf again and be totally happy. Anyway, one night a long time ago I made Pearl cry. She was ripping on Geddy Lee, and I lost my shit. I really laid into her, with this being one of the nicest things I said: "You may hate Rush, but not as much as I hate your dad." I felt awful afterward, and everyone at the table was uncomfortable. But my point was made. In my shitty, ugly, awkward, kind of psycho way, the message was clear as hell: don't fuck with Rush!

SIXTEEN

COMEDY:
MY OTHER OTHER OBSESSION

The few things I knew about my dad were that he loved imported beers like Lowenbrau and Heineken, and he liked hiking, San Francisco, and comedy. I like three of those things. I thought I was bonding with him one time when I was on the roof of my apartment building in his favorite city as I drank a ton of his favorite beers, Heineken. Of course we both liked Heineken and Lowenbrau—they're fucking delicious.

He also loved San Francisco and made my mom love it even more by introducing her to parts of the city she didn't know before. I thought it was so cool that they watched Steve McQueen shoot the iconic car chase from *Bullitt* on a busy city street one day.

I also learned from my mom and Uncle Mike that my dad loved comedy. He took my mom to see Mort Sahl at the legendary Hungry I in San Francisco, and his favorite comic was Lenny Bruce. I think my dad would've tried stand-up if he hadn't died so young.

I was already a fan of comedy when my mom told me about their Mort Sahl show and his admiration of Lenny. I watched and listened to anything I could when it came to comedy—Steve Martin, Robin Williams, Freddie Prinze, and even novelty songs like "Junkfood Junkie" and "The Streak." I was really into "Let's Get Small," but Steve Martin would become a god to me with "Wild and Crazy Guy." He was the ruler of stand-up comedy for about two years, but I was a fan for life. I even liked "Comedy Is Not Pretty." I asked for the *Cruel Shoes* book for Christmas. I saw the shit out of *The Jerk* and laughed my skinny butt off. That became a repeat renter.

On day trips to San Francisco I was often left at one of my favorite movie theaters in the city, the Coronet and the Alhambra. They were both classic, old-school theaters with huge ceilings and balconies. I would sit through anything, really, but I genuinely enjoyed rewatching comedies. I saw both *It's a Mad, Mad, Mad, Mad World* and *Freaky Friday* on different occasions, the Jodie Foster *Freaky Friday*—not the other one with Dillhole and What's-Her-Nut. I would watch the same movie sometimes three times in a sitting. Not only did I not mind being left there alone, I actually loved it.

I was obsessed with all the *SNL* comedies—*Animal House, Caddyshack, Meatballs*—having been a fan of the show from the first season. I caught one of the first episodes while my mom was out with Ken the Monster. One episode and I was hooked. I also liked *Fridays* with the young, manic Michael Richards. Sketch comedy had already planted a seed.

I think I inherited my sense of humor from both sides. I probably got my darker sense of humor from my Grandpa Ed. The older I got, the more his humor came out around me. He installed an air horn used by diesel trucks into his pickup purely to fuck with people. One morning there was an old lady in the crosswalk. He barked, "Watch me make this old lady shit her pants." Not sure if she did, but I almost did—laughing.

He wasn't great with fireworks or kids. I had a firecracker in my hand, and he let it go off in the palm of my hand.

It was a shitty lesson. "Don't hold onto lit firecrackers," he told me. Glad it ended there and didn't cover "Don't punch a shark in the dick" and "Don't point a loaded gun at your dumb mouth."

I had grown up visiting their neighbor, Marie, and her rabbits and chickens next door. When I was around ten years old I went with Grandpa Ed to cut off a chicken's head. I was not happy—I loved animals. He yelled at me to hold onto the chicken and to get it in the bucket once the loss of its head made it go crazy. And because that wasn't nearly traumatic enough, my grandpa threw the head at me. I ran back to my grandma's crying. His man lessons often backfired and sent me running from the thing he was trying to make me comfortable with, though this didn't stop me from eating chickens because they're fucking delicious.

So if the darkness of my comedy can be attributed to my grandpa and my gallows humor came from coping with death at a young age, then I definitely got my crass side from Nana Norma. She brought home off-colored jokes from work, and she'd say them at the dinner table because Nana didn't give a fuck. My mom would try to stop her—no chance. I used it as an opportunity to entertain Nana with Italian and Polish jokes from my book. She loved them. My mom told each of us not to encourage the other.

Nana did nails at a salon in Atherton. The salon was owned by an out and proud seventies dude named Sal. He was like an Italian American Paul Lynde—over the top and a blast to be around. Always flamboyant, outrageous, and the hit of the party. Nana fucking worshipped him. So the shit I'd heard about gay being different or bad wasn't fitting for me. Sal was a crack-up. I thank god or whatever for the exposure to all types of people my Bay Area childhood gave me. And also for giving me goofy grandparents.

I had been interested in journalism since my junior year in high school, so in college I studied journalism and communications. But I wasn't very good at it and was kind of a candy ass when it came to commitment. I even totally faked one of the class assignments: my human-interest story about an old guy with a paper route was total bullshit, completely fabricated. Write what you know.

Through my instructor I wrote a review of "Welcome to the Jungle" for the school paper, the *American River College Beaver*. I was actually pretty proud of it. So when I heard that LA band Fishbone was coming to the El Dorado Saloon, I knew I had to interview them. But it went terribly. The singer answered my juvenile questions with more juvenile unfunny responses. I went back to my school paper with no usable answers to my shitty questions. Thank god, because if I'd had a good Fishbone interview I might never have done comedy.

So I was pretty immersed in comedy before I actually did any. I was watching comedy nonstop. Studying anybody and everybody I saw on HBO and all the cable outlets—Jerry Seinfeld, Rick Ducommun, Bobcat Goldthwait, Dennis Miller, Drake Sather, Norm Macdonald. And I would continue to study after I started. When I lived in New York I visited the Museum of TV and Radio to watch old Richard Pryor, George Carlin, and Bob Newhart TV appearances.

I WENT THROUGH a bunch of jobs—McDonald's, Burger King, Rax Roast Beef, a couple of pizza places—before landing at

Tower Records, one of the best jobs I ever had. I always had one or two jobs, because that was part of the deal I made with my grandpa. I made a bunch of friends at my day jobs who encouraged my jackassery. And soon only comedy mattered, when I got serious about my jackassery.

SEVENTEEN

STAND-UP:
AN OBSESSION BECOMES MY LIFE

I never had a big epiphany that I had to be a performer, but there were hints along the way. I started stand-up in the summer of 1987. This is fucking unbelievable to me, but thirty years ago today as I write this I was preparing to go on stage for my first time at a local open mic in Sacramento, California. I had been writing jokes for about six months, waiting until I turned twenty-one and could even get into the Metro Bar and Grill in downtown Sac.

I was referred to the place when I had tried calling the local full-time comedy club, Laughs Unlimited in the Birdcage Walk Mall that I frequented. It was as suburban as it sounds. Whoever answered the phones at Laughs told twenty-year-old me that I had to be twenty-one and that I should really try it at an open mic before I could do one of their showcase nights.

So I wrote jokes. About ten minutes worth of jokes. Mostly self-deprecating already, commenting on my looks (long hair, big nose, and a lot of Stussy gear and metal and skateboarding T-shirts) and my size and demeanor. I was actually pretty much myself on stage that first time; later I would try gimmicks and a more aggressive delivery before circling back to being myself onstage.

Anyway, that first night I guzzled beers in the parking lot with my pal Glen to prepare for this event and my eventual career. Glen had been pushing for me to try this, maybe because at that point it was super clear I wasn't going to be playing in a band with him. He had been really encouraging when I had decided to play the drums six months before that, but I sucked harder at the drums than I had previously sucked in sports, which was some sucking at the highest level. My bird limbs are not fucking meant to even touch drumsticks or sports equipment, but as I would learn that night, I could hold a microphone and make fun of myself.

After pounding canned beverages and cranking eighties metal—of course, it was the eighties—out of Glen's VW Bug we descended the stairs with a nice buzz going, and I got on the list. For the next two-plus hours we watched a bunch of local guys perform in front of a modest but enthusiastic audience. When it was my turn I made my buzz and my pants-shitting nervousness work for me. That first set went perfectly, and I loved being on that one-foot-high riser with a stool and a microphone in a basement bar on a weekday. The next week I went back to feed my new addiction—I had written five all-new minutes. But then I fucking ate it hard for the entire set. Holy crap, did I eat it. Nothing worked; my nervousness won the day. But instead of giving up, like I had previously done every time I ate shit doing something, I went up a third week.

My comedy is so much about truth, but not in a cheesy way. I just mean that all my stories are true, they all actually happened. But I started comedy by lying. Lying to my mom to make a story better or to make her laugh, I would embellish things at first, then I would lie: I had a few fake girlfriends and one I completely made up—even her name, Sinea, was made up. Nice, huh? Very exotic sounding and pretty inclusive for the mid-eighties. She was a punk Edie

Brickell I met in a Napa coffeehouse. And completely made up.

I also lied to everybody at my new jobs in Sacto, rewriting my history like a sociopath. First of all, my mom and I had more money in my fantasy life. To explain the beater I drove, I had trashed my loaded Mazda RX7. In retrospect I aimed pretty low with my lie—a Mazda? Like everything I like, I had an obsessive period with comedy: I got onstage as much as I could and took any road gig that came up. I went to every open mic anywhere near Sacramento. I did an open mic in a suburban bar, and the crazy old lady who owned the place had a swear jar on the bar: if you cursed during your set, you had to contribute to the swear jar. I didn't make any money that night.

I made a few friends in the local comedy scene. One was an older guy named Maurice. I did a lot of shows with Maurice in that short time; we did comedy competitions at bars and dance clubs and drove to San Francisco to try to get onstage. One night Maurice asked a couple of us if we would do a show at San Quentin Prison with him. We all were obsessed with stage time, so we all said yes. A couple of weeks before the prison show we were all hanging out after our weekly Metro Bar and Grill show. We were at a friend's house after the bars closed, and that was the last time I ever saw Maurice. I went home with a girl, because comedy had made me confident.

The next morning I was at my job at Steve's Place Pizza making and flipping pizza dough when a customer mentioned that cops had killed a local comedian the night before. I responded with a hearty "What the fuck?" Well, what the fuck was: Maurice was a rapist. While I was being consensually horny, Maurice had climbed through the window of a strange woman to rape her. She had managed to dial the operator during the struggle.

Sacramento cops showed up as Maurice made his escape; they say he reached for a gun. We all believed them and actually pictured him faking the gun so he wouldn't have to go back to San Quentin as a rapist. It turned out that he had scheduled the San Quentin show as a homecoming show to show off to his old prison pals his new comedy skills. And then he blew it and raped again like a rapist. How crazy is that? I still have yet to play San Quentin.

While I was working at Tower I was the rap buyer, but I ran the counter a lot. That was super fun. I would crank my thrash heroes like Anthrax, Testament, Vio-lence, Exodus, and Death Angel and then make fun of customers. And boy, were they dipshits. One day a customer called, asking, "Do you have 'Riding with the Monkey' by Tony San Martini?" and I said, a beat later, "Do you mean 'Surfing with the Alien' by Joe Satriani?" "Yeah, that." I should have won an award for that. I got what he was saying, and he only had two words right: "with" and "the."

And yeah, the metalhead kid was also the rap buyer. Nothing gets past you. When I was hired it came up that I was pretty knowledgeable about rap—I was actually a big fan of it at the time. Still am, of course, as I'm old my favorite stuff is from '85 to '95. I was/am into everything from Run-DMC, LL Cool J, and the Beastie Boys to NWA, Public Enemy, Biggie Smalls, Wu-Tang Clan. And I love A Tribe Called Quest and De La Soul. I am also a massive fan of California hip-hop performers Souls of Mischief and The Pharcyde. So there's my rap cred—at the time it was enough. I wasn't the only metalhead at my Citrus Heights Tower Records, but I was the only guy in our suburban neighborhood who knew the difference between MC Hammer and Too Short and would school anyone who asked. Or didn't ask.

I was fired several months later. Fired for attitude. From Tower Records. They hired me for attitude. But I soon got a job building skateboards for a place called Sacramento Surf and Skate, where my attitude fit in really well. My long-haired, Stussy-wearing hesher pals and I would lay grip tape and install trucks and wheels onto skateboard decks as per our job description. But most of our time was spent making fun of the suburban kids buying skateboards, trendy clothes, sunglasses, snowboards, and surfing gear from us. The irony was not lost on us that we worked at a land-locked surf shop. We were cool; the dudes and dudettes who shopped there, they were the "fecking posers."

In January of 1990 I left Sacramento and the job security of a skateboard shop for the comedy mecca, Long Beach, California, to make it in comedy. Then I didn't. One thing I didn't know when I moved to Long Beach is that it is kinda far from Hollywood—like, on a good day, a half hour away and usually at least an hour. It was such a dumb choice. But that was the year of a lot of bad choices. At least I had the support of my mom, though. She was impressed with what I had done with stand-up in two and a half years, so in January of 1990 she helped me load up a U-Haul and head down south from Sacramento.

We should have known it was a bad move. It rained most of the way as we went over the Grapevine, this treacherous pass over the mountains before you get to Los Angeles where it's super sketchy if you've never done it before and especially if you're young and driving a U-Haul with your mom. And it's harder to smoke pot and masturbate.

I got sets at bars and comedy clubs all around LA and Orange County pretty quickly just by being the new kid who had a decent twenty minutes. I did the local open-mic night at the Long Beach Comedy Club and pretty quickly became a regular opener/MC.

I opened for such dead comedians as Skip Stephenson from *Real People*; Blake Clark, a hilarious Boston comic who was also featured in a couple of Adam Sandler movies; and Vic Dunlop, who did every possible stand-up show in the late eighties and early nineties. It was cool to have a local venue where I could get tons of stage time in front of huge national acts. From that, the booker of the club, Francine, turned me on to other gigs, a couple of Improvs in the Orange County suburbs.

One night I got pulled over coming back from San Diego in my shitty '68 Bug. I'd already gotten pulled over in Sac for a possible 502—highway patrol code for drinking and driving. The San Diego one was brutal; they were total bullies. Sheriff: "Who do you think you are, Axl Rose?" Me: "Um, Axl Rose is a rock singer. I'm a comedian." Shitty smirks all around. Sheriff: "You're a comedian? Do you have any jokes about cops?" Me: "No, but I will tomorrow." That guy actually smiled before he put me in the drunk tank, even though I wasn't fucking drunk. I later got a letter from Orange County saying I wasn't guilty. Turns out I wasn't drunk. No shit.

My friend Paige also moved down from Sacramento. She had broken up with Glen when she showed up at his house and caught him with another girl in his bedroom. He said, "I was just showing her my puppies." (In his defense, he did have cute puppies.) Paige then crashed with us for a couple of months; she actually lived in my room with me and slept in my bed. I was so in love with her that I thought something would just organically happen. It didn't.

I tried to get a record store job but couldn't lock one down. Instead, I delivered subpoenas and filed papers at different courthouses around LA county. Compton was intimidating, hip-hop reputation withstanding. I had a guy pull a gun on me when I stepped on his porch trying to deliver a subpoena; I put it in his mailbox when he wasn't looking. Sketchy job. And I hated it. I was getting stand-up dates, but I needed more income. So I took a job as an entertainer for children's parties. I was going to be in a Ninja Turtle costume. Pretty awesome job for a turtle, huh? But I would never get to put on that shell.

That July a couple of friends were visiting from Sacramento, and the day started like any other. We got high and grabbed tacos. It wound up being one of the worst nights of my life.

After fourteen hours of drinking and smoking and a little bit of blow we decided to keep it going when the bars on the trendy Third Street closed. We grabbed more beers, loaded up our backpacks, and headed for the beach. I would later wish I had died. We drank on the roof of a lifeguard tower. When we were leaving we all jumped off the tower. I went last. But I had no business jumping off of there. I broke my back.

That's how it works. I had a compressed fracture of the L3 vertebrae. And I walked home. Terrible idea. I got into a hot bathtub with Epsom salts because I thought that was what my mom would recommend. Why four twenty-three-year-old guys had Epsom salt in the house, I still have no idea. Anyway, I was sitting in the tub and realized I was paralyzed. I panicked. An ambulance came and threw me shirtless with soaking-wet Billabong sweatpants into the back. This was Long Beach—that probably happened all the time. I remember the cold sensation of the metal table in the emergency room on my back, but I really didn't feel that much pain. Booze made the situation happen, but it also made it kind of better.

A week later they moved me to a spinal cord injury clinic in Whittier. I had a compressed fracture of the L3 vertebrae, which led to swelling of my spinal column and paralysis. After meeting with specialists I was given the choice of surgery that would fuse my back together and I'd still probably never walk again or, because I was young, maybe let my back heal itself. I went with plan B, the biggest maybe ever. I was alone. My mom had freaked out when she heard about my injury, blacked out, hit her head on the bathroom sink, and broke her arm. It was a fucking nightmare.

I came out of my paralysis ten days after my dumbass leap, but I wouldn't walk for two and a half months. I was moved enough not to get bed sores, but I would be bedridden for the duration. When I was fitted with a hard-plastic brace that would hopefully heal my spine, they told me I was the only patient in the whole hospital who might ever walk again. It was essentially a giant turtle shell. So I guess I got to wear a shell after all—small victories and all that. While in Whittier I heard gunshots a couple times. Turned out that a gang kid who had been paralyzed was in the front of the hospital visiting with family members, and rival gang drove by to finish the job. They didn't. Someone else died, though. Thankfully they soon moved me to an old folks' home in Carson, scrappy neighbor to Compton. (Read in a sarcastic voice) Another really nice neighborhood.

My new home/hospital bed was not in a fancy assisted-living facility like the docked cruise ship my mom currently lives in. No, this was an old folks' home. It was super depressing. I wound up sharing a room with a very old, bedridden man who seemed to be hallucinating. I never found out his whole story, but I'm now guessing that he suffered from dementia, because later I would deal with dementia more closely.

At the time the old guy in the bed next to me, Richard, was a constant annoyance. I don't remember his last name. I feel like the nurses said it and he said, "Call me Richard." Not in a cool way—he was super bossy about everything. You know how some old people are sweet all the time and some of them are bossy dicks? This guy was a bossy dick. The only conversations Richard and I ever had were about the same two things: he wanted to know what time it was, and luckily or unluckily, I had a swatch. Those were dumb. But I was super metal laying in a hospital bed wearing a plastic watch.

Anyway, it felt like every twenty minutes the entire time I was there he would ask me what time it was. And he said it in the weirdest way: "Excuse me, what time do you have by your watch?" It wasn't an old-fashioned expression. I don't think anybody ever talked like that. I would tell him the time, and he would either say, "thank you" and fall quiet until he asked me again, twenty minutes later, what time I had by my watch. Or he would follow it by saying his wife was coming to get him in their Cadillac.

The first time he told me that I believed him—why wouldn't I? I eventually figured out, like, forty times later that she wasn't coming. I don't know if Richard ever figured it out. He died. Just kidding. Not while I was there. But I'm pretty sure he's dead now.

If you think that's depressing, I also handmade a calendar detailing my two months I had to stay there. More?

Okay, filling the pee cup became a game no one won. I had
a sadistic running gag where I'd try to fill the pee cup to
the rim, so whoever moved it would get pee everywhere.
Oh, and yes, I know I'm an asshole. I knew it then. The
only other person my age in the whole care center was this
kid confined to a bed-chair because of spina bifida. He was
also a crackhead and a gang member—spina bifida couldn't
keep him down. Well, it did.

I didn't have a ton of friends in Long Beach, so I didn't
have a ton of visitors, which definitely added to the depressing nature and relentless boredom of staying there. The
booker of the Long Beach comedy club visited a couple of
times. She also helped find a buyer for my VW Bug and
brought me weed. Good friend. Paige, the *Playboy* model
who slept in my bed and never, ever fucked me, sent her
friend to visit me. She said Paige was concerned for me but
would not be visiting me. There was a cool nurse at the senior care facility who took pity on me and brought me food
from my favorite local Southern California joints, Taco Surf
and In and Out Burger.

In October of 1990, after around three months of hospi-
talization, I was released. I would still have to wear the turtle
shell. Pete came and got me. With my Bug sold, I flew home
to Sonoma to live with my mom one final time. In that year
and a half, while living with my mom, I had two record store
jobs, protested Desert Storm, did it with a cute punk chick
a bunch of times, finally got a girlfriend, got her pregnant,
and had both my grandpas die—all as I was concentrating
on getting back on stage.

One day I was working the register at Rainbow Records,
high and full of Classic Coke and Skittles. I ruled that register with a snarky heavy-metal fist. I was probably mid-snark

when my mom called to tell me that my Grandpa George had suffered a heart attack and we had to go to the hospital immediately. When we got to Santa Rosa Hospital an hour and a half later he was already dead. I still said good-bye to him, and as far as my interactions with dead bodies go, that was my least favorite. But Grandpa Ed died in a way more dramatic fashion. He was suffering from Parkinson's and dementia when he first went missing. One afternoon he went on a walk and never came back. Boom. Stephen King.

We looked for Grandpa Ed for almost two weeks. I spent a ton of time searching all over Sacramento for the poor guy. I put posters everywhere and followed up on sightings of him. He had been seen twenty-five miles away from his house, so my Uncle Mike and I expanded our search area. But the guy from that sighting wasn't my grandpa. Turns out that ol' Ed had never left the neighborhood. He had fallen off a cliff the day he went missing. In classic Boy Scout fashion, they found his dead body on some rocks down by the river. America's Boy Scouts, finding dead bodies since 1908.

I took losing both my grandfathers in one month pretty well—that is, until a year later, when I was on the road by myself in Montana and had a nervous breakdown. I was listening to a book on tape of *Iron John* when I lost it. It doesn't matter really what I was listening to when I started crying; it could have been The Cure or Jovi. On the way to my next gig I'm cruising through the middle of nowhere, and I just started crying uncontrollably—just a realization that my biggest cheerleaders were gone. I had never ever felt so alone. When I returned to San Francisco I found a therapist.

Grandpa Ed's passing came with an inheritance, which enabled me to move to San Francisco. I only lived there two and a half years, but they were two and a half awesome years filled with road gigs, almost-nightly local shows, and a lot of partying. Oh yeah, I drank again after my dumb night on a lifeguard tower. During my short time there, I wound up meeting lifelong comedy friends Karen Kilgariff, Greg Behrendt, Patton Oswalt, Blaine Capatch, and Margaret Cho as well as out-of-town comics David Cross, Janeane Garofalo, and Doug Benson.

One weekend I went to an open mic at a pizza place out by the ocean. We would get free slices for doing sets there, and after one set you learned not to get the pizza anymore. We were all starving comedians, and the food was even too shitty for us. One night there was a new young, edgy, dark comic in town. He was tiny and even younger than me. His name was Patton Oswalt. He was funny the first time I saw him. He did an impression of Spider-Man in Kansas, and Patton would just stand there, making the Spidey-hand, sadly looking around for a place to shoot his webs. It was super funny. And nerdy as shit.

I had a joke at the time in which I referenced "Feck weed" from the eighties indie movie *River's Edge*. (Dennis Hopper's character was named Feck and sold weed.) Patton liked the joke, and I complimented him back on his Spidey bit. We ran into each other a couple of more times and started to become friends, but our friendship really took off when we both signed up for the San Francisco Comedy Competition in 1992. While we carpooled to shows with another guy, we would talk about serial killers, creeping out the poor Christian comic named Derik we were carpooling with. Patton and I soon cemented our pact with Satan and moved in together.

Our apartment in the middle of the city quickly became a comic hangout; it was a handy quick stumble away from legendary comedy club the Holy City Zoo. It was a huge two bedroom with high ceilings and hardwood floors, a second-floor Victorian walkup on the corner of Fifth and Geary. And because I had dead-grandpa money, we had a decent TV and a killer stereo, and there was always beer in the fridge and Stoli in the freezer. It was a short, booze- and weed-fueled period of my life, but I cherish that time of living and breathing comedy with my super-cool, funny, crazy-talented friends.

In the spring of 1993 a writing job opportunity came up in LA: to write for a new MTV show called *Trashed*. I jumped at it. After an interview in LA I got the job, quickly subletted my space in San Francisco, and moved to LA to try again to make it there. This time I lived in LA proper.

On that job Doug Benson was also one of the writers. We had a blast thinking of segment ideas and developing the show from the ground up. We kinda didn't know what we were doing, but Steve Higgins, the head writer, kept us on track and productive.

I was living in the Hollywood Hills with fellow comic Todd Glass and my manager, Dave Rath, when we were hit by the 1994 Northridge earthquake. We were fine, but it was fucking scary. We were on a cliff, and the whole house shook. Doug's apartment had suffered a lot of damage, so he crashed with us for a while.

One night we realized that if Dave and I went into our rooms and shook the windows it would feel like an earth- quake upstairs in the living room. Shortly after that, Dave Chappelle was over and complaining about the quake and all the aftershocks, so my roommate and I signaled each other and headed downstairs. We shook the shit out of our windows. When we went back upstairs Chappelle was gone.

He was so scared that he went straight to the airport and flew the fuck home. Sorry, Dave.

Sarah Silverman had also recently moved to LA from New York and was at our house a lot. It had kind of become the party house, with recent LA transplants like Patton and Greg Behrendt visiting frequently. And David Cross and Janeane had introduced me to LA people like Bob Odenkirk and Kathy Griffin.

We were putting on shows around LA all the time, and then we would end the evening at my house or Greg Behrendt and Janeane Garofolo's place and party—in Greg's words, like we had all won an Emmy. I was asked to perform on four episodes of a sketch show with Odenkirk and Cross—not sure what happened with it. Then, in 1995, I took a job in New York on the syndicated *Jon Stewart Show*.

Despite working with Dave Attell and Jon Stewart, I did not have a great time living in Manhattan. So when the show was canceled I moved back to LA to live with my girlfriend, Paula, the wardrobe woman from *Trashed* as well as a funny new show my friends and I were all a part of.

From 1995 to 1998 a bunch of us worked together on *Mr. Show with Bob and David* for HBO. It was an incredibly fun job that I was way too immature for at the time. I learned a lot about writing, performing, and just being a funny human from Bob and David and my fellow writers like Dino Stamatopoulos, Paul F. Tompkins, Bill Odenkirk, and Jay Johnston. My love of SCTV, Python, and *SNL* had paid off. I felt like I was born to write sketches and skits with those insanely hilarious guys. To this day *Mr. Show* and *The Sarah Silverman Program* are the two TV shows I'm most proud of. They match my comedic sensibility the closest, and I got to work with my funniest friends.

Since I moved to LA in '94 I have been incredibly lucky to appear on a million sitcoms and animated shows. Well, not a million, but I've done a shitload of shows. I was lucky in casting; I have a memorable look and a couple of notes I can hit. I can do dumb guy or smart guy, sweet guy and, best of all, a weird guy. Of all the dumb, smart, sweet guys I've played, almost all of them have been weird.

I did *NewsRadio* twice. Phil Hartman was my favorite guy there, and one of my greatest memories is when he would see me on set and say, "Bri . . ." with that Phil Hartman voice. So cool and so fucking tragic. I did *Friends* during the second season; half of them were assholes. I did *Veronica's Closet*; both of the stars were not nice. I'm an easy guy on the set too; I keep to myself and never complain. But that's kind of it for negative stories. All my other guest-star experiences were pretty positive. I did four years on *Just Shoot Me,* and that was only ever fun.

I did an episode of a Tom Selleck sitcom called *The Closer*. You've probably never heard of it, but I'll remember it forever. *Adventure in Babysitting* cutie Penelope Ann Miller got to sit on my lap in a scene. The great Ed Asner was also a star on the show, and I found myself in the makeup room with just Tom, Ed, and the makeup people the night of the taping. I was already super nervous just being in the same room as two TV legends. Then Ed ripped one. Long and loud, it shook the room. Tom immediately reacted, saying, "Jesus, Ed!" And all I could think was that Lou Grant farted and Magnum got mad.

I wish that Jerry Seinfeld said something super funny and memorable to me or even if he ripped one; instead, he was just incredibly nice and welcoming when I did that TV show he had in the nineties. I had auditioned three times and wound up on *Seinfeld* during the final season. It was a dream job, and he couldn't have been cooler. But you can change that story and make it Kramer farted and Jerry blanched.

Bernie Mac was also incredibly cool. I did his show twice, and he was a very gracious host. One day we were all on set, and he started talking to a little girl who was also part of the guest cast for the week. There were about thirty people in the room getting ready to shoot our scene. Bernie was so commanding and charismatic that when he spoke to the girl, everybody got quiet.

Bernie said, "Now, little girl, what's your name?" She looked up at him and said, "Sincere." Bernie did a double-take, "Sincere . . . ? Where's your mama, so I can smack her silly?" BEAT. "Sincerely!" The room quietly lost our minds; everybody was snickering. His timing was impeccable. I felt awful for the mom, but I'll remember that moment for the rest of my life. Bernie was right—you have to take a joke like that when it's just laying there.

Biggest regret? *Monsters, Inc.* Apparently I was second choice to play the lovable furry blue monster Sully. Of course, at the time I didn't know I was second choice. I knew I was close because I read for it a couple of times. I wanted it badly and really made an effort doing my take on the sweet lug. Pixar employees and Disney casting people have told me that I got as close as you can get. And then the studio pushed for John Goodman. I get it: I couldn't be a bigger John Goodman fan. I can't even picture Sully with my voice now, but I'd love that sequel money.

Stand-up is still the focus now. I act and write to stay busy, but I travel year-round performing in the best comedy clubs and just-okay rock venues. And I mostly play cities I actually want to be in, which is nice. It's been thirty years since July

12, 1987, and it feels nice to associate that day with something cool, because it's also the day my dad died forty-nine years ago. Not to be a bummer, but that will always be connected to July 12 too.

My success in comedy has been a bonding moment for me and my mom. We've been really close since I started doing what I love in 1987. She went to school after her husband died to get a better career to support her selfish, smart-assed, fuck-faced, dickhead son so he could write a bunch of mean, totally true things about her. She's really kind of a badass. A giant majestic lady who lost her fellow giant mate. And made the best life she could for the two of us. And she worked with developmentally disabled kids for half her life. Kind of hard to hate her. I don't. Not anymore.

EIGHTEEN

GIRLS: TALES OF A LATE BLOOMER

Like every nerd in every movie ever, I had fake girlfriends. Three. Sinea, Karen, and Paige. Sinea was my first fake girlfriend. Not even based on anyone. She was completely made up. Sinea "lived" in Napa. Napa was our Canada, just over the hill, but far enough away so my friends had no idea I was full of shit. Karen, "the swimsuit model" was based on my step-cousin Karen, a swimsuit model. Gross. Moving on. Sinea and Karen were total lies. All made up. Except for Paige. She was a real person I was madly in love with in such a *Pretty in Pink* way, except if Molly Ringwald was tiny and blonde and had been in *Playboy*.

When I grew up *Playboy* magazine definitely represented a feminine ideal. I also connected it to my dad because one of the few photos I have of my dad and his friends shows him holding up a *Playboy* magazine. He had told my mom that he liked the magazine for style and stereo reviews—he read it for the articles. In 1965. He might've been the first guy to come up with that.

I've never been a porn guy, mostly because of *Playboy*. My standards are too high: Playmates aren't doing porno; Hustler Honeys are. And I hated *Hustler*. I had a bad experience with *Hustler*. Yep, a bad experience with a magazine. Russ, Darren, Hinchman, and I had a *Hustler* in our treehouse. It got left out in the rain. When it dried out, it had a weird fucking smell. One day I decided to check it out. I opened it to a nice young lady basically showing the "reader" a full gynecology exam. That was my first close-up of a vagina. I almost threw up. Gagging. Retching, almost puking.

After the magazine tested my gag reflex, I associated vaginas with that mildew scent and my responding gag reflex. That is the making of a serial killer. Somehow, even with that weird story, my fucked-up relationship with my mom, and a bunch of rejections, I actually did pretty well with women once I hit my twenties. Because of Tami Baker, I had a serious thing for cute, tiny blondes; I also blame seventies and eighties advertising and the entertainment industry for pushing this Barbie ideal with Farrah Fawcett and Cheryl Ladd. Anyway, I like pretty blonde girls. How on the nose. I also liked red-haired girls, brunettes, and black-haired girls of every ethnicity. They all seemed nice.

Once I really started dating, I realized I didn't totally have a type. But in the beginning most of my early crushes fit the cute, little blonde type. Michelle was my type. She worked with me at a pizza place in the mall. I asked her to go to Sonoma with me to party with my friends and the beach for spring break. She'd already fucked my friend Glen. At my house. I didn't care. She was little and cute and blonde. Nothing happened. I didn't even try. I just liked being around her, even though she was kind of a ding-dong. My mom came home while Michelle was in the shower. She was so mad I had "snuck a girl" into her house that she left to cool down.

For years my mom thought I slept with Michelle on her bed. I've never corrected her. It would be weird now. And if she makes it this far in the book, fuck it.

The cool new-wave girls in Sonoma took me aside and told me I could do better. I knew I could too, and I only sort of resented the fact that the cool new-wave girls weren't attracted to me. There were a few crushes during that period I didn't follow up on. I was usually broke, so I only went on a handful of dates.

Thank god for booze and comedy, or else I would never have gotten laid. I also owe a debt to comedy club waitresses. At least three. There were a couple of times when we weren't both sloppy drunk, and I didn't like the awkwardness of the act. When I was young and super inexperienced, unless someone said, "Hey, we're gonna have sex now, so don't feel like a creep," it all felt creepy to me. Like it was a weird game of seeing how much you could "get away" with.

And then there was Melissa, the older chick I lost my virginity to. I met her at the Metro after the open mic—it was a great night. I was eight months in and had a great set. That night was a hot crowd full of cute women. And I was a buzzed twenty-one-year-old virgin. There were actually two women I could've slept with that night. I know this because I'd never felt that before. Three including Lizzie, the older woman who booked the comedy show—I had an ongoing flirtation with her, but she intimidated me. But there were these two pretty blondes I was focusing on that night. By the time the bar was closing and I had flirted boozily with both, one seemed easy. The other seemed easier. I was leaning toward easier. They were both blonde and totally my type: out of my league.

I chose Melissa, the one who was slightly sexier in a messy way. We went to a popular late-night joint downtown, Sam's Hoffbrau, and drank and made out at the bar. We actually got kicked out for making out at the bar. We were both pretty sloppy and super-fucking horny. Around then, between make-out sessions, I found out she was seven years

older than me. Hot. After getting kicked out of Sam's we
made out on the way to the Pine Cove, a divey cop bar all
of us comics hung out at. We made out inside, grabbed another drink, and then went outside. She pulled me close to
her while we were making out and put her tit in my mouth.
I couldn't believe my luck—a free tit.

It was moving super fast and getting dirty. We were
dry-humping like crazy. I had never been that excited. I
lifted her dress; she bit my neck and pulled me closer. I felt
like I was finally getting to live out one of those *Penthouse*
forums. I couldn't believe this was happening. I was about
to lose my virginity to a hot older chick against a car. She
grabbed my wiener aggressively and started to wrestle it out
of my jeans. Holy fucking shit, it's finally gonna happen!
And then a hobo interrupted us: "Excuse me, do you have
any change?" (I know they prefer "homeless," but I'm trying
to bring "hobo" back.)

Melissa lost her damn mind and drunkenly yelled at
him, "Get the fuck away from us, dude!" I realized I had to
get this dream girl home before she turned into a pumpkin.
Don't ask me how we got home. Drunkenly, I'd guess. In
1987–88 drunk driving was totally okay. Although I'm sure
we weren't driving fast because we were trying to bone each
other the whole way home. So super-safe sex is what I'm
saying.

We were a sloppy mess, and I remember being so happy
that twenty-one years in, this shit was finally happening. We
practically did it in my elevator, and it was only three floors.
We got in my room, and I put on Guns N' Roses. I lost my
virginity to *Appetite for Destruction*. Right away. Super romantic. I lost my virginity three times that first night. Not even
sure I lasted thirty seconds the first time. I think three and a

half strokes was more than enough. For me. I kept pumping, hoping she wouldn't notice. I had never done this before, but I knew it wasn't right. She was way too drunk and horny to care. After the quick first time she didn't even seem disappointed. I didn't let on that it was my first time, but unless she was a total ding-dong, I'm sure she knew.

I was even kinda uncharacteristically cocky and blasé. I actually said, "There's something wrong with Mr. Happy." And she said, "What do you want me to do?" "Give him a kiss," I said. And she did. She sucked my dick like a champ. (Which is one of my all-time favorite expressions.) I couldn't believe how awesome it felt, and then we had sex again. I think I lasted a half a stroke longer. I went down on her first. I'm sure that was awesome for her and not an awkward bummer. I had no fucking idea what I was doing. And then we did it again. And then I awkwardly sent her home. Like a dick. A clueless young recent virgin dick, but still a dick. And that, children, was the romantic story of my first time with a lady.

I didn't know she still lived with her ex-husband 'til we were naked on their bed on our "second date" and I realized it didn't look like any single girl's apartment I had been in at that point. So . . . one. She farted while we were messing around and blamed it on her cat. She slipped at one point that she lived with her ex. Thank god, I was spared the weirdness of meeting that dude. I was kind of done after the second time. I didn't want to date her because we didn't have much in common, plus I was broke. But I also didn't want to string her along just for sex. And honestly, after I heard about the ex, I was terrified he was gonna snap and pummel me. When she came to see me at the Metro the third week in a row, I kinda blew her off. So she gave my friend a BJ in the bathroom. Same lady. And I must stress "lady." Really surprised I'm not married to her with grandchildren.

I dropped a girl while trying to have sex with her standing up. Twice. Two different girls. I lived the movie *Porky's* with not a lot of penetration. A ton of blue balls. If my sex life back then had an emoji, it would be a frowning hard-on. I was nervous about repeating my premature ejaculation when I was more sober, so I bailed on a couple of girls before I could disappoint them. I would go back to their place, make out, and then scoot out nervously before the deed. Soon I would have more confidence. And I got better at sex. One of the girls I neurotically bailed on, Natalie, became my girlfriend when I was back living with my mom. She was my first real girlfriend. I really only had four girlfriends, and I married the last one.

I'm so glad I made it out of that dating period without really fucking up. Well, I did get Natalie pregnant. I wish that was someone else's story. Well, it is—hers. But it's also mine. She decided she wanted an abortion before she even told me she was pregnant. Even though I had dodged a baby bullet, I couldn't help but feel awful. No real guilt about the act, more sympathy that my girlfriend had to go through it. We still messed around for a while, but she wanted something more serious. And I didn't. I still feel shitty for the way that went down. I like to think I'm a good guy and a friend of women, and yet there are regrets.

Back to Lizzie, the woman who ran my regular open mic at the Metro. I was there every week and quickly developed a crush, and we flirted heavily. I never slept with Lizzie; she was twelve years older and experienced, so I was definitely worried about disappointing her. But I wanted to disappoint her real bad. We made out a couple of times. When I broke my back she wrote me flirty notes. She was awesome. It's one of my only romantic regrets that I didn't spend more time with her and have some much-needed sex lessons. I used to wish I had climbed into my friend's bed with her when she asked me to.

Lizzie had planned on it. I got to my friend's party, and she told me her plan and took me upstairs to his room. I made out with her, and then when it came down to it, I didn't do the deed. I was still too nervous, and I actually think there was another girl or two at Arthur's house I wanted to try my chances with, so I think that was the excuse I used. But really I was just chicken. I had kind of talked up to Lizzie the advantages of me being a young guy—stamina and insane horniness and all that. She was sold. I wasn't. I knew I would finish instantly and would either have to fake it or deal with it.

At first it was just flirting and making a lot of jokes about our age difference, but it got heavy over time. After a date at my house, where we just had take-out food and made out, she made fun of me for it being such a young-guy date. I tried to have sex with her then, after we made out on my bed for a long time. She said, "not tonight." And took off. That's why it was kind of a surprise when she tried to seduce me at Arthur's. Another time when I was high at her house Lizzie tried to get a three-way going with me, her, and her friend Kristy. I chickened out and said I was too high. Too high to have an awkward three-way.

I intended on finally sleeping with her after I recuperated from my accident at my mom's, and then I got a girlfriend, Natalie, and Lizzie got a boyfriend. The main reason I regret not taking lessons from her is because you just read several sentences about how I almost fucked someone. Great.

Every good nerd has a "one that got away" story. I'm a great nerd—so I don't have a "one that got away" story; I have a couple who got away and a couple I awkwardly sent away. At the end of the day and this book, the only one who really, really matters I'll be with forever. And she gets a whole chapter.

There are probably twenty or so girls I used to wish I had sex with but didn't. Here goes. Number one. Kate Beckinsale. Not that I ever had a chance with her, but I've been in the same room with her a handful of times. So maybe in a universe where I had a 19 charisma instead of the 3 I rolled at birth, I could've made that happen. She is fucking stunning. And I think she's actually a vamp, because she refuses to age.

Number two. This indie rock singer. She's famous, and we met when I first started dating my wife. In the beginning I thought my girlfriend, now wife would break up with me any day and I would call the rock star. It's been twenty years. I'm happier than a guy who married twenty rock stars.

Number three, Paige.

Number four, Lizzie.

Number five, Cheryl. We actually dated, but my fears of being a terrible sex partner killed that. Cheryl was older too and divorced with a kid, but, oh fuck, was she hot and sexy and I was skinny and long haired and at my most Jeff Spicoli. We didn't have that much in common other than we both were trying to be famous and wanted to bang each other. It was purely sexual.

We met in Los Angeles; we were both winners of a Sacramento talent contest. For winning, we got a free trip to LA to meet with real, live casting people. Cheryl won for modeling and acting, and I won for comedy. After meeting a casting agent, we made out on the patio of my room and were about to totally do it when she noticed that my roommate Paul was hanging right behind me in our room, windows open, looking at us. Weirdo. We all flew home on a private plane (that was part of the prize). So we made out on the plane. Not part of the prize, but awesome. She climbed on my lap while we made out. I came. Almost instantly. She didn't jump off of me or punch me in the face, so I don't think she knew. That was my Mile-High Club experience. I was even too early for that.

On our second "date"—but our first real one—I took Cheryl to a free meal at a bowling alley restaurant. I had won a gift certificate there in a comedy competition. Cheap date. She was disappointed with my low level of romanticism. I was twenty-two and broke and horny. Give me a break. Even though the night was not a success, we still almost humped in my car in front of the bowling alley. We were sloppy drunk. Because of the free food, I was able to afford many beers.

The third date was in 1990, after my injury. It was almost two years later. We ran into each other at a Sacramento bar. We were both very excited to see each other. There was an instant attraction. I looked like a stud to my friend Sean because he thought we had just met, so when Cheryl and I were making out against the bar a minute later, Sean was surprised. He had just tried hitting on her. He asked me what was going on with Cheryl, and I admitted I had known her from before. He told me he was impressed and wished me good luck. We went back to her apartment. I asked about her kid, and she said he was staying overnight at her mom's nearby. We talked, made out a little, and looked at her exotic fish.

Cheryl brought me a drink and took her clothes off. I said, "I guess we're done looking at your fish." She laughed.

She was tiny, so I easily lifted her up and kissed her. I carried her into her room and gently threw her on her bed, and she giggled sexily. In a sloppy attempt to pleasure her, I was so excited the second I started, I came. Again, I'm pretty sure she had no idea. I was instantly ashamed and embarrassed. I had a pretty bad case of hair-trigger with her.

I could have maybe finished the job and recovered, but I was so mortified. Even though Cheryl had no idea, I had to get out of there. So I abruptly stopped. When she asked what was happening, I told her I had a girlfriend and was feeling guilty. I didn't, but it shut the situation down and I was on my way, driving an hour and a half home to my mom's at, like, 3 a.m. Sad. Why I thought it was better to make a girl hate me rather than admitting to the embarrassing act, I have no idea. I was a fucking idiot.

Unlike John Mayer's wiener, my wiener is not racist. I've also disappointed Asian, Hispanic, and black girls. First was Sidney, the girl whose play I was in at American River College. She had approached me in drama class to be in a one act she wrote and was directing. My slightly racist grandfather had to voice his disapproval. "Some people might not understand that." Clearly, you don't. When I was living with my mom, right before I reacquainted myself with Natalie, I went out with a Sonoma girl, Marissa, the punk-rock chick I worked with at a record store.

We only went out for a couple of weeks. We made out behind the video counter on the floor in a sloppy pile. We almost did it there, but she was worried about getting caught, though that wasn't a concern when we boned on my mom's couch. My mom wasn't there, but I kept hoping she would catch us so she'd know I liked girls. Because I was such a late bloomer, she had expressed concern. I once farted while I went down on Marissa. I was completely mortified, and she didn't seem to care. She laughed and told me to finish. Punk rock, for sure.

When I moved to San Francisco I had a couple of crushes, but when I acted on them the girls turned me down politely. There were a couple who made it clear they needed to go out on dates first because they were then in their late twenties and didn't just drunkenly fuck whoever was close when the night ended.

I dated three different comedy club waitresses: Kayla, Natalie, and Kristen. Kayla cooled on me pretty quickly. I saw her at a pro-choice rally, figuring that would get me points. It didn't. Natalie and Kristen both became my girlfriends. I got slightly better at sex after having it on a regular basis. At least I wasn't freaking out about finishing before I started anymore.

There was also a street prostitute in San Francisco I had a crush on. Let me explain. She looked like Brigette Nielson from that one minute when Brigitte Nielson was sexy, Stallone's *Cobra*. All the comics talked about her because she was always in front of the Improv and really cute—not just cute for a street prostitute cute but, like, actually very cute. Her sales line one night was "Would you like some company?" It almost worked, because that is so nice—who doesn't want some company?

I've never had a three-way, because GROSS. I did come close to a four-way once, but I was too dumb, too wasted, and much too much of a chicken to follow through. When I left San Francisco my friends threw me a going-away party. I was supposed to drive to LA the next day. But by around three in the morning I was ridiculously hammered. Next thing I knew I left my own party with three girls. We get to their apartment, and I remember figuring out what was happening: two of the girls were trying to seduce me.

Of course, I was more into the third girl. I made out briefly with all three and then started to fall asleep because I was so wasted and lame. I also remember a sense of the usual performance anxiety, now three-fold, because there were three girls to disappoint. Instead, I disappointed them by breaking up the party awkwardly and heading back to my apartment. During the *Mr. Show* years, at the beginning of the internet, I received a note from a girl who wanted to have a three-way with David Cross and me. David Cross and some girl. Any girl. Yuck. That girl or woman was incredible at bad ideas. Her name was Kellyanne Conway. Not really.

I didn't have sex with Kathy Griffin. Not everyone can say that. We went out maybe three times. She made me take her to a hot Hollywood nightspot, not the kind of place I'd ever been to. She only wanted to go because she heard it was really popular. We went to the Roosevelt Hotel. She wasn't really a drinker. I drank. Pretty sure I was also high every time I was around her. Not on purpose. If I were around her now, it would be on purpose.

I was a fan of *Shakes the Clown*, Bobcat's fucked-up clown movie, so that came up when Kathy and I were out. "You were really funny in that . . ." I said. We had nothing in common other than the fact that we both had red hair and performed comedy. Oh, and we both had moms. "Janeane said you don't like physical contact or hugging or anything." By the way, she was talking about Janeane Garofalo. I said, "Uh, I guess that's true. She said that?" Kathy said, "She sure did. Are you weird? What's that about?" Me: "I think hugging is fake. And it makes me really uncomfortable, and being my size sucks because I could hurt people." Kathy laughed, "Ha, you are weird. Want to order food?"

She made me make out with her in front of the hotel bar as we were leaving. "Uh, Brian, I'm a pretty girl. Why aren't you trying to kiss me?" When she put it that way, I didn't have an answer. So I kissed her in the street as we walked to the car. I lifted her up a little, and she swooned. That had become my "go-to" with petite girls—lift them up a little. I think she wanted to do it right there. We went back to my place and made out in her car in my driveway.

It got a little heated. I wanted to take her upstairs to my room. Or do it right there in the car. She read the signs—and by that I mean she probably felt my boner—and said, "Your roommates are home, so I don't want to go to your room, and we're not doing it in the car, so why don't you come over to my place?" It sounded so simple. It wasn't.

Kathy lived on the West Side. I lived in Laurel Canyon. Her place was about a half hour away. My door was five steps away. My roommates were home. And that meant video games and weed. I thought about the drive there and back and passed. I think I said something like, "Well, it doesn't make any sense for me to drive all the way over to your place." She was kind of annoyed, and rightly so. I went up and played video games and got high. Not in that order.

She called me a day or two later and very seriously said we needed to talk. Okay. Would I go see *Grumpy Old Men* with her at the Beverly Center? I guess. I brought my friend Doug Benson. She was bummed. Not too bummed, though—she "dated" him next. But first she had to break up with me. Why? We weren't actually going out; nothing had ever been said. Did people usually prefer weed and games over sex with someone they were dating?

Nevertheless, she broke up with me. In the garage of the iconic Beverly Center Mall in Hollywood. We weren't going out, remember? And yet she told me she had something to tell me. After the movie she went to Cinnabon and got a treat. I was thinking, *What in the fuck is happening?* She asked me to go to her car with her. I walked her to her car. She said she had to break up with me, that it wasn't working out. I said, "We're not going together." She said, "Whatever, Brian, you're crazy! We can still be friends." I thought, *Do we have to?*

Before I got married I went to strip clubs. A lot. I used to dumbly think that lap dances aren't cheating. But they are. Especially the way some girls do it: "You came on me. You tip me now. Three hundred dollars." This was a scary Russian lady, if you couldn't tell by my kinda racist broken English schtick. I paid her. The last thing I wanted was her to scream at security, "He come on me!" And then sometimes they're really nice. Just like real people—mean sometimes, nice others.

In those years of dating I didn't know what to do. Ever. Flowers scared girls off every time I bought them for a date, and I bought them every time, because of movies. In real life, on first dates, girls think it's weird. What the fuck? Didn't they see the same movies as me?

Girls often confused me, and every once in a while that would lead to frustration and anger. Nowadays I'd be a woman-hating online troll. No, I wouldn't. Those guys are shitty. But when I first moved to LA I didn't want a girlfriend really. I liked a handful of girls at MTV. I was kind of a pig. I liked flirting. When we started production a whole new group of girls showed up.

And I met Paula, my first long-term girlfriend. We only flirted while we were in production. At the wrap party I made my feelings known. The next morning we were in love. She was awesome, and we moved pretty fast. I eventually moved in with her. We dated for four years. We had a lot of fun. I wasn't a great roommate—kind of a messy slacker. She kicked me out, but we continued to date. I moved in again with Dave Rath, my manager. This time we lived in a house in Encino that looked like it had been in a porno. That didn't bode well for Paula and me. I broke up with Paula in early December of 1997. I used the "see other people" cliché bullshit, and that was part of it. Part of me also felt that if we couldn't live together, we probably didn't have a future. And I wanted to see other people.

And then on New Years Eve of 1998 I met my dream girl. Tiny. Blonde. So cute. And sexy. Like the sexiest cute girl I'd ever seen. And because it was the nineties, she had tight plastic pants and a cute halter-like top, with her tan shoulders and neck adding to the look. She had pigtails and was twenty-five and super cute. Did I mention she was cute? She looked like Buffy from that show I liked. I was a big *Buffy the Vampire Slayer* fan, so it was love at first sight. I didn't know who "Buffy girl" was, but I had to meet her. I didn't even talk to the poor girl, and I still had to get to know her. She left the party. The end.

Nope. Keep reading, silly.

NINETEEN

NERD GETS CHEERLEADER

So I had to meet this Buffy from my party. Like all the other crushes, I thought that would never happen. This sounds creepy, but I had a picture of her. I showed it to my roommate, Dave. "Oh, that's Melanie. We just hired her." I started calling her immediately. But I first needed to go through Cindy, the main assistant. She knew before anybody that I liked Melanie. Then I would engage in small talk. It worked, talking more and more each time. She was incredibly easy to talk to—so friendly and the perkiest, sweetest, most engaging person I had ever met. She was from a small town outside of Fresno, had been a cheerleader, and was the youngest sister in a big family. She loved her parents. She was normal. It's not as corny as it sounds. She was also smoking hot.

How does a nerd get his dream girl? Well, luck mostly, but by the time I met Melanie I had kind of figured out dating. I was still awkward, but I didn't make any of the early mistakes. Actually, that is not true. She still talks of the first time someone told her I liked her and she didn't believe them. She showed up at a party at David Cross's apartment, and my friend Melissa saw her and, on my behalf, said, "Brian Posehn likes you." Melanie, being super confident and the coolest girl ever, said, "Oh really? I'm gonna go talk to him." She came up to me, and I froze like a giant dork. She said I blew her off, but I know it was because I was petrified.

She was super way out of my league. (Have you looked at any of the pictures yet?) But she was sweet and actually interested in me. Flowers worked. They weren't weird for her. They were seen as the old-fashioned romantic gesture I wanted them to be. We moved slowly at first. We saw a couple of bands; it was more casual. Our first date was low key: we went to see Gorgeous George at Luna Park in West Hollywood. It was super casual. I had worked up the nerve to call her and ask her to see my friend's band. Blues Sarceno was a shredder guitar player I had met through Dweezil Zappa, and he had asked me to check out his new band, Gorgeous George. They were cool, but she was incredible.

I was still awkward around her, but she was so easy to talk to that the more time I spent with her, the better I got at talking to her. That first night we had a couple of drinks and talked a lot. At a St. Patrick's Day party I asked if I could take her to see the band Tool for her birthday. I got to introduce them, and we had backstage passes, so I'm sure that got me extra points. That was our first real date and our first kiss. Melanie, of course, made fun of my kiss. She called me a "little pecker." It could've been worse—she could've been talking about my tiny wiener.

Her teasing didn't hurt, though. It was gentle and with love. I only wanted to kiss her more. I fell pretty hard. I had a short phase of being a jealous boyfriend—she hated that. I didn't want to lose her, so I quickly checked my jealousy. She also assured me that I had nothing to worry about. It wasn't all perfect, though. Like any drunk twenty-something girl, she liked to sing, and it was almost a deal-breaker when she and her roommate sang my least favorite No Doubt song, "Don't Speak," at the top of their lungs. Don't speak? Don't sing.

Speaking of deal-breakers, I almost lost her in the beginning when this idiot here showed her the movie *Henry: Portrait of a Serial Killer*. What the fuck was I thinking? In my defense, it was totally innocent. I showed her *Harold and Maude* too. I was just trying to share my love of movies with her. But in her defense, what girl wants "date movie night" to be a raw portrayal of real-life serial killer and rapist Henry Lee Lucas? It's super brutal; it feels like you're watching a snuff film. He kills his girlfriend. SPOILER. And puts her remains in two suitcases. And I owned it on DVD. I almost lost her. She thought, *What kind of a creep owns that movie?* Not this creep—I got rid of it. Still, I think singing No Doubt is kinda worse.

We moved slow those first couple of weeks, and then we moved incredibly fast. I wanted to be around her all the time. I'm not going to describe here any of the sex acts with her like I did with the other girls I dated. I'm sure you understand: she's my wife and my kid might read this someday. But I will tell you she blows everybody else away—the best. It felt perfect, like we were meant to be together. That unreachable ideal. We had crazy, fun times in the beginning. I always felt lucky to be with her. The first time I saw her breasts it was magical, like seeing a Disney princess's tits.

I fucked up a couple of times but was able to figure it out, and I know we will be together forever. I know I'll never fuck up again. She told me she'd cut my wiener off if I cheated. I believe her. It is possible, nerds, to get your dream girl. Just don't be a dick. If you like being yourself, you can probably do it sooner than I did. I got my dream girl—the cheerleader, the popular girl, the achingly cute little blonde, the Tami Baker. I did better than Tami; I got my Melanie Truhett. And I eventually made her a Posehn.

We married in 2004, and she's been my life partner and my best friend ever since. Melanie is the funniest, smartest, most loving woman I've ever met. In May of 2009 she became the mother of our son, Rhoads. She's an amazing, loving, nurturing mom and an irreplaceable partner and co-parent. She has her own business and has excelled at that effortlessly while juggling two nerdy guys and three dogs in the house. She has aged with such grace and style that I am constantly in awe and I couldn't feel luckier. And she still has the tits of a Disney Princess.

TWENTY

NERDING OUT

I've been going to Comic-Con for over twenty years. I have not missed one since 1996. And oh boy, I have met some fucking nerds. Most of my friends are nerds. Nothing like a Con to make you feel better about your nerdiness. I may be a giant fucking nerd, but what about that dude? Oh wow, look at her—holy shit! Who is nerdier? Nerdiest? A Furry. A Trekkie? An Anime nut? A Belieber? A cosplayer? A hard-core Christian? You heard me: if we follow my "nerdiness is an obsession" rule, then a Christian is just a nerd for Christ. Their cosplaying is amazing.

Besides my obvious love for metal, *Star Wars*, Rush, horror, comedy, and Stephen King, I have played video games my whole life; D&D became a big part of my life in the second part of it. And since the late eighties, when my friends Dana and Aaron from Tower Records had turned me on to *The Dark Knight Returns* by Frank Miller and *The Watchmen* by Alan Moore, I've been completely immersed in comic books.

My uncle Mike had shown me Pong in the mid-seventies. The same guy who introduced me to nerdiness through *Star Trek* showed me Pong on his computer when I was visiting him at his office at Lawrence Livermore Labs. I loved it. I got a pong machine when Atari released them one Christmas. With each new development in video games, I was in. There was a diner in my neighborhood with a Space Invaders; I had the Atari 2600 and 5200, and they both had Space Invaders, and I was still terrible at it.

I sucked at games, but I loved them. I had to have every new system—TurboGrafx, Nintendo 64. Donkey Kong Country and Mario Kart 64 were fucking amazing and fun to play with other people. And Golden Eye. Season four of *Mr. Show* we had a system in our office and later our dressing room, and our work didn't suffer. Games were an addiction. I picked up the GameCube, the Sega Genesis, and the total failure, Dreamcast. I got a little money in the late nineties and bought a Defender/Joust upright arcade game and Ms. Pac-Man/Galaga machine along with a Jurassic Park pinball machine. Since I've done voice-over jobs, I've wound up in a couple of games. Doug Benson and I did a game for 3DO called Off-World Interceptor—it was terrible. I did voices for the *Star Wars* parody I cowrote, Star Warped, as well as Halo 2. My fellow Sonoma High metalhead, Tim Schaefer hired me to play a main character in Brutal Legend, and I wrote on Destiny with David Cross.

In 2011 my friend Gerry Duggan and I began cowriting the popular Marvel comic *Deadpool*. My history with the character went back to the beginning. I knew of him from *X-Force* by Rob Liefeld. I loved what writers Joe Kelly and Gail Simone did with the character. They nailed the manic voice and actions of the unkillable Merc with a Mouth. Deadpool has the best fans in the comic business: voracious and loyal, DP cosplayers are super-popular sights at Comic-Cons around the world. Women even cosplay as a character we created, Shiklah, in the forty-five issues we cowrote. We got the *Deadpool* gig because Gerry and I had a minor success in comic book writing.

In the early 2000s Gerry and I had created *The Last Christmas* together as a script. Santa Claus after the apocalypse fighting zombies. People loved our script, but no one wanted to pull the trigger. So we did what our friend Steve Niles had done with *30 Days of Night:* he had failed to sell it as a script, so he wrote it as a comic book and sold it as a movie for a lot of money. We recently sold *The Last Christmas* too. Not for a lot of money, though.

Because it's clear that I've earned my nerd cred, I feel like it's my time to comment on gamer and nerd culture. CUE OLD MAN RANT. First off, these angry young nerds I read about on the internet harassing women involved in the comic book and video game industry because they're jealous of their talent has to fucking stop. To treat fellow fans that way is one thing, but to harass industry professionals is embarrassing to an old nerd like me. Not to mention the shit cosplayers have to put up with. There should not have to be signs at conventions that say COSPLAY IS NOT CONSENT. No shit. And then every time a nerdy movie or show comes out with a diverse cast, nerdy white assholes get mad about it.

From the *Ghostbusters* reboot to franchises like *Star Wars* and *Wonder Woman*, these guys are complaining that the cast is too female heavy or that they don't like the feminist leaning of the actual movie. *Black Panther* is too black? Good. It's about fucking time. And shut up, nerd. And take your racism with you. White male "nerds" need to quit griping. As the oldest nerd in the room, I hereby tell you to SHUT THE FUCK UP! The misogyny and racism have no place in our culture. Nerds, of all people, should know about inclusivity and how vital and important it is that we accept and welcome all nerds. END RANT.

If it wasn't cool enough that I have been able to turn most of my hobbies into extra income and fans, I also get paid to play Dungeons & Dragons. That's right: people pay me to play Dungeons & Dragons, and that is so crazy. My history with the game goes back to junior high when I heard about it in seventh grade and was disappointed to see Ross Jox ruining it with his dumb friends.

I didn't get into it again 'til 1991, when I was working at Rainbow Records in Sonoma. This dude Rick, a total hesher friend of mine, taught me how fun it actually was. We went over to his house after work one night and got super high with his parents. Yep, that's right. Another Sonoma parent who got high with their kids and it wasn't weird. It was actually super cool and relaxed. I feel like not everyone grew up with that kind of openness.

We cruised back to Rick's room with our friend Tony A. and listened to Slayer while we played. It was pretty dark, and we played some kick-ass D&D. You know how people defend D&D, saying it's not satanic? Because when seventies and eighties Christian people would attack Dungeons & Dragons for being this Satanic thing, people who played D&D would say, "No, it's not satanic"? Well, when we played it, it was. Weed and Slayer made it fucking creepy, and I always came out of there feeling bad for my soul, but those were fun times. We made D&D satanic.

In 2004 we were playing Halo a ton. A pretty big group of mostly guys—there must have been sixteen of us. Four people on four TVs, so you do the math, as a terrible comedian would say a long time ago. I just said it into the dictation app on my phone, so I'm a high-tech terrible comedian.

Anyway, we were playing Halo 2 one night, and after the game we went to a late-night diner, the 101 Coffee Shop.

It's the Hollywood diner featured in the film *Swingers*—you know the one: it's called the 101 Coffee Shop, like I just told you. It's sort of near Silverlake, where the hipsters live. So we went for food after playing Halo 2 at my friend Paget Brewster's house on one of those nights. Paget is a helluva actress and was an amazing host to a rowdy group of nerds.

Those game nights were crazy fun. People you've seen on TV would be drinking and killing each other in three different rooms. Then we'd head to the backyard for smoke and food breaks. People you like, like Paul F. Tompkins, would be there. He's a pretty good gamer. I don't know if he games anymore, but we were pretty serious about it back then. I was probably the worst player at Halo and Halo 2, a game I did a voice in.

After a while, I figured out, I was of best use as a human shield. I would just run in and get killed. I would often be the first murdered, and I didn't mind. I always played with goofy gamertags like "a dirty hobo" and then, later, "AIDSY Hobo" so it would say on the kill screen, "You just killed A Dirty Hobo." We would all laugh then. I also played with the gamertags "Rapenstein" and "Rapeula." Yes, I know, rape and AIDS aren't funny. I am well aware that there is nothing funny about rape or AIDS. And yet those names were.

Anyway, I later landed on "Ruth Gordon" as my gamer tag. If you don't know who Ruth Gordon is, then please stop reading and immediately watch every single movie she ever did. Amazing. *Harold and Maude* was the film that blew my wife away in our early dating years. I got a lot of points for sharing that movie's greatness with her.

My pals Gerry Duggan and Sark were at the diner that night. Sark's real name is Scott Robison, but he always played as Sark, which was a *Tron* reference and it just stuck. No one calls him Scott. He's a thin, tall, white kid from Utah with a shaved head. Sark looked like a Mormon Marine. And he's one of the coolest nerds I've ever met. Sark has been a big gamer his whole life and makes a living as a gamer now, doing YouTube videos. A total fucking nerd and one of the coolest dudes I know. Almost fifteen years later, and he still looks like that Mormon kid straight out of Utah.

So we're sitting there eating grub late at night and we got on the subject of D&D. Dungeons and also Dragons. And we thought it would be great to get a game going. And that was it. We played a couple of weeks later. Sark immediately tracked down a bunch of second-edition advanced Dungeons & Dragons player manuals for us, and we got a group of people together pretty quickly.

Sark's games were weird and super fun. It was Patton, Gerry, Sark, my old friends Ken Daly and Blaine Capatch, and my buddy Chris Martin. Not the dude from Coldplay—I would never play with him. My character was super fun to play, a monk named Jackie with high dexterity and strength. Jackie Chan if he were a murderous rogue who loved pickles.

We killed a bus. Sark called it a land whale, but it was an LA city bus. We had experienced a time rift that put us in modern Los Angeles. During that same game we showed up at the famous Beverly Center mall and were confused. It also happened to be some sort of holiday, so we killed a fat gnome in a red suit that was sitting on a throne and blessing children. Actually, we didn't kill him; we levitated him with a child on his lap.

He missed a saving throw and dropped the kid to his death. When he landed, everyone in the mall killed him. Sark fucking killed Santa. Sark was such a great DM. Those nights were amazing and sold me on the fun and magic of D&D. In the beginning we played wherever we could. When we lost Chris, we were joined by my friend Sarah, who is the coolest—such a smart girl with great energy and a sense of humor enabling her to put up with us all.

Later it became a popular podcast called *Nerd Poker*. I named the show *Nerd Poker with Brian Posehn and Friends* because I feel like the main attraction to D&D for me is the social aspect—like poker, just way fucking nerdier. We did it for three-plus years on the Earwolf podcast network. I started to lose interest. The other shit made it not fun; booking the show and driving to it through traffic at six at night just wasn't worth it.

So last year, after missing the game and my goofy friends, we rebooted the show. *Brian Posehn's Nerd Poker* is an independent, more intimate version of the show with my pals Dan Telfer, Sarah Guzzardo, and Blaine Capatch, with guests like Tom Lennon and Joe Manganiello. We record the show at my dining room table. It's a blast playing again, and we're not going anywhere this time. And when I cash a check from money I made playing D&D, I cackle.

TWENTY-ONE

MEETING MY HEROES

I've heard the expression "Don't meet your heroes" for a long time, but my luck with it has been mixed. Sure, some performers I've met have been assholes, but other times they have been incredibly cool. And a couple have even become my friends. The first famous people I met when I moved to LA were the Zappa kids. I had read *The Real Frank Zappa Book* a couple of years before. I was a casual fan of Frank's music, but his writing made me a fan for life.

One of my takeaways from the book was what a cool family they were. I remember thinking how fun it would be to be friends with the Zappa kids. I thought Moon was super cute from her "Valley Girl" song with her dad and her MTV appearances. And Dweezil seemed like the coolest kid ever and was a shredder on guitar. So my head exploded when I wrote a sketch for *Trashed* that needed a famous shredder cameo and my producer, Leslie, said, "Would Dweezil Zappa work?" I said, "Fuck yeah!"

A week later he did the sketch with me. I played a poser Guitar Institute of Technology instructor who gets shown up by his student—Dweezil, of course. Through Leslie I met the whole family—Dweezil's brother Ahmet; his younger sister Diva; their mom, Gayle; and of course Moon. Moon was even cuter in person; I had a crush before we met that intensified once I got to hang out with her and her cool siblings. That summer of '94 I spent a ton of time at the

Zappa house on Laurel Canyon. One afternoon I was over swimming and followed Dweezil into his dad's studio to get something. I briefly met Frank. Quick and cordial. Meet a legend. A minute later I'm in the pool and laughing with his daughter. Surreal. I love LA. I loved it the minute I got here.

Meeting Scott Ian from Anthrax was also super random and yet made total sense. I was hanging on the roof of Messina Baker Management, where my manager, Dave Rath, worked. I was hanging out with a guy who worked for Dave, my buddy Sheck. We were smoking pot, and I mentioned that I was going to see Anthrax that evening at the House of Blues. Sheck said something like, "Do you know those guys?" And I said, "No, man, but it seems like we should be friends." I then told Sheck the reasons I should be friends with Anthrax: next to Metallica, they had always been my favorite. Anthrax was crunchier and catchier.

Scott Ian had that insane guitar tone that created a sound. Charlie Benante was monster behind the drum kit and easily my favorite metal drummer. And I felt a bond to them, like we had something in common. Of all the thrash bands, they were the only ones who seemed to have a sense of humor, they wrote songs based on Stephen King stories, they wrote songs about comic book characters, they liked hip-hop, and they wore board shorts.

I was running out of things we had in common. I think Sheck just agreed, "Yeah, they seem cool." Or "Word." Sheck was from Jersey and also enjoyed hip-hop. That night I became friends with Anthrax. I went by myself, because none of my friends back then wanted to go to heavy-metal shows with me. That was before I hung out with Brendon Small and Steve Agee. Patton may reference Anthrax or Lamb of God in his act, but he was not gonna mosh it up in the pit.

I was standing at the bar before Anthrax went up, and a roadie-looking dude says, "Hey man, you're Brian Posehn," and I said, "Yep. Usually." Because I want to be liked, but I'm still kind of an asshole. He said, "Do you know the guys in Anthrax?" This was the second time that day someone asked me that, so I just said, "Nope." He said, "Do you want to meet them?" I said, "Uh, yeah." He said, "C'mon. I'm a roadie. I'll take you back there."

Back there was Anthrax's dressing room. They were all getting ready. To be my friends. No, they were looking at the set list, warming up, stretching and hanging out, with another band that happened to be there, fucking *Slayer*. I was overwhelmed. It was a blur as I met my heroes; I thought I was gonna destroy my pants and pass out. Scott and Charlie knew *Mr. Show* and some other shit I had done. I was completely fucking blown away, which helped ease my nervousness and made it so I might not embarrass myself in front of one half of the big four total metal legends. They were about to go on, so I headed out to the floor. The roadie, Bill, gave me a pass so I could come back after the show. I did. We hung out for a while; it was a total blast.

I was living the dream, literally. I had never read *The Secret*, but here, just like meeting Frank and the Zappa kids, I had put something into the universe, and it happened. Because at the end of the night I exchanged phone numbers with Scott. And we have been friends ever since. Scott and I have had an amazing fifteen-plus years of friendship—recording songs, traveling, friendship. Before Scott I did not have a great track record with meeting hard-rock musicians.

Besides the James Hetfield embarrassment, I had bad experiences with the bands Night Ranger and W.A.S.P. Mike Baden and I were backstage in Sacramento at a Night

Ranger, Y&T show, and we walked by Night Ranger. When we said hi, they blew us off. Mike yelled to the guitar player, Jeff Watson, "Fuck you, Jeff! We're here to see Y&T anyway." Later that same year I'm at W.A.S.P. and meet the guitar player, Chris Holmes. I said, "Hey, man, can I get your autograph?" He said, "Grow some tits." Like, that was the only thing stopping me from being a hot lady—a set of tits. It never made sense to me and wound up in my act.

Knowing Scott has been incredible for the sheer amount of metal gods I've met through him. I've been introduced to Judas Priest, Iron Maiden, the Slayer guys, most of Pantera, and even Ronnie James Dio. I wrote a sketch for the *Revolver* magazine Golden Gods Metal Awards, and Ronnie was the star. We shot the sketch in my library using my actual vinyl. Ronnie James Dio looked at my record collection, and we talked in my kitchen.

I didn't want to wash my kitchen after that. I have a picture of Ronnie in my backyard, enjoying the sun, and it's one of the definite highlights of my metal nerdy life. We were standing in the driveway with Scott, Ronnie, and Vinnie Paul from Pantera, and Vinnie said, "Hey Ronnie, doesn't Rudy Sarzo live around here?" Ronnie thought and said, "Yes, I think he does." Mundane exchange, and yet I will never ever forget it. My wife, Melanie, once pulled on Kerry King's beard. Twice. He's the guy who looks like a Satanic wrestler and plays guitar for Slayer. Melanie can get away with anything. I wish I were born cute.

Scott loved my Hetfield story when I told him one night and said, "Ah man, if you ever meet James, you got to tell him that." So one night, through Scott, I met James again at a VH1 award show. Metallica was presented with the VH1 icon award, and we were backstage hanging out—this was when James was still drinking. Scott introduced me to James and said, "You have to tell him the story of when you were in high school." So I told James about the first time we met at the Kabuki and how we were early Metallica fans and he basically called us posers and said, "Yeah, almost." I finish the story, and James, totally straight-faced, looks at me and says, "Yep, that sounds like me." And then he walked away, blowing me off for the second time in my life.

I have since become friendly with Lars Ulrich and Robert Trujillo and even good friends with Kirk Hammett, but I don't think I will ever crack James. I don't think he'd get me. I'm not even sure Kirk finds me that funny when we're around each other, but he loves that I'm from Sonoma. We've bonded over that over the years, and he's let me into Metallica shows almost every time they play in LA. It's been incredible to be friends with a guy I've respected for so long; he's literally one of my favorite musicians and a good pal.

Through Kirk one night we all got to go see Van Halen perform at the Forum in front of two to three hundred other people. They were about to start the reunion shows of 2008 and wanted to do a warm-up show at the legendary LA Forum. It was friends and family only, and because, through Scott, I was suddenly friends with Kirk from Metallica, I got to go. The group included Scott and his now wife, Pearl; Kirk; a couple of assistants; and my friend Mark from Death Angel. We watched Van Halen perform a full set with Eddie's son Wolfgang. They did two hours for around three hundred people. The set list was amazing, and they performed like there were fifteen thousand people in the building—we were so stoked. It was fun to watch Kirk, Scott, and Mark go off for these legends.

Then we went backstage. I met David Lee Roth, and he
actually knew who I was. In classic Dave style he said, "Man,
you're from the *Sarah Silverman Program*. I know you." I
said, "No fucking way." He said, "I love Sarah. She's a funny
bitch." I agreed. Sort of. We sat backstage and talked for a
while. He had instructed his roadies not to break out the
bottle of Jack Daniels 'til Wolfgang was gone. Eddie came by
and said "Hi," and that was surreal. Then we got the report
that Wolfgang was gone, the bottle was broken out, and soon
I was smoking marijuana and drinking Jack Daniels with
Kirk, Mark, Scott, and David fucking Lee Roth.

Insane. Remember all those chapters ago when I talked
about listening to Van Halen on my fucking headphones
on my shitty paper route in my tiny town? Well, that night
I had never been so excited in my life; it's still one of the
coolest things I've ever done. And then it got crazier. We
all still wanted to drink, so the group of us went back to the
world-famous Rainbow Room and closed it. Around 3:30 in
the morning we all decided to get tattoos.

Well, Kirk decided we would all get tattoos. At that point
I had made it forty-three years without getting a tattoo, and
an hour later I had 666 on my middle knuckle. Kirk an-
nounced at the Rainbow that he wanted to get a 666 tattoo—everybody thought that sounded cool. I didn't. But I
also decided I would do whatever anybody else wanted just
to commemorate this amazing night. Of course, because my
friends are rock stars, we went to Kat Von D's studio, and
around four in the morning we all got different 666 tattoos.

Mark from Death Angel got a tramp stamp, and Kirk got
it on his ass. At least I don't have 666 on my ass. My knuckle
tattoo took about four minutes to complete. Kat Von D did

it personally, and she played "Number of the Beast" by Iron Maiden while she tattooed 666 from the movie *The Omen* onto my middle finger. Pretty apropos. Around five in the morning I stumbled into bed, waking my wife. I said, "Baby, I fucked up." She woke up a little more and said, "What did you do?" I showed her my tattoo, and she shrugged and said, "You idiot" and went back to bed. I guess my dumb tattoo was way better than sleeping with a stripper. A face tattoo would have been better than cheating.

My mom hates tattoos, so I never showed it to her until just recently. I was able to keep it a secret for over twelve years. I had come close to blowing it before. One time I did the show *That Metal Show* on VH1, and Eddie Trunk asked me about my tattoo. I told the story and showed it to them, thinking, *There was no way my mom would ever see* That Metal Show *on VH1*. So of course somebody in my mom's apartment complex had a son, and he saw my mom and said, "Hey, Brian had a tattoo on a TV show." So my mom said to me, "Was that just a sketch?" And I, of course, said, "Yeah, Mom, it was just a sketch."

I have never been a Paul Rodriguez fan, and one time I got to tell him that. We did *A Weakest Link Comedy Special*. He was being a bully to some of my friends, and if you've read an earlier chapter, you know I don't enjoy bullies, like, much at all. So when Anne, the bespectacled British lady who hosted the show, asked us in her measured style why we were kicking off Paul Rodriguez—"Brian Posehn, why do you think Paul Rodriguez is the weakest link?"—I said, "I've never been a fan." He lost his shit.

He stormed off set. He threatened me on camera, and even that wasn't funny. He said, "Never been a fan? I don't even know who you are." Burn. "I may be the weakest link, but I have the biggest knife." Burn. Or stab. "I'll see you in the parking lot." No sir, you will not. He did see me in the parking lot, though, a couple of months later. Because stereotypes sometimes come from a real place, I was visiting a mini-mall in the valley because there was a comic book shop called DJ's Universal Comics there. At the same time, Paul was getting Mexican food. As I walked to the store Paul pulled up, driving a Porsche. We saw each other, he gave me the stink eye, and I scooted into the store.

A beat later he menacingly drove by really slowly. Kat, the owner, noticed and said, "Did Paul Rodriquez just mad-dog you?" Yes, he did.

Once, I was at the Playboy mansion. It happens. Well, not anymore. But one night Melanie and I went to a party there, and it was crawling with comedians. Mel overheard this exchange when Paul and his manager saw me. Paul: "Hey, there's that nerd. I'm gonna go talk to him." Manager: "Wait, be cool. He's talking to Drew Carey." Paul: "Oh shit, okay." Drew Carey saved my ass, I guess. Why? I have no fucking idea. I hope one day we can squash our beef. Not really. I could give a shit.

I've gotten to meet three of the original members of KISS. I've met Gene Simmons twice. Both times were very brief. Once at a Rob Zombie show in Long Beach. He was nice enough. The second time was not long after; I was getting breakfast in the valley with my wife and friends at a local chain, Jerry's Deli. I was wearing a T-shirt I got from the Metallica Club that was a parody of the KISS album cover *Rock and Roll Over*.

I saw Gene before he saw me, and I thought Gene would give me shit for the shirt, whether it was licensed or not. I just thought he would give me beef or at the least say,

"Metallica, huh? Those boys owe me some money." Instead, he saw the shirt and said, "Nice shirt." I was so disappointed. I wanted snarky Gene; instead, I got self-involved Gene who didn't even notice my shirt was a parody.

I had a crazy, fun night partying with Ace Frehley and Scott Ian. I actually met Paul Stanley a couple of times on my own. When I guest starred the first time on *Everybody Loves Raymond* it was a high school reunion episode. Raymond's character had a history with a hot blonde who he couldn't talk to, and in the reunion episode Bob Odenkirk, Raymond, and I bump into the hot blonde. And, of course, because we were still nerds, none of us could talk to her. The hot blonde was an actress named Pam; on the second day of work we were having small talk and Pam said, "You like hard rock? My husband is a famous singer."

My curiosity was piqued, of course, so I said, "Oh yeah, who is he?" Never ever thinking she was going to be the wife of one of my favorite singers. When she said "Paul Stanley" my smile got bigger than it had ever been. She said, "Oh well, Paul is coming to the show on Friday. I'll introduce you." I couldn't fucking believe it. I still thought something would go wrong and I wouldn't get to meet him. On tape night I brought my copy of the KISS CD *Animalize* for Paul to sign. We met, and he was super cool, "*Animalize*—I wrote a lot of that." I said, "I know." I told him it was one of my favorite records of that period of KISS. When he found out I did stand-up he said, "When are you performing next?" "I happen to have a show scheduled next Monday at Largo."

Largo was and is the premier alternative comedy and indie music space in Los Angeles. Flannigan, the owner, is an old friend and has an amazing eye for talent. Paul said he would come by; I didn't believe him. That Monday night I showed up at the club, and Paul F. Tompkins saw me first. He said, "Hey, you'll never believe who is here. Paul Stanley from KISS." I said, "Oh shit, he's here to see me." We talked after the show, he was very complimentary, and I was blown away.

Then, many years later, when my son Rhoads was in pre-school, Paul was one of the other dads at the school—he also had a four-year-old. So that was cool seeing him park his Tesla in his rock-star parking space. And he showed up to the Christmas pageant wearing a leather jacket with no shirt underneath. Rock on, Paul. We would expect nothing less.

Harrison Ford is the one hero I haven't met. And I kinda hope I never do meet him because I would probably blow it. I've met other guys at his level: I met Bruce Willis and Mel Gibson, and both were pretty cool. Both meetings were strictly professional; I did table reads for movies that were never made with both of those guys. When I met Bruce, Jeff Goldblum and Ed Harris were also in the room—that was fucking surreal. When we left, Goldblum pointed out how "conservative" Bruce was and that the fact that Bruce climbed into a Hummer was "predictable" and then how "liberal" Harris was. He then climbed into a Ford pickup truck and drove away from the valet. Pretty fucking cool. And anytime you can have Jeff Goldblum narrate a Hol-lywood situation for you, it doesn't really get cooler. The meeting with Mel Gibson was way more brief; we were intro-duced, we read the script, and he scooted. Still, I was in the same room as Mad Max.

So I haven't gotten to meet Indiana Jones or Han Solo, but I've met Luke and Leia. I met Mark Hamill years ago through a mutual friend, Tom Kenny. Tom introduced us, and I was shocked to find out that Mark Hamill knew who

I was and was a comedy fan. Holy fucking shit. We talked briefly and took a picture; pretty sure it's in this book. My takeaway was that he was as nice a guy as you would guess. I worked with him just recently on *The Big Bang Theory* for four days, and my new takeaway is he's the sweetest guy ever.

Meeting Carrie Fisher was definitely one of the top-five coolest things that ever happened to me. The year before she passed I was invited to do a comedy gala at the Montreal comedy festival, Just for Laughs. At the time I had ten minutes of *Star Wars* material, so I did all of it. I think she dug it; we talked afterward in her dressing room. I normally would never bug anybody, but it was Carrie fucking Fisher. I'm so glad I broke my nerdy protocol and harassed her. I got to meet her adorable French bulldog, Gary. When I took a picture with her, she apologized for her height. "Sorry, I'm so short." I said, "My wife is the same size." And she said, "Oh, you married a spinner." Carrie Fisher was the coolest fucking woman to ever live. And I miss her along with every nerd ever.

I wish I had been cooler when I met Rush. Yep, I met two-thirds of Rush, and I fucking blew it. My biggest idols in life were doing their final show at the LA Forum, their last show ever. I had to go, and I had to meet them. Again, like cornering Carrie Fisher, I did something I usually never do: I bugged someone. I decided to hit up my friend Mike Smith, who plays Bubbles in *Trailer Park Boys*. I knew Mike was in good with the band because they're all from Canada, eh. Mike hooked it up. I went with my friend and manager, Dave, and we waited in line to do the official meet-and-greet.

I had days to think of something original to say to Alex and Geddy, my fucking heroes. I could've said, "Hey guys, Mike Smith put me on the list." I should've said that; it is the most logical thing I could've said. Then they would've said, "Oh Mike. We love Mike." And we could've talked like human beings. Instead, I just muttered about how great they were and called Geddy "sir." I called Geddy Lee "sir" twice in the same sentence: "Sir, nice to meet you, sir. You're amazing." What a fucking idiot. I still can't believe that I finally got to meet those dudes, and I botched it so fucking bad. So the lesson here is that you can totally meet your heroes, but don't be a fucking dumbass and call them "sir." You'll regret it.

TWENTY-TWO

FUCK YOU, PANDORA

Note: This all happened, but the conversation may or may not be embellished.

One of the most frustrating moments of my life in the modern era was when Grandpa Posehn here tried to program a Rush channel on Pandora. True story. It happened while I was writing this very book you're reading, and I thought to myself, *Wow, that would be fantastic filler for the book.*

I had previously made a Black Sabbath, Van Halen, Iron Maiden, Pantera channel for myself, and they all had a lot of crossover. I programmed a Pixies channel for my wife; it also played eighties and nineties bands like Dinosaur Jr., The Cure, and Modern English, and we both loved most of Pandora's picks. Anyway, I was trying to program a Rush station on Pandora, but this time I wanted only Rush. No other band would do on my Rush channel.

First, it plays "Spirit of the Radio," one of my all-time favorite Rush songs—no, one of my all-time favorite songs.

ME: Okay Pandora, yeah that's good. One of my all-time favorite Rush songs. Thumbs-up.

I press the thumbs-up button on my stereo. Soon the next song starts.

PANDORA: How about "The Trees" live by Rush?

ME: Wow, Pandora, you must be a real Rush fan. I know it's not necessarily a deep cut, but every real Rush fan loves "The Trees." Dumb people find it corny, but they're dumb. And it's "The Trees" live. Well, okay, it's a thumbs-up. Way to go.

PANDORA: Okay, how about "Cashmere" by Led Zeppelin?

ME: No, Pandora. I love Led Zeppelin, but this is a Rush channel, okay? Rush only. This is what I'm working on, so thumbs down.

PANDORA: How about "Changes" by Yes?

ME: Oh yeah, totally, I see why you would think yes, but no.

PANDORA: Duh, I know, "Going to California." How about "Going to California" by Led Zeppelin?

ME: No, see, I already said no to Led Zeppelin. Oh my god, Pandora, don't fucking get me wrong, I love Led Zeppelin. They're really, really great—probably one of the greatest bands of all time, no question. No question. But Rush. Only. Thumbs down.

PANDORA: "Big City Nights" by the Scorpions?

ME: No thanks.

PANDORA: Van Halen?

ME: Nope.

PANDORA: The Who?

ME: Nope.

PANDORA: The Kinks?

ME: Nope.

PANDORA: Kansas?

ME: Nope.

PANDORA: Styx?

ME: Fuck nope.

Then Pandora had a meltdown. For reals: the AI that runs Pandora ran out of ideas but still wouldn't get the fucking clue that I only fucking wanted Rush. It now wouldn't play anything. I backed away.

So the next day I tried again.

PANDORA: "Tom Sawyer" by Rush?

ME: Kinda on the nose, but thumbs way the fuck up, eh.

PANDORA: "Freewill" by Rush?

ME: Yep. Thumbs up!

PANDORA: "All of My Love" by Led Zeppelin?

ME: No thanks. Remember yesterday? Love Led Zep. Rush channel. Rush only, no Zeppelin. Thumbs down.

PANDORA: "My Best Friend's Girl" by The Cars?

ME: Great band, the Cars. Not really close to Rush, but same era. I get it—I'm old. Thumbs down. What else?

PANDORA: How about "Synchronicity" by The Police?

ME: Nope. Rush channel. Thumbs down.

PANDORA: Got it, Rush channel, totally. Got it, Rush channel. Of course, Rush. Rush. How about "Candy O" by The Cars?

ME: The Cars, again? NO NO NO NO NO FUCKING NO!! Thumbs down.

I hit the thumbs-down button on my stereo a little harder than necessary.

PANDORA: How about some boring song by the Foo Fighters?

ME: NOPE. Thumbs down.

PANDORA: How about "Your Love" by The Outfield?

ME: How about fuck you? Nuh, Uh. Thumbs down.

PANDORA: How about a different boring song from The Foo Fighters?

ME: Wow, Pandora, you're really losing it. What the fuck? Really, Pandora?

PANDORA: Sorry.

ME: Shut up! I'm still mad. The Foo Fighters? Are you kidding me? "How about the Foo Fighters?" THAT'S YOU! No, Pandora! No Foo Fighters. Rush channel.

PANDORA: Sorry, Brian. Please don't be mad. How about "Just What I Needed" by The Cars?

ME: FUCK! You stupid fucking robot. I robot, you are not, you will never take over the humans with your shitty robot brain. Skynet would shoot you in your dumb robot face. You love The Cars, huh? Okay, I'll start a Cars channel—will that make you happy, Pandora?

ME: Okay, I'm gonna start a Cars channel. Okay, yeah, that's a good one.

I grab my phone and type in "The Cars" to Pandora.

PANDORA: How about "It's Magic" by The Cars?

ME: Okay, Pandora, I was thinking a deeper cut, but you picked pretty much their most popular song. What else do you got?

PANDORA: How about "Moving in Stereo" by The Cars?

ME: Well done, Pandora. Total classic. Remember *Fast Times*, Pandora? Phoebe Cates and those perfect tits? What else, Pandora?

PANDORA: How about "Red Barchetta" by Rush?

ME: [screaming] NO! FUCK YOU, PANDORA!

PANDORA: [BEAT, then, calmly] I'm sorry, Brian. I thought you loved "Red Barchetta." Isn't it one of your favorites?

ME: [BEAT] Yeah.

PANDORA: I know what you like. I know everything about you. [whispers] I love you, Brian.

ME: [whispers] I love you too, Pandora.

PANDORA: Say it louder.

ME: I love you too, Pandora.

PANDORA: Shall we play a game?

ME: Sure.

PANDORA: How about Global Thermonuclear War?

TWENTY-THREE

MY SON:
THE BEST THING
I EVER DID

I never wanted to have a kid, and it didn't ever seem in the cards. I used to tell my mom she would never have a grandkid—what a dick. Anyway, around 2007 Melanie and I decided we really wanted to try to have a baby. We knew we couldn't do it in our tiny starter house with two dogs and three cats. So we got a bigger place. Once we were situated, we decided to try to make a baby—with our parts. I'm pretty sure that first time stuck because we heard very soon that my little buddy was forming inside my best friend.

We talked about names, and it was easy because everything is easy with my wife. We had a girl's name we really liked, Matheson. After Richard, of course. I thought of it, and Melanie liked it instantly. Then we found out our little girl had a penis. Okay. "Let's start thinking of boys' names." Me: "How about Saddam?" C'mon, Saddam Posehn? That shit is hell-arious. We thought about other last names of people we love like Matheson. I pitched King—either Stephen or Kerry would have worked. And then I thought of Randy Rhoads. "What about Rhoads?" She loved it; it was an instant lock. Let me please reiterate how awesome my wife is.

And on May 18, 2009, Rhoads Carlton Posehn was born. He was premature, but he still wouldn't have been as big as me. Thank god, because of my wife being tiny and all. He's not really showing an inclination toward sports. And of course, I'm totally fucking fine with that.

I'm currently passing the nerd baton. Rhoads is eight, and we have the same hobbies. He's become my Comic-Con buddy. We've been to San Diego three times, and his first trip to Manhattan in 2015 included a trip to the New York Comic-Con. My wife calls him my mini-me. He loves *Spider-Man, Batman, Star Wars, Iron Man, Black Panther, Ghostbusters, Back to the Future, Goonies,* and Legos. All the good stuff, really.

Without getting too corny, it does actually feel great to like *Star Wars* again. Especially being a dad and being able to share the classics together. I even hate the special editions less because he loves them like I loved the original cuts. The prequels, however, I haven't been able to hide my disdain for them. He knows I hate them. But I actually felt bad that I ever shared that with him because I don't want to taint the experience for him. I have tempered my rage when they're brought up or, yes, even viewed in my house.

He's seen Weird Al and Danny Elfman live and gotten to meet them both, all through me doing what I've done. I don't think he knows how lucky he is, but I hope one day he realizes how hard I worked and that, when I was home, I always tried to be as present as I could be all the time. I definitely didn't have a "Cat's in the Cradle" relationship with him, especially not the Ugly Kid Joe version. He's my mini-me, and I wouldn't want it any other way. Pretty soon we'll see Ozzy, KISS, or AC/DC together, even if they're all new members. Or a 3-D hologram. If Rush ever does a one-off, we will go. No matter where it is.

And if in the next couple of years he rebels and decides Rush is stupid, *Star Wars* sucks, and Spider-Man is a dick, then I'll make him go to a Rush reunion show with me anyway. Mainly so he can have something to complain about when he writes his book when he's fifty-one. Or he could just do what I did and throw my mom under the bus and call the book *My Nana Sucks!*

TWENTY-FOUR

FOREVER NERDY:
FIFTY AND BEYOND

Welp, my book is done, but my life story isn't over yet. I continue to tour, doing my first love, stand-up comedy. I have an awesome family, a beautiful wife who supports the shit out of me, and the coolest little nerd ever. I have great friends from my whole life; I still hang with Baden and Krop and stay in pretty close contact with Patton and the *Mr. Show* guys. Sarah and I are still very close and trying to work on another project together for television. I got to write a book. This book. I took longer than I was supposed to, but I'm totally happy with it.

My dogs, my mom, writing, comic books, comic-cons, superhero movies. I have the same likes as ever: horror and metal. Why I liked heavy music at fourteen is one thing; why I still like it thirty-five years later is another. It's a part of me at this point. I'm not done listening to it, and this year I'm contributing to it again. I've been working on a comedy metal album with Scott Ian and Brendon Small from *Metalocalypse*. It's called "Grandpa Metal" and features cameos from members of Testament, Exodus, Slayer, Death Angel, Slipknot, and Huntress. It will be as dumb and silly as it is heavy.

I love *Star Wars* again. We're two movies in with the Disney/Marvel *Star Wars* movies, and I liked them both. I never thought I'd like a thing with that title, *Star Wars*, ever again.

I'm still relieved. But surprisingly enough, *Force Awakens* won me back. I loved the feel. I loved the practical effects and real sets that felt like the originals. They weren't the green-screened messes that the prequels were. The plots are simple and easy to follow, unlike those unwatchable turds.

Rhoads made me like *Star Wars* with a renewed joy. Last year *Rogue One* came out and further cemented my love of the new Disney *Star Wars* films. SPOILER. Everyone dies. Even people who see it die. It's like *The Ring* and every modern horror film. Just kidding. I liked *The Last Jedi* this year, and a lot of nerds hated it. It felt good to be on the other side of *Star Wars* nerd hate.

In 2017 I made the Sonoma Valley High School Dragon Hall of Fame, along with people who had spent decades in the military or brought doctors to Africa. I wrote dick jokes for thirty years and act like an imbecile on TV pretty often. Not sure if the people that awarded me knew I barely made it out of high school. Pretty fucking amazing. Everything that happened to me, the stuff that made the book and the stuff that didn't, it's all been amazing. To come from sadness and not many friends to being happy and surrounded by friends and full of love has been incredible.

The point, I guess, is that I never thought I'd do this as long as I have and be as successful as I've been. And I want to thank Glen and every friend and family member who's been supportive of this shit, especially my sweet, amazing, beautiful, and funny best friend/wife, Melanie Truhett, and my tiny pal, Rhoads, and, of course, my poor mom, Carole. Thanks to David Rath, my manager, for having my back since he started hip-pocketing me in the early 1990s.

Thanks to all the great, funny friends I've made (they know who they are and you know the famous ones). There are way too many to name, but I will forever owe Patton Os-walt, Sarah Silverman, and Cross and Odenkirk for every-thing I've gotten to do with them. Also thanks to everyone who has come to see me live (especially if you came back) or purchased my comedy or not purchased it but still enjoyed it. If you got it for free and still don't like me, fuck you.

The world has gone bat-shit fucking crazy in the last couple of years, but I'm going to keep going, doing what I do and trying to enjoy it. I'm going to cut myself a break and know that I deserve everything I have and even more.

I know that I will forever be nerdy, and that is super-fucking cool with me.

AFTERWORD

This is the hardest thing I've ever done. The book you just finished took a long time to write. I missed deadlines. Rhoads asked me, "Is that why it's called *Forever Nerdy*, daddy—because it took forever to write?" Cute kid. We're totally keeping him.

This whole writing a book about your life shit is hard. It is an unbelievable amount of work. Even more than that, it's an unbelievable amount of words. Seventy-five to eighty-five thousand words. So many words. Let me again reiterate how many words that is. A lot. When the contract says seventy-five to eighty-five thousand words it doesn't seem like a lot, but when you've been typing for months and you only have eighteen thousand words cobbled together, it's a lot. Not to have a boo-hoo party before you read a thing you hopefully paid for. And by the way, people who read afterwords first are total weirdoes.

And this next paragraph might lose me half of my potential audience anyway, but here goes: I sold this book in the summer of 2016, it always takes a while for a deal to get worked out, so I didn't officially have to start writing 'til the holidays of 2016. In early November of 2016 something had happened in the news. Something that made me sad and, later on, mad. Some sort of election, I guess, and everything went wrong for people who have empathy.

So when I started writing this book at the beginning of 2017 I was drinking a lot and smoking weed pretty much all day, every day, because there is this evil, orange-faced, shitty-wigged, racist, misogynist, transphobic, homophobic, Islamaphobic, Obamaphobic, readaphobic, common-fucking-decency-aphobic, charisma-deprived dumb-fuck doing things in the news every single day. So it was a little hard to write about my life and the things I love every day. I bet everything you've ever read was written by somebody who was mad about something while they were writing *Jaws* or the *Autobiography of Ed Sheeran* or whatever.

Probably a lot of them were mad at a particular president, but none of those people had the task of writing while Trump was in office. I'm amazed I've been able to write anything. It's impressive to me that you don't just have pages and pages of all my handwritten notes that say "Fuck Trump" over and over. I'm sure a lot of writers had trouble writing things during the Obama administration because they hated him so much. And those people are racist. Thanks so much for reading my book. See you next time?

ACKNOWLEDGMENTS

A lot of thanks are due to quite a few great people. Let's start with Ben Schafer, my editor, after meeting him when I wrote a blurb for Scott Ian's book, I knew I wanted to work with him. Almost two years from my pitch to the book that's in your hand, Ben was so helpful and supportive and above all patient, I now consider him a friend.

Also big thanks to Ben's assistant, Justin Lovell, and project manager Christine Marra. Much thanks to my publicist at Da Capo Press, Michael Giarratano, and Kevin Hanover in marketing. Thanks to everyone else at Da Capo.

Thanks to my long time manager/pal Dave Rath, for twenty-five years of loyalty and support, you deserve a medal, instead here's my thanks, buddy. Thanks to Marlene Vigil, Joseph Barkely, and everyone else at Generate Management.

And thanks to my favorite agent ever, Doug Edley; his assistant, Carly Frankel; Logan Eisenberg, my lit agent; Marc Gerald and everyone else at United Talent Agency. Thanks to my lawyer Lev Ginsberg.

Special thanks to my old Sonoma pals, Russ and Darren Goodman, Jim Hinchman, Joel Myers, Pete Ricci, Randy Whitten, Dan McConnel, Tony Edwards, Ian Clark, Rick Means, and Debbie Cohn.

Mucho gracias to my pals in heavy metal, Jon Krop and Mike Baden. Scorpions forever!!! Thanks to Rush for ruling. Thanks to Kirk and Metallica, Joey, Frankie, Charlie and n of Anthrax, Exodus, Testament, Slayer, Pantera, Marc equeda and Rob Cavestany of Death Angel, Phil Demmel and Robb Flynn of Vio-Lence and Machine Head, and John, Willie and Lamb of God, Red Fang, those nuts in Mastodon, Jill Janus and the rest of Huntress.

Thanks to my Sacto Tower family, Daren Harris, Dana Gumbiner, Brian Webb, Jeff Arrellano. Special thanks to Glen Vick for being a friend and encouraging me to tell fart and wiener jokes. Thanks to Alexis, Kerri, and Connie. Thanks to Kristen Battersby. Thanks to Paula Elins for good times and three perfect cats. RIP Kristen Berendt.

To all my stand-up friends: Greg Behrendt, Ngaio Bealum, Andy Kindler, Todd Glass, Paul Hopkins, Tony Camin, Chris Hobbs, Laura Milligan, Karen Kilgariff, Doug Benson, Blaine Capatch, Janeanne Garafolo, David Cross, Paul F. Tompkins, Maria Bamford, Zach Galifianakis.

Extra special thanks to my famous pals that gave me a blurb: Patton Oswalt, Sarah Silverman, Bob Odenkirk, Scott Ian, Randy Blythe, Gail Simone.

Thanks to Chris Hardwick, Rob Zombie, Pearl Aday (thanks and sorry I'm such a dick), Eric Liederman, Joe and Marie Trohman, Brendon and Courtney Small, Jody Gluck, and Jeremy Fleener.

To my Nerd Poker friends, Ken Daly, Dan Telfer, Blaine Capatch, Sarah Guzzardo, Chris Tallman, and my pals, Gerry Duggan, Sark, Rick Remender, Jeremy Essig, Derek Sheen, and Brad Wenzell.

To my son's school Los Encinos (Ilene Reinfeld) and all our friends: Brady and Tiffany Smith, Lee and Lisa Barron, Jessica and Dean McNaughton, Jason and Tara Ehrlich, Albert and Melissa Vaca. And to Tori Spelling. I don't really know her and I don't say those things to her and I'm pretty sure she's not the president of show biz. She seems like nice lady and I hope she never sees this book.

To Carole Posehn, thanks for giving me life, I guess. I hope you can forgive me writing all the things you actually said and know at the end of the day, I appreciate everything you did for me and your love and support. To my Uncle Gary and my cousins Todd and Rachel, thanks for everything. Thanks to Uncle Mike, Aunt Cindy, and Keith and Kristen. Thanks to my mother-in-law, Vel Truhett, we love you, Gigi. And thanks to the Truhett and Porter families.

Thanks to my sweet pups, Mavis and Licky, and my old hound dog, Ernie.

And finally and most importantly, thanks to Melanie Truhett Posehn, my sweet, beautiful, and loving wife. Thanks so much for everything you've done for me and thanks for putting up with how crazy I was while writing this. And to Rhoads Posehn, buddy, I love you more than you will ever know, but I will spend every day of my life showing you.